Transforming Choral Singing

Transforming Choral Singing

An Activist's Guide for Choir Directors

CHARLES W. BEALE

Oxford University Press is a department of the University of Oxford. It furthers
the University's objective of excellence in research, scholarship, and education
by publishing worldwide. Oxford is a registered trade mark of Oxford University
Press in the UK and certain other countries.

Published in the United States of America by Oxford University Press
198 Madison Avenue, New York, NY 10016, United States of America.

© Oxford University Press 2024

All rights reserved. No part of this publication may be reproduced, stored in
a retrieval system, or transmitted, in any form or by any means, without the
prior permission in writing of Oxford University Press, or as expressly permitted
by law, by license, or under terms agreed with the appropriate reproduction
rights organization. Inquiries concerning reproduction outside the scope of the
above should be sent to the Rights Department, Oxford University Press, at the
address above.

You must not circulate this work in any other form
and you must impose this same condition on any acquirer.

Library of Congress Cataloging-in-Publication Data
Names: Beale, Charles, author.
Title: Transforming choral singing : an activist's guide for choir
directors / Charles Beale.
Description: New York, NY : Oxford University Press, 2024. |
Includes bibliographical references and index.
Identifiers: LCCN 2023033941 (print) | LCCN 2023033942 (ebook) |
ISBN 9780197657782 (paperback) | ISBN 9780197657775 (hardback) |
ISBN 9780197657805 (epub)
Subjects: LCSH: Choral singing—Instruction and study. |
Choral singing—Social aspects.
Classification: LCC MT875 .B405 2024 (print) | LCC MT875 (ebook) |
DDC 782.5071—dc23/eng/20230809
LC record available at https://lccn.loc.gov/2023033941
LC ebook record available at https://lccn.loc.gov/2023033942

DOI: 10.1093/oso/9780197657775.001.0001

Contents

Preface	vii
Acknowledgments	ix
1. Four Principles	1
2. Defining Your Purpose	25
3. Vocal Sound	46
4. Pulse, Rhythm, and Groove	69
5. Improvising	86
6. Programming, Repertoire, and Show Design	99
7. Teaching and Learning in Rehearsal	127
8. Directing and Leading a Choral Community	152
9. The Daily Practice of Equity and Inclusion	173
10. An Activist Vision for Choral Singing	199
11. Calls to Action	218
Singer and Choir Appendix	223
Bibliography	227
Index	233

Preface

All jobs teach you about yourself. For seventeen years, I directed two leading choirs in the LGBTQIA+ choral movement: first, the London Gay Men's Chorus, later, the New York City Gay Men's Chorus. A glutton for punishment, in 2022, I recently joined a third, the San Diego Gay Men's Chorus. The experience of leading all three has profoundly affected my sense of who I am as a choral director, what I stand for, and the good I can do in the world through my music-making. It gave me a much deeper sense of how music functions, and revealed how my choral practice could help others and be a powerful force for change. Now is the time for me to share that insight with others.

I believe singing is an act of radical change, and an act of education. It changes us, empowers us, makes us more aware of ourselves, and teaches us who we are. It is also a catalyst that brings people together, and empowers them by giving them a voice. It has a civilizing effect on society. By its very nature, it creates the possibility that we bond in messy common humanity and understand each other better. In the process, authentic stories are told and transforming choral art is created—art of the dark, and art of the light.

My hope is that this book will create a path to increased participation and engagement in choral singing, and better art of all kinds. More than that, it is time to clear away some outdated practices, and replace them with a clear focus on the potential that choral singing offers today. If only a few are inspired by this book to use their music-making for the good as I have been, then sharing this vision will have been worthwhile.

Acknowledgments

Thanks are due to all those teachers who inspired me to be more stylistically open, and especially to Nick Moor, Andrew Worton-Steward, Chris Rathbone, Helen Davies, Barbara and Malcolm Pointon, Stephen Johns, Scott Stroman, Pete Churchill, Simon Purcell, Keith Swanwick, and Lucy Green. Also to the hundreds of members of the San Diego Gay Men's Chorus, New York City Gay Men's Chorus and the London Gay Men's Chorus who taught me what love is in choral singing.

Special thanks to those who collaborated with me artistically in all the projects mentioned, including Jeff Lettiere, Jason Cannon, Johnny Atorino, Peter Criswell, Steve Kurowski, and Damian Kington; also to Jane Ramseyer Miller for showing me what was possible; also to Clarence Patton for keeping me humble, and Steve Smith for his support during the writing process.

And of course to Yuwrajh, my husband, for putting up with all my nonsense.

1

Four Principles

Only connect . . . Live in fragments no longer.

—E.M. Forster, *Howards End*

All art MOVES people. It connects and therefore changes them. Art offers new and transforming insights that lead us to see the world, ourselves, and others in new ways. It says something truthful, that has impact. The better the art, the deeper and more truthful that impact is. This book is about choral singing and its ability to move, connect, and change us. It too is art.

For seventeen years, I was lucky enough to be the director of two large choirs. Both were about change. Both were activist choirs. Unlike the majority, their art grew directly from the lived experience of their community, in this case the LGBTQIA+ (or queer) community. The very reason for their existence was to be that community's voice, and to change perceptions of who they were. The needs and aspirations of that community gave the art of both choirs resonance, vibrancy, and relevance, and this enabled their singing to speak to all people, gay and straight, and to move and change them. In my view, being strongly grounded in a community made their art better. As I grew as a choral director, I learned that I too had become an activist, an agent for change through choral singing. Gradually, I began to find other choral art less satisfying. In many cases, I knew the music was pretty, and gorgeously sung. But what was it *for*?

This book is not about queer choirs. It is about *all* choirs. It offers several challenges. The first is to choirs, their directors, and the wider choral singing community. What is your singing *for*? What is its purpose? Whose voice does your art represent, and to what extent does what you sing resonate with the wider audience you serve?

Every group sits within a wider community of singers, listeners, and other stakeholders. Yours may be a school choir, a college choir, a church choir, a community chorus, or some other kind. But what does your choir's community need to say? What are your community's joys and struggles? What change does it seek in the world? What are the urgent insights about your community's life experience, that you feel you *must* sing about? Conversely, what do you need to say *to* that community? Then, does the music that you sing broadcast those insights truthfully, cogently, and innovatively? Does it grab today's audiences, compel them, and enable your singers to commit with passion and joy? Is it truthful, impactful, relevant art?

I decided to write this book because much choral singing today leaves me puzzled. Fantastic work continues, but at times I am no longer sure what it is saying. The art we produce is beautiful on one level but for me lacks engagement with the world on

Transforming Choral Singing. Charles W. Beale, Oxford University Press. © Oxford University Press 2024.
DOI: 10.1093/oso/9780197657775.003.0001

2   Transforming Choral Singing

another. I want it to meet people where they are, to be more grounded in the musical experience of most people, to represent them all, and to reflect their lived experience. It often excludes many of the marginalized people who most need it. It needs a new rationale.

This book, then, is about the purpose of choral singing. It offers a provocative and potentially transforming contemporary vision for the whole field. It proposes a paradigm shift, grounded in a return to first principles, which has profound implications for why we sing, what we sing, how we sing, and therefore how choral directors conduct, lead, teach, and rehearse. Too few choirs and choral directors see what they do as having purpose beyond music alone. I believe that they should, and my experience is that the practical tools and strategies in this book can transform their art, re-energize their sound, bond their group,[1] expand their audience, and vastly increase the impact of their work.

This transformation of choral singing begins from four principles. All four require us to see our art as a catalyst for change: *social* change in our singers, in audiences, and in society; and *musical* change in the goals, themes, repertoire, and activities of choral singing itself, and of its pedagogy. I believe this change is needed across all choral singing. I also believe that because they are artists, choral directors are, one way or another, activists, and to ignore that aspect of our work is to fail to fulfill our potential. I return to the concept of activist choral singing in earnest toward the end.

The principles set out in this first chapter underpin the whole of the rest of the book. Subsequent chapters then implement these principles by offering practical solutions in the form of workshops, suggestions, and tips that you can use with your singers and share with others who support you in leading your choir. These solutions cover many aspects of our work, including how we define our purpose, the way in which we design performances and choose repertoire, how we facilitate singing and conduct, how we lead choral communities, how we manage teaching and learning, and how we integrate the daily practice of equity and inclusion into every aspect of what we do.

We begin with the central premise, which is that we need to rethink the primary function of choral singing—what it's for.

Principle 1: Connection

As I write, COVID-19 has been sweeping the globe in waves for nearly two years. It has cruelly and indiscriminately been taking our loved ones, destroying key parts of our economic and cultural life, and, through social distancing, depriving us all of basic social contact with each other. Suddenly we have no choice but to be alone, or risk death. During the pandemic, we have become more aware than ever of our deep need for human intimacy, friendship, and connection.

At the same time, new forces of division and authoritarianism are silencing voices of many kinds across the globe. We are suffering a crisis of empathy, and becoming more and more divided as we witness the unraveling of our social fabric. Funding for the arts in the UK is in decline,[2] and in the US remains subject to the whims of philanthropists and corporate donors. Music education provision grows patchy in schools[3,4] and the number of students doing music qualifications at all levels is shrinking. According to the UK's Musicians Union,[5] in late 2020 one in three musicians was thinking of leaving the profession. Our art form is under existential threat, and so is the connection and cohesion it facilitates.

At the same time, you can't have missed the extraordinary outpouring of singing on social media during the lockdowns of 2020 to 2022. As I write, amateurs and professionals alike have been furiously belting out their favorite songs, sharing their top ten albums, and dancing manically around their socially distanced living rooms. All ages, all backgrounds, and all cultures are compelled to share with their communities. All of us are ravenously consuming theater, music, singing, dance, writing, and the visual arts, hour after hour and day after day. Our Netflix subscriptions and social media accounts have become prized possessions. Even more fascinating, more of us than ever are creating new content. Why? We have time on our hands, granted, and are enabled by technology, but I believe lockdown has reminded us of something more profound. Again, it is our deep human need for connection.

Alone, it is as though we don't exist. It is through human connection with others that we express our love, and experience the love of others. Connection gives us agency through awareness of others. We see someone, they see us, and we both know we are there. At its most basic, day-to-day connection comes through a Zoom call, a simple hug, or perhaps a face-to-face chat over a meal. Creating and consuming art is in many ways no more than a particularly intense and expressive version of that same connection, albeit in a larger group.

Like a Zoom call, art connects creator, performer, and listener.[6] The best art can connect a larger number of people, and embodies those universal stories and those feelings of love, fear, joy, and sadness that we all share. When a piece of art is really resonant, an audience applauds. In doing so, they of course validate and thank us artists as human beings, but in their applause, their laughter, and their tears, they also signal that they recognize themselves in the art we create. Our story becomes theirs. In this disconnected world, we as choral directors use singing to connect people.

Connection, Identity, and Belonging

I lived in New York for many years, so I rode the subway. Most mornings I'd see people listening on their phones, and often, because headphones leak, I could tell they were listening to singing. I would also see all kinds of people sing, dance, and perform live on the trains and platforms. So many people sing. But why do they do it, and what is so special about it?

4   Transforming Choral Singing

Whatever our age, singing expresses especially important things about who we are. For teens, it expresses the adults they aspire to be, and their values as transgressors, full of youthful energy and life. We adults will sing the songs that give us joy, or make us cry; or we'll perform the songs we heard when we got married, fell in love with that special person, or went to a new school. We remember the songs our mother sang, to send us to sleep as a child. There is that song that reminds us of the death of a loved one, of the struggles we face, or of our spirituality. Singing often puts older people in touch with what has been most meaningful in their lives. In dementia,[7] the speech disappears, while the singing sometimes stays, sparking long-buried memories. All of this singing connects us with what is most important to us, to our identity: who we are, who we love, what we believe, and where we belong.[8]

It can be unbelievably powerful to find someone who likes the same songs as you do. My colleague and co-conspirator Steve won't mind me telling you the story of the time we first met at a choral conference in the early 2000s. We were both music educators, total strangers, but both coincidentally the only people giving talks there on groove-based choral singing. After we had presented, we went for a drink together. I remember so clearly the moment when we discovered we both had the same obscure albums in our vinyl collections. Later that night in a club, we drunkenly belted out the same backing vocals to equally obscure pop tracks from the '80s. One African American, one white British, choral directors brought up on different continents with wildly differing life experiences, identities, and opportunities, we nevertheless changed by singing together, magically bonded, from that moment. We have stayed bonded, the closest of friends ever since.

To be in a choir, big or small, can be similarly mind-blowing. It exponentially multiplies the experience of connection Steve and I shared, and potentially offers a whole new way of seeing yourself in the world. Previously alone, singers in choirs are bonded and unified through a single sound; they become part of something bigger than themselves. In singing together, they share what's important, and in doing so they connect, and at times achieve transcendence.[9] To sing the same song as another is to be in the same musical space, but it is also to be in the same social space. It makes us feel good about ourselves, and it makes us feel good (or at least better!) about those around us.

The increased level of belonging and connection that choral singing provides is electrifying, life-transforming, precious indeed. It is why I do what I do. For some, singing in my New York choir was like coming home for the first time. Others said it was like church. They felt comfortable, they felt powerful, they felt healed, they felt they belonged, and they felt that they were able to be fully themselves, sometimes for the very first time. This was not because they were all in *any* big group together. The unique connection of choral singing had changed them. I have a saying, that my choir became bored of hearing me use at our shows: "It is hard to hate someone you just sang a song with." Choral singing is a radical, change-making act, because, in the words of Ken Burns, from a "me" and a "you" it creates the potential for a new "us."[10]

Principle 2: Impact

In his groundbreaking book, *Good to Great and the Social Sectors*, corporate strategist and nonprofit expert Jim Collins identifies a qualitative difference between what he calls "business" and "social sector" organizations, such as those in the performing arts. He writes: "In business, money is both an input (a resource for achieving greatness) *and* an output (a measure of greatness). In the social sectors, money is *only* an input, and not a measure of greatness. . . . In the social sectors, then, the critical question is not, "How much money do we make per dollar of invested capital," but "How effectively do we deliver our mission and make a distinctive impact, relative to our resources?"[11]

Impact is hard to define. Here I use two starting points to attempt a definition of impact in choral singing: first that the best impact is deep and lasting, rather than superficial and momentary; and second, that singing can be impactful in three main ways: personal impact, community impact, and societal impact.

A choral performance can affect me personally by making me think or feel differently about myself: who I am, what my identity is, and where I fit into the social fabric. As a gay teen in a high school choir, for example, I can sing a song like Pasek and Paul's "This Is Me," which tells a story in "I" language about proudly being who you are, however flawed you feel. Likewise, African American friends and colleagues tell me that James Brown's "Say It Loud, I'm Black and I'm Proud" has deep resonance going back to childhood, and reminds them of who they are. Both songs empower the singer and express their identity to them. In both, the lyric has a personal "me"-based impact on them, and so does the music itself. The music works directly on the emotional level. The song becomes an analogue for the singer's identity and inner feelings. It enacts them. I, the singer, can find myself laughing or crying out loud as I sing, in recognition of a feeling or situation in the song that relates directly to my own feelings or situation. I become more aware of myself, and I feel recognized. My feelings have been articulated. I feel more powerful, in myself.[12] I feel less alone. This is the personal element of the radical power of choral singing.

Community is a problematic word in some ways, and I return to it later, particularly with regard to inclusion and equity. For the purposes of this introductory chapter, however, we can say that community impact, perhaps bonding, begins when I sing my song with others. As I did with my friend Steve, I feel bonded when I sing. A community is created, who agree through singing together that they all feel the same. I discover that others feel or think the same as me, and this discovery feeds, nurtures, and heals me as I sing. Bonding happens directly through the simultaneous acts of singing together and hearing sound. I feel heard in the literal sense, because others hear my voice. I also feel heard at a deeper level, because I experience their voices singing along with mine. I know now that I am not alone in my situation and feelings, and so does everyone else in the group. I find myself, and at the same time lose a portion of my individuality as my voice becomes part of the group whole.[13]

Listeners who hear a whole choir singing have the experience of a wall of sound, perhaps a group proudly and powerfully singing an anthem. They also experience singers bonding in the moment, directly in front of them, and liberating themselves from day-to-day loneliness, oppression, and division. The music bonds and liberates those listeners too. Gospel choirs, LGBTQIA+ choirs, and church choirs function in this way all the time. Singers in school choirs often come to the experience of group singing for the first time, and for them such group bonding, liberation, and empowerment can be especially powerful. Some singers may already feel liberated, while others are quite literally in the process of psychologically freeing themselves as they perform. Watching that freedom develop in the moment makes such performances especially compelling.

What an audience sees and hears has an impact on them too. Through encounter with choral singing, they are led to their own liberation, and to their own ownership of a song's emotional and social message. They too feel heard, articulated, and empowered. They are educated about the singers' personal situations and feelings and those of their community, in a way no spreadsheet or PowerPoint presentation can achieve. They empathize with the message, and they become aware of the singers' needs, feelings, and identities. Through this new awareness, I have seen and heard firsthand how listeners' behavior or language can change as a direct result of hearing a choir sing.[14] This is the community element of the radical power of choral singing.

Third, over time, our choirs have an increasing impact on wider society. When I became a choral director, I remember feeling my role shift. In choosing "This Is Me" and then conducting my group singing it, I discovered that I had become an agent for change. Suddenly my artistic work had wide and palpable social impact. Previously just a conductor (itself an achievement), now I was leading my singers in making a public statement of our values, of who we were, as a community. If done well, that musical statement had power to create change in the world beyond music-making. My work as a choral director and leader had new purpose.

Sometimes music's social purpose is obvious. Choral groups of this kind are all around us at a range of levels: from Croatian choir Le Zbor's antifascist songs[15] to Hanoi's groundbreaking Diversity Choir[16]; from the Trans Chorus of Los Angeles to Canada's "Choir! Choir! Choir!" drop-in project[17] and the UK's "The Zimmers."[18] Each has its own unique social purpose, and a way of singing that embodies it. Yet looking back, I realize that all the choral singing I led since my teens has had similar but often unacknowledged social impact. All that singing directly improved the lives of the people who were involved in it and heard it.

The musical and social impact of singing has been identified in so many different domains. One is physical and mental health and well-being,[19] crucial in our fragmented post-COVID world. Singing can also be therapy,[20] healing, and rehabilitation for those in the criminal justice system.[21] Likewise, singing can be of massive general educational benefit in the development of cognitive function, academic performance, and emotional abilities, in children and adults of all ages.[22] It is central to self-actualization, literally bringing your full voice to life.[23] We know too that it can help those with dementia[24] and Alzheimer's[25] and those who stutter[26] to communicate. For older people generally, choral singing can have impact on both physical and mental health.[27] In the endnotes, I have left starting point references for further research in all these areas. Such wide-ranging impact is intrinsic to the work of every choir every time they sing. All choirs have such power. That is the impact of choral singing.

Saying Something

Just as the potter's medium is clay, a musician's medium is sound. As a young choral director, I was obsessed with that medium for its own sake, and immersed myself in the materials of music. I became absorbed on multiple levels. As a thinker, there was something about systems of harmony, melody, rhythm, timbre, and sonority that made me curious, and as a performer I found myself actively exploring those materials in my practice. I was also nerdily eclectic from very early on. I loved the Byrd Masses, the Magnificat and Nunc Dimittis from Howell's *Collegium Regale*, Mahler symphonies, and the chords of Messiaen's piano music, but even then, I also adored the rhythms of South African jazz, the vocal stylings of Nat "King" Cole, and later the fiery improvisations and melodic and sonic innovation of Kenny Wheeler and John Coltrane. I played in orchestras, sang in choirs of many kinds in jazz clubs and cathedrals, and directed big bands. My dating music was the Human League and Howard Jones '80s synth pop of early gay clubs. Even at age eight, I was immersed in the Emerson, Lake and Palmer and Led Zeppelin prog rock obsessions of my teenage brother and sisters. Definitely a child of privilege, my 1970s school owned a Mellotron, so I got into tape loops early too. I greedily consumed music of all kinds.

How meaningful can all those fascinating systems and structures be, if they only have an audience of one? It has been my journey to discover that, again like a Zoom call, music's primary purpose is to connect performer and listener. There is something about the presence of that listener, the person communicated to, that is crucial to our process as musicians. Of course as performers we listen very intently, and understand, analyze, and emotionally engage with what we do in many different ways. We have to be self-critical, own our obsessions, love music for itself, and understand and revel in the intrinsic qualities of its processes. But if others do not listen equally intently, our work has little or indeed no power. As a composer, I don't really know whether my piece is any good until someone else hears it. Likewise, as a performer, I imagine listeners as I practice. However complex and perfect the structure of a piece, I have often discovered I was wrong about something I played or conducted, when the impact I had imagined did not materialize. Music is intrinsically a social activity. We musicians need our work to have impact in the world, and that impact requires other listeners.

8 Transforming Choral Singing

In social media terms, we want our art to go viral. It should say something important that resonates with others, and makes them like and share it. If I hear applause, or read praise from the critic I hoped to please, it makes my work more valuable and more meaningful, and I feel valued, both personally and as an artist. All the "great" art of the past did that at some point soon after its first performance. We know what we *intend* music to mean, but meaning is only really created when art "says something" to others, and they acknowledge and feed that back to us. Only then, when that feedback reaches us, is our process complete.

Some choir directors see themselves as purists. They argue that the choral singing they make has no social and political purpose, beyond that of sound itself. "We just make beautiful music," I hear them say. I was trained to think that way myself. After over twenty years in activist choral singing, now I would challenge them on that. Let's begin with community. While you were working on your pure art, how many of the singers in your group developed deeper friendships through singing in it? For how many people is singing that pure art in your choir the highlight of their week, regardless of what is sung? For how many professional musicians does music-making provide the very reason for their existence? Doesn't music also have spiritual impact for some of your singers, expressing a feeling of coming together, or of creating something bigger, greater, and more uplifting than they could create on their own?

It is also worth double-checking whether the music your choir sings had a direct social purpose when it was written. A work like Vivaldi's *Gloria* can seem innocuous, gorgeous in itself, but is definitely saying something about the glory of a certain sort of God. Between one-third and one-half of the choral repertoire in Western Europe and the US is Christian, after all. I am no longer a person of faith, but I see how it embodies in sound the awe-inspiring power of that Christian God to (guess what?) change the world. It too is activist music. Choral singing was the ultimate social media asset of its day. It was written for listeners, to express their concerns, to have shared impact, to change people's hearts and minds, to bind them to a community. It told powerful Biblical stories that advocated for a set of very specific social values that were the norms of the time. Of course, that same music remains beautiful to us middle-class, educated Westerners; it is well-written and refined. It does that job of legacy extremely well. But beware! If you ignore the social and political purpose of the music your choir sings, you may find yourself passionately advocating for a social cause you do not believe in.

Some more examples: A piece like Ola Gjeilo's *New Year's Carol* articulates another universal truth, about the turning wheel of time—what he calls "the frostbite of pain and loss giving way to the flower of hope and renewal." Likewise, while the melody is jaunty, the Beatles' "When I'm Sixty-Four" says something dark and unsettling: "What will it be like when I am older? Will I be lonely?" Sondheim's "Another Hundred People" is also an amazing musical construction, but it is *about* the bustle and anonymity of the big city, and paints a paradoxical picture of the spectacular togetherness and simultaneous loneliness of New York life. Aretha Franklin's "Respect" is complex too. On one level it is about human rights, and on another it is an uncompromising personal statement and expression of pain, about her own unique experience of *dis*respect as an African American, and as a woman. All of this music is satisfying, structurally intricate, and intrinsically worthwhile as music. All of it also tells stories about human experience. All contain truths about life outside music that have impact and purpose. All of it is "saying something."

Choral music, indeed all art, always has this power to "say something" to the listener. It is inseparable from the work of all choral directors every day, and it is often the central function of what they do, whether they realize it or not. Many choral directors ignore this function for many reasons, but I believe it is time to acknowledge it, and to use its power intentionally. A choir is at its core a glove puppet, a communication tool. The art of puppetry is important, and puppets can be beautiful, but the glove puppet needs something to say. Your choir needs to own the story its art is telling. The job of the choral director is then to use their musical expertise to enable that story to resonate the very best it can to the largest number of people.

But what should your choral music "say"? What do you believe your choir's singing can do in the world? And do you need to have a strong social and political position to be a choral director? That depends on your mission, on how you define your purpose, which is the subject of Chapter 2. Activism is in that sense a stance, an idea I return to in the final chapter. To see your work as activist does not define what is changed. That definition will vary from group to group. My starting point is not that you have to take any particular position. But you do have to decide what your unique position is, and sing with intention from there, in order for your art to have impact.

Returning to the quotation on "inputs and outputs" that opened this section, Jim Collins's book is about moving arts organizations from good to great, and about how we know we are improving. For choral directors, then, it is about how we measure the "great"-ness of a choir, and its choral performances. Is it in the quality of the choral sound, or the beauty of the repertoire chosen? Is it perhaps the quality of the conducting, or the sense of authority and relaxed expressiveness of the voices? Is it perhaps having amazing school facilities, a big congregation, fantastic fundraising, great administrative capacity, an efficient production team, kick-ass marketing, a sympathetic principal, or the most well-managed business operation that always comes out in profit?

To paraphrase Collins's simple but powerful idea, a choral performance can have *all* of these qualities, make all the money in the world, and still not be "great." Instead, it is only through its connection and impact that we should measure the "greatness" of all choral art.[28]

Principle 3: Social Justice

On his personal website, Francisco Nuñez, conductor of the Young People's Chorus of New York City, writes:

> During this pivotal time in our country's history, I, along with our board and our staff, am looking deeper into our work and evaluating whether it has been enough. Is it enough to be diverse? Is it enough to sing together, to create music together at the highest levels? Or is it our responsibility to dig deeper, and frame the conversation surrounding the importance of our diversity—namely, empathy, cultural awareness, sensitivity, and respect? I believe the answer to this last question is yes.
>
> This is the time to make hard decisions, and challenge and expand our models. . . . Diversity is a major step, but true equality is the goal, and equity and education are the vehicles by which we attain it. I will continue to challenge myself, and I invite my fellow conductors to do the same.[29]

My first two principles were about the function of choral singing. They establish change through connection and impact as the major driver of all our work. The third and fourth concern what *kind* of change is needed in the 2020s. They set out the means by which we as choral directors can best increase our connection and impact today, and so improve our art. I believe we do it by focusing on the role of the artist as commenting on society, as saying the unsayable, and as holding a mirror up to the world. Artists reveal the core issues of their day, and present a set of values that can lead society forward. So my third principle is social justice.

Of all the issues facing Western society today, social justice is the most obvious, the most clearly articulated, and also one of the toughest. In his influential TED talk, choral director Anthony Trecek-King puts the challenge before us as follows: "In order to really change, you have to look deep inside yourself, and get uncomfortable."[30] There is no easy way to say this. Thanks to our colonial past, inequality and marginalization are everywhere, and they are rife in choral singing. There is a dominant culture. With honorable exceptions that are notable by their rarity, we are a mainly white, mainly older, mainly straight-acting artistic movement.[31] Our repertoire remains mostly written by white men of the past. We sing in churches or other faith spaces, or in schools, colleges, and concert halls, very few of which are free from similar bias. Much choral repertoire is overtly Christian in content, and the Christians, especially old testament ones, have a 2000-year-old reputation for smiting all kinds of people(!), including foreigners, non-Christians, and, many would say, LGBTQIA+ people. All of this is embedded in choral culture, such that even when we try to change it, it is present anyway. To face this lack of social justice and this inequality in most choral music-making should indeed, in the words of Anthony Trecek-King, make us uncomfortable.

Right away, I want to get specific, and ask you to think about your own choir or chorus through three lenses. The first is race and ethnicity. How many members of your choir come from black, indigenous, and people of color (BIPOC) backgrounds? (Also sometimes known as black and ethnic minority, BAME, in the UK.) And how many of those BIPOC people would you *expect* to be in your group, given the demographics of your area? Your group may be in a BIPOC community context and have its own point of view, and I admit here that I am assuming a white gaze. Many choirs in the US and Europe are mainly white. I am calling them "mainstream" throughout, which is no reflection of what I think the mainstream should be. I will hazard a guess that the audience for this book will be mainly white too. This is also not a criticism, but at this point merely an observation. However, it leads us directly to the question of why mainstream groups may be failing to connect and have impact with BIPOC singers and listeners. Could their purpose and how they define it have something to do with it?

The second lens is gender and sexuality. How many in your group are open members of the LGBTQIA+ community? Many mainstream choirs are full of LGBTQIA+ people. No, really, they are *full* of them! But how many feel comfortable to be 100 percent open about their personal lives and the people they love? Some choirs are better than others in this regard. School choirs often fill up with LGBTQIA+ singers, who find them to be safe and empowering spaces, at least in comparison to the cruelties of the playground. So too do church choirs, ironically. Even so, the chances are that you are massively under-counting your LGBTQIA+ folks, and not connecting with them as well as you think. They have learned not to make themselves visible, even where there is some welcome. Choirs, like churches, can seem loving and compassionate, but for many, they feel like deeply unsafe, judgmental places. It is often safer to remain hidden, and they can be very skilled at hiding. Again, is something about your choir's purpose preventing them from feeling comfortable being their full selves?

Finally, age. If you run a community choir, what is the average age in your group? Many currently skew older. About one of my choirs, an audience member and later personal friend commented, "You look fine when you're singing, but it's when you all bow that the grey and the bald patches show!" Is your community choir connecting and having the impact it is capable of with younger people? And if not, as is statistically likely to be the case, what is driving that, do you suppose?

I've opened by mentioning just three groups often seen as underrepresented in mainstream choirs and their audiences, but there are many more. In 2017, there were, for example, 42.8 million people in the US with a disability—that's 13.2 percent.[32] Likewise in 2016, 1.4 million adults identified as "transgender,"[33] including 0.7 percent of under-twenty-fours and 0.5 percent of over-sixty-fives. Many more are not comfortable to self-identify. Are they represented in your choirs? If not, why not? Likewise, we could, for example, see the work of choirs through the lens of socioeconomic status, mental health, neurodiversity, learning style, or citizenship status. More on these lenses to varying extents later.

My hunch is that those in your choir and its surrounding communities face at least one of these challenges. You may even have identified it. Faced with our busy lives and many priorities, how, then, do we as choral directors make a systematic attempt to solve these endemic issues? It can seem overwhelming. Being great at welcoming queer people is no guarantee that your group will be equally welcoming to people, say, from a range of races or ages. Intersectionality is complex, and bias is built into our musical processes.

12 Transforming Choral Singing

My experience is that most in the arts are at least well-meaning. Many are kind, compassionate, and open. To make good art at all, there has to be some emotional honesty. In singing, we all make ourselves vulnerable to each other and our work requires us to take a stance. It reveals insights about the new, the "othered," or the different, and offers us a means to better understand each other. As a gay man, this function certainly made me feel safe when I first became a musician. The performing arts gave me a safe-ish space to express who I was, and to grow. Choral artists *should* be great at this, because the values of social justice are in this sense intrinsic to our artistic process.

At the same time, there are real challenges. We tell ourselves we are welcoming and singing is for all, but in doing so, recent history shows us that we hide baked-in *in*justice from ourselves. We want to stay comfortable, so we fail to follow through. We argue that we have to work with the singers that show up, or that the singing we do is beautiful "in its own terms." Nothing needs real change here.

In doing so we make a number of false assumptions: first that everyone is encultured as a Westerner; second that everyone has the tools to take part in the choral singing we like; and third, that everyone should. We return to assumptions later in Chapter 9, but for now, can we agree that none of these are especially inclusive starting points? In 2022, all are only true for certain people, who, let's face it, tend to be white, middle-class, often cisgender, straight, and musically educated in a certain way. To be clear, many kinds of people are not showing up to take part in our choral work because we *are* excluding them, through our artistic practices and the way we run our communities. Is this what we intend? Sometimes the answer is unfortunately yes, but in the main, most choirs are not overtly discriminatory places. My hunch is that the majority of real exclusion is unintentional. That does not make it justified.

Back to my personal story. Twenty years ago, I would have been much less proactive in my approach. As a gay man, a bully victim in school, and someone who was often picked last for a team, I experienced some exclusion myself. Full disclosure, I am white and identify as male, so I am clearly privileged in so many other ways. My well-meaning heart has always been in the right place, and for me that used to be enough. Earlier in my career, I would have said something like, "Isn't it enough just to say in our mission statement that we must all be respectful and nice to each other?" As a jazz musician, I had worked with all kinds of players from South Africa to New Zealand, old and young, gay and straight, black, brown, and white. I was a musical purist, and argued that the purity of the musical process made it an especially safe space for conversations about inequality to play out. Social justice was important, but not my main concern, I said.

Since then, I've learned that our music-making is a direct expression of our social and political values as human beings. I may think I am well-intentioned, and I may *assume* I am not racist myself, but because bias, prejudice, and stigma are systemic, we are, in the words of the *Avenue Q* song, all a little bit racist. And so, often, are our choirs. Well, actually, more than a little bit . . .

We are also all a little bit homophobic. Because it has been my lived experience, I can attest personally to the intensity with which LGBTQIA+ folks are marginalized and oppressed, and carry inside ourselves the homophobia we are taught by society. As a result, even when society sees itself as freeing us and our choirs tell us they welcome us, we will oppress ourselves. In fear, we hide and tell ourselves we should be ashamed. Queer people are hiding in plain sight in choirs of all ethnicities, even in "welcoming" choral groups. Again, our choirs' self-examination does not go deep enough, and we don't put in place concrete steps to ensure equity, comfort, and welcome. We are not persistent, and we give up too easily, because systemic change is hard.

Now here's the hardest part. As choral directors, we have to face the fact that mainstream choral music is at base a music of privilege. Because they are dominant, it is therefore the special job of white, straight, cisgendered people with privilege to acknowledge this, and actively do something about it. If we just let it be, the issue will not solve itself. Instead, like it or not we will be actively contributing to it. Without purpose, further transformation is simply not possible.

To summarize, then, my third principle is that the art of *all* choirs is saying something about social justice. At the risk of repeating myself, choral singing is *by its very nature* a uniquely powerful tool that creates change through saying something every time it takes place. Storytelling that expresses social values is intrinsic to our artistic process. Are we telling the right stories?

A crucial factor limiting the impact of our choirs is that they are actively excluding BIPOC people, queer folks, and many other marginalized people of different ages, classes, abilities, and backgrounds from equal connection and belonging. We do not tell their stories. Simply examine who is not in our groups, and not in our audiences, and you cannot miss how racism, homophobia, ageism, and other kinds of exclusion are clearly present in our choirs. This is bad for our art, because it makes it narrow, backward-looking, and less impactful and relevant. But it is also bad for our societies. There is healing to be done, and real anger out there, because the lives of individuals in marginalized communities, many of whom are our neighbors, fellow singers, and audience members, are under direct threat. In order for that healing to take place, these individuals have to be in the room when we sing. Chapter 9 focuses on these issues.

We majority-white choir directors and our organizations, the majority of choirs, have to ask ourselves some hard questions. We have to actively debate why we sing, what we sing, and how we sing. We have to change ourselves, so that we root out the inequality that is baked into our work,[34] so that our impact can increase. We have to transparently set out our principles, and apply them persistently. The path is not easy, but in the process, our choirs will transform and become beacons of hope, our art will align with the times, and we will begin to contribute to the solution rather than the problem. We will become change-makers.

Principle 4: Stylistic Openness

Last year, I had the privilege of spending some time in Singapore with my gorgeous, then-nine-month-old great niece, Sreya. Predictably, "Baby Shark" was her favorite song. Not yet able to speak a single word, she was nevertheless to be found bouncing infectiously up and down on the couch in time to the music. She would immediately start to cry if the music was turned off, and I found myself grinning inanely along with her chuckles of delight, my head nodding as she bounced. It was almost involuntary for us both. We heard "Baby Shark" many times that day.

Duke Ellington memorably said, "There are simply only two kinds of music. Good music, and the other kind."[35] When all of us hear *any* music, we respond. Unless there is an *extremely* rare (like 1/200,000) cognitive or hearing issue, research shows that tone deafness is very unlikely,[36] and effectively all human beings are what Doug Goodkin calls "musical beings."[37] Likewise Katie Kat describes singing as a "necessity," an "incredible gift we *all* have."[38] We are all wired to respond to music on some level, just as we are to speech and other sounds.

I am not proposing here some kind of 1960s liberal utopian world view, where music is somehow a "universal language." The level and type of your individual response will vary, depending on your age, skills, culture, and musical experience. Ten thousand hours really are needed for mastery of any worthwhile skill. People also respond to different styles in markedly different ways. Sometimes we dance (or bounce!), sometimes we sit still and cry, sometimes music is to our taste and sometimes it isn't. But we do all respond to all music, because we are human beings. At this crucial basic level, all music is equally valuable, regardless of style. I certainly felt connected to Sreya as we bounced together.

This is not how music is presented to us day to day. Musical culture is not a level playing field. Those with power control what we hear and how often we hear it, and effectively manage how deeply we respond. This plays out in a number of ways. First, let's agree that if music were a running race, common practice classical music (by which throughout this book I mean Dowland to early Stravinsky) has a massive head start. Some classical musicians, educators, and programmers are open to other styles too, but my experience is that this is not often the case. Indeed, many of the classical music educators I have worked with in universities and conservatories have appointed themselves as the gatekeepers of musical culture itself. They see themselves as the owners of the secret sauce of music as a whole. Really—*all* of it!

These classical exceptionalists consider their music (by which we mean the music of eighteenth- and nineteenth-century white Europeans) more refined, more considered, more complex, more imaginative, capable of deeper expression—just somehow better overall.[39] My Cambridge director of studies told me firmly that Duke Ellington's music (of all things!) was "not worthy of study."[40] At two of the universities I later taught at, I found it impossible to teach even quite tame pop music in choir, because I was told by the head of department and by vocal teachers that it would "ruin their voices." There are also many who profess stylistic openness as a goal, but know inside that classical music is somehow just better. None of this makes any sense.

Again, let's start from the premise that we want our singing to connect people, to have impact and to facilitate social justice. The best singing has always done that without us even trying. Common practice classical music does connect some people, but like all music, it is written in code, and only those able to read its code, mainly white and middle class, will ever truly be connected by it. It has deep impact for a privileged few, and some impact for all, as does "Baby Shark," but for full effect it requires a particular sort of advanced education. This is often what classical exceptionalists mean by "refinement," and other similar terms. They mean that there is really only one way to be truly refined as a musician, and that is to learn that one specific code, regardless of your identity and culture.[41] Of course, much common practice classical music is incredibly beautiful, complex, and the result of hundreds of years of a particular sort of musical development. It is possible, though less likely, for BIPOC people and those of other cultures to become encultured in these ways of thinking and feeling about music. That does not make classical music's impact somehow universal. While simply singing classical music because it is beautiful "in itself" is an honorable position, it is also a minority one.

I am here to assert from my lived experience as performer, educator, and academic in both the classical and popular fields that many other styles can be equally impactful. Many styles can also be just as structurally complex, *and* can be sung with equal refinement.[42] We return to this in Chapter 3. Meanwhile, the codes of popular music, jazz, folk and indigenous musics, musical theater, and other styles are readable by many more, so their potential for impact and connection is much wider. Sreya's response alone reminds us that music is capable of more than this.

It is especially puzzling that these highly specialized classical musicians with their exceptionalist views are supported by virtually the *entire* education system, which in 2020 still foregrounds the Western European art music of the eighteenth and nineteenth centuries as somehow more worthy. This is a huge structural problem. If formal education suits your learning style and budget, there are great conservatory programs all over the world that now teach jazz, popular music, musical theater, and non-Western music with real excellence. Incomprehensibly, very few students get the opportunity to take them, even though some have now been going for fifty years. Some of the most musically complex and pedagogically demanding non-Western musical trainings are thousands of years old. UK-based beginner assessments in jazz for seven-year-olds[43] are now available in the UK, the US, Canada, Singapore, Malaysia, Hong Kong, Australia, and New Zealand. So are many formal and informal trainings in non-Western styles, from Balinese gamelan to Indian ragas. Self-evidently, there is simplicity and complexity, compositional skill, sophisticated musicianship, cultural depth, and pedagogical integrity to be found in all these styles.

Vocal education has also moved on. Scientific research into how the vocal mechanism works has conclusively proven that singing musical theater, jazz, and popular music is in no way less safe than singing opera, oratorio, or church music. Vocal teachers and choral directors teach people to sing with great subtlety and nuance in all these styles. Specifically on the issue of vocal safety, good opera teachers will quickly tell you that unsafe singing exists in classical music too. Yet the baked-in

16 Transforming Choral Singing

myths persist in choral education, and singers are still often excluded from choirs because they use their voices in ways seen as forbidden, or naive. We return to this too in Chapter 3.

In my twenties, I ran an innovative college-based foundation course for jazz and pop musicians wanting to return to the education system. What I found was that these students were very musically able in many respects. On entry, they often had playing, composing, and improvising skills to a level well beyond many degree-holding classical musicians, and, having learned informally, had sometimes already been around the world playing and singing in bands. They could pick up complex melodic and harmonic material by ear, were often great at embellishing and improvising melodies, and had fantastic rhythm skills and the ability to interpret and communicate through music with power and authority. They were nevertheless unable to get access to the first rung of an undergraduate university degree because they did not know classical music theory. Others needed an initial qualification in the history and analysis of "music," by which was meant the list of Western classical greats from 1600 on. Worse, even the most knowledgeable and experienced non-classical performers felt inside that they must somehow be lesser musicians, because they did not have "classical" skills. Like the queer people hiding in plain sight mentioned earlier, they had internalized messages about their own lack of self-worth as musicians, and then acted accordingly.[44]

As with people, styles such as jazz, musical theater, and pop music continue to be "othered," marginalized, and treated as somehow less valuable or "serious," both inside and outside choral music education. While pockets of excellence exist, the narrow curricula and power structures of formal music education have created many barriers to progression for those who are not already encultured in classical music. Meanwhile, the conservatory doors open for those choral singers and conductors who already read music, sing using a certain resonance, or learned a Western classical instrument before the age of ten.[45] As a result, the vast majority of the singers and conductors who make non-classical music do it in other places and learn it in other ways, ignored by the education system and its elites. Very few of those talented and expert singers will end up in our choirs, and fewer still will become choral directors.

Another structural problem preventing stylistic openness is that our choice of music is presented to us by streaming services and multinationals. This gives some music in this stylistic running race a head start. These powerful organizations devise algorithms that expose us to some music much more than others. As a result, we are encouraged into passive listening, and we do much less live performance than in previous generations. We can choose only from the narrow, commercially skewed selections we are offered. Again, there are problematic demographic issues. The pop music we are presented with online is heavily skewed in favor of younger people, for example. White people also tend to have control of who hears what by a long way, even when those organizations offer us the music of BIPOC people. Non-Western music and the music of LGBTQIA+ people are off on their own, on separate websites deemed less commercial. So too are the more specialized classical offerings. I could go on. Often, the most interesting and relevant voices are the ones the algorithms make it hardest to hear. It is much harder to be presented with music we have not yet "liked." Instead, we sit powerlessly in our software-generated bubbles, passive listeners to Spotify playlists, that paradoxically we have compiled ourselves.[46]

Since Victorian times, singing itself has transformed, but mainstream *choral* singing has hardly changed at all. The repertoire, themes, vocal styles, and educational approaches of many choirs would often not be out of place in the 1880s.[47] Back then, our forefathers (and mothers) defined for themselves a fundamentally unified repertoire and a "good" way of singing. In the West, we placed closed boundaries around that repertoire, canonized it, and have broadly stuck to it ever since.

While choral directors live in a stylistically unequal world, outside choral singing that world is much more stylistically open. The huge cultural changes of the late twentieth and early twenty-first centuries have transformed attitudes, repertoires, and the place of music in our society. Pop music, jazz, and musical theater are now people's primary means to connect through song across much of the globe. New hybrids like Bollywood and K-pop spring up continually alongside indigenous styles.[48] Outside choral singing, whole new communities of transgender singers and performers are well established online, writing and producing innovative, relevant, and insightful singing.[49] In the West and elsewhere, music is no longer primarily experienced unamplified in drafty churches or massive concert halls. Instead, it is consumed on devices and distributed online, via YouTube and the broadcast media. Attention spans, we are told, have shrunk, and while huge amounts of complex and refined art is going on, a scarcity of music education of any kind means that fewer listeners and musicians are "artistically literate" in the old-fashioned sense.

While some would say choral singing is doing fine in its own small way, increasing numbers of singers and audience members are not even considering joining choirs and choruses, either because they feel excluded socially, or because the styles being sung no longer have impact for them. This is particularly true in schools, where choral directors mostly trained in classical artistic practices are finding that they have to include increasing amounts of pop music to keep their students engaged. At times, they feel disgruntled by this.[50,51] Singers and listeners feel increasingly disengaged with the musical language of the choral music presented to them. They are dissatisfied both with what it is trying to say, and how it is saying it. In my view, this is both our failure as choral directors, and the failure of those who trained us.

There are three main stylistic issues to address around choral music. First, while choral music can function to connect all kinds of people, it currently only connects those who are encultured in some styles, and I will name the main one as common practice Western classical music. With honorable exceptions, choral singing is also fundamentally recreative, a music of the past. It has massive potential to connect a much wider range of people. Indeed, it used to do so, and the evidence is strong that it could easily do so again, as people outside choral singing clearly still want to sing in large numbers. I believe that it should. To do so, it must engage with the music of the present, and indeed, create the music of the future.

Second, current choral singing will never have the impact of the music we are surrounded by today, until it rediscovers its full purpose. That purpose is likely to involve not only beautiful singing, but also storytelling of relevance to the lives of today's singers and listeners.

Third, choral singing is inequitable. Its stylistic bias excludes too many. The solutions to this are complex and deep-rooted. They are in part around our musical practices—our art, our repertoire, and our ways of rehearsing and performing. They are also in part around our educational practices—how we teach singing, define styles as worthy of study, separate easy from hard, and how we organize and enact repertoire and musical concepts in our curricula and our pedagogy. And they are in part around how our choral communities operate socially, and how they are led. We return to this issue in Chapter 8.

My fourth and final principle, then, is that choirs should take a radically open approach to musical style, both in terms of their repertoire, their performance practices, and the contexts they perform in. Here, stylistic openness is not simply a vague and spineless liberal concept, but a principled, activist position that equitably prioritizes well-performed group singing of all kinds, as long as it connects people and centers openness, eclecticism, and musical authenticity in a disciplined and persistent way.

We need to ditch the classical canon as the primary driver of repertoire choice. Instead, we should always sing creative, innovative, risk-taking artistic work that focuses on present-day concerns and expresses those concerns in musical language that mainstream listeners know how to decode, because they are encultured in it and it means something to them. This could still include some common practice and contemporary classical music, but only where it is resonant and meaningful to singers and listeners.

Choral singing will only have maximum impact in the world if it truly embraces all styles of music in its programming, its approach to the voice, and its teaching. It is long overdue that we clear away outdated assumptions about the absolute value of classical music and its associated ways of singing and presenting concerts. High-level and low-level singing exist in every style, as does good and poor storytelling. You can "say something" without necessarily being "excellent." Level and function are not the same thing. Tastes change, and we should be able to sing whatever we like, wherever we like, as long as we do it well. If classical music is so great (and I believe it often is), it can surely compete with other music in a stylistically open world. Choral quality and musical style are different things, and you can find well (and poorly) written choral material in any style.

It seems like common sense to say that all music is equally valuable as long as it is good. This was certainly Duke Ellington's view. Strangely, though, to integrate that seemingly simple principle of stylistic openness into choral singing turns out to be a radical proposition.

This Book

Choral singing, then, facilitates change by its very nature, and is also in need of change itself. It has the potential to transform, and is itself in need of transformation. Choral directors are change-makers, and the more change they make happen in the world through their work, the better choral directors they are. This book, then, proposes a paradigm shift, a rethinking of what counts as good choral music, why we do it, how we do it and what makes it good. It focuses on the radical power of choral singing to bring human beings together and change their lives in concrete ways. It proposes that choral leaders use that power every day persistently, for the good of their art form and for the good of society.

It asks, "What would a transformed choral singing look like, that started from this place of purpose?" It invites us to reimagine our entire artistic process, including the vocal sound that we aim for, our approach to rhythm and improvising, the way we teach, the themes we sing about, our programming strategies, our repertoire, our approach to rhythm, the way we present ourselves, the venues we sing in and the audiences we sing to. It demands a similar revolution in choral music education, and proposes a reimagining of the way a choral director leads and manages their group, and conceives of its music and the relationships that music generates. All these proposals stem from a single core idea, which is that we need a clearer, simpler definition of *why* we sing.

The scope of this book, then, is exceptionally wide. For that reason, it does not aim to be comprehensive. Also, while my writing is at times theoretical and is underpinned by scholarly perspectives, it also reflects my experience as a choral practitioner and educator who understands that books about choral singing need to be practical and useful. This is by no means a research text, nor is it quite a choral methods book, or an autobiography. Instead, containing elements of each, it argues for a new direction of travel.

Each of the following chapters takes the same format. An initial discussion is followed by a series of tried and tested workshops, suggestions and tips from my long experience working with choirs. My hope is that together, each chapter will provide you with both the theoretical tools and the practical techniques and strategies for embedding these principles into the artistic and social practices of your group. Both are in dialogue with stories from my personal experience as a choral director, which I hope will add color and illustrate the points made. In an attempt to keep the main text simple and clear, endnotes underpin and comment on the more theoretical ideas, and offer avenues for further reading, research, and practical exploration with your choir.

Taking a sociological approach, there are some key terms that I will be referring to throughout. First, I will be referring to the *musical practices* of choirs and choral directors (and at times *vocal practices*), by which I mean what they say and how they act in their music-making. This covers everything from repertoire choice and programming to vocal pedagogy, rehearsal technique, performance style, musical terms used, what singers wear, how they stand, and so on. I will also be referring to their *social practices*, which I am using here to refer to what singers, directors, musicians, and others say and do *around* their music-making, in, for example, the language they use and how they behave with each other.

Here then is a diagram (Figure 1.1) representing our four principles, and the two sets of practices through which they are implemented throughout this book:

The arrows indicate that I am treating the social practices and the musical practices of choral singing as linked and overlapping. While I acknowledge they are a separate domain, I am also treating the practices of teaching and learning as embedded in a choir's musical and social practices, so they are not separately noted here.

All four principles are implemented in every aspect of the work, but to differing extents. So, for example, the principle of social justice might be implemented in two overlapping ways in any choir—by singing anti-racist songs (musical practices) and by implementing a policy around its auditions that facilitate a wider range of ethnicities to be socially successful (social practices).

Chapter 2 starts from WHY we sing, and a set of workshops on how to develop an energized and relevant artistic and social mission for your group, that will revitalize your art and help you define your purpose clearly. There is also help on your choir's artistic strategy. Then we move on to HOW we sing. To perform in a range of styles and create entertaining, compelling, and inclusive shows, choirs need access to a more stylistically flexible sound palette. Singing one style using only one set of vocal colors is like only driving your car in second gear. It is possible, but fewer people will join you, you won't get very far, and you are missing out on massive potential to visit many more destinations, and so have more musical impact. The chapters on HOW we sing cover three areas: first, sound and vocal production (Chapter 3); second, groove-based choral singing (Chapter 4); and third, vocal improvising (Chapter 5).

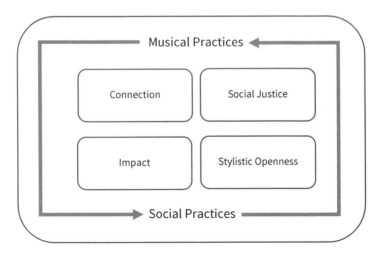

Figure 1.1 Four principles.

Chapter 6 focuses on programming as the engine for artistic and social innovation and change, while Chapter 7 covers the pedagogical specifics of teaching and learning in rehearsal.

Best practice choral singing does not occur in a social vacuum, and as the book continues, the social practices of choral singing are increasingly foregrounded. We turn in Chapter 8 to the challenges of conducting and leading a stylistically open group, while Chapter 9 offers specific strategies for managing your group as an equitable and inclusive musical community whose social practices articulate principles of social justice. We finish with Chapters 10 and 11, which draw together the various strands from earlier. Chapter 10 defines a new activist vision for what choral singing could be, and explores the concept of the activist choral director. Chapter 11 closes the book by returning to our four principles and proposing a series of concrete calls to action. These are things you can do tomorrow to improve your choir's current work.

At this stage, you may not yet be convinced that change is what choral singing is about. Even so, read on, because I am sure you would at least agree that choral singing has huge power and is vitally important to society. The ultimate goal of this book is to support the creation of more successful choirs. These choirs understand better why they sing, the purpose and potential of singing, and how to do it really well in today's world.

So, follow me on this journey back to the fundamentals of choral singing. My hope is that you will be inspired and perhaps challenged, cast off a number of old ideas about what choral singing is for, and emerge freed, refreshed, and stimulated. My aim is to equip you with a new rationale for what choral directors do, and to give you the practical tools to implement that rationale, so that your choir can sing better and do more good in the world.

Notes

1. For more on "bonds" through choral singing, see also Pearce, Launay, and Dunbar (2015) and Suttie (2015). Dafydd Evans's article on the Trelawnyd Male Voice Choir in Flintshire, Wales, talks movingly about the "very special bond" singing produces in Welsh male voice choirs. As the father of one singer puts it: "It's an incredible community—a community of men who have a way of looking after each other and the challenge that one has when going into old age. . . . These are very emotional songs, and I think there's . . . a real power in these men singing about beautiful things."
2. Harvey (2016) states: "Local authority investment in arts/culture has declined by £236 million, 17 percent since 2010. While English local government still spent £1.2 billion on arts and culture in 2014/15, the cuts remain significant and are likely to continue. London boroughs saw the largest cuts in arts and culture spending; 19 percent between 2010 and 2015."
3. For more on the decline of US music education, see Burrack, Payne, Bazan, and Hellman (2014).
4. For more on the decline of UK music education in schools, see Bath, Daubney, Mackrill, and Spruce (2020).
5. Beaumont-Thomas (2020).

22 Transforming Choral Singing

6. Such connection can occur in all styles. For example, in a memorable Boston Philharmonic master class with a violin student playing Saint Saens, Ben Zander points to a smiling audience member and entreats his technically brilliant student, "Your job is to light up his face ([timestamp] 10:30). . . . Never play from the fingers. . . . Use your violin to communicate with *people*" ([timestamp] 20:32) (Zander, 2015).

7. Osman, Tischler, and Schneider (2016).

8. Sloboda (2010: 493–514) has shown in his psychological research how his subjects achieve "synchronization," a sense of belonging and shared values, for example in aerobics classes.

9. In Stone-Davis's (2015) groundbreaking study of music and transcendence, she discusses the capacity of music for "world-making," which she defines as "attempts to make sense of the human person, the environment in which she is situated, and the environment between the two" (126). Music "can be understood as a border or liminal practice due to its reliance upon thresholds" (129).

10. A great example of a choral conductor whose mission is around community building and cultural development is Hussein Janmohamed, cofounder of the Vancouver and Canadian Ismaili Muslim Youth Choirs. One of the most thorough and nuanced examinations of community building through music is the UK-based community music project report by McKay and Higham (2017), which covers artistic practice, repertoire, community, pedagogy, digital technology, health, and therapy. The report also explores community music policy and funding, and what impact looks like in the field.

11. Collins (2005): 5.

12. Hesmondhalgh (2013) argues that music encodes human emotion (12), discusses music's power for "self-realization" (21) and related ideas of sexuality, sex, gender, sexual desire, and what he calls "vulnerable needs for attachment." He also suggests music, and in particular "funk" can lead to the "healthy integration of different aspects of our being" (53).

13. Roderick Williams (2017) says that when one sings, one is also losing oneself to some extent, almost as if choir members blend in to one massive creature.

14. Throughout, this book draws on the ideas of Higgins et al. (2012), working in the fertile and burgeoning domain of community music, and in particular his influential concept of "musicking."

15. Prtoric (2016).

16. For more on Hanoi's unique Diversity Choir, which welcomes and celebrates all genders, all races, all ages, all sexualities, and all backgrounds, see Nhan Dan Online (2019).

17. https://choirchoirchoir.com/.

18. The Zimmers were one of the UK's first choirs advocating for older people, appearing in *Britain's Got Talent* in 2012, and in a famous YouTube clip, singing The Who's "My Generation" https://www.youtube.com/watch?v=zqfFrCUrEbY. For more elders' choirs and choruses, see also the New Dementians from Burnaby, British Columbia, and the Silvertones Senior Choir, Fort Collins, Colorado.

19. Youth Music (2017).

20. de Botton and Armstrong (2013).

21. Crossick and Krasynska (2016).

22. See, for example, Gersema (2016), and the UK organization Sing Up's great work applying their concept by integrating choral singing into every aspect of the UK's primary curriculum, from songs about "Chocolate" and "People of the Past" to "Buildings" and "Resilience."

23. See Barbara McAfee (2015).

24. Osman, Tischler, and Schneider (2016).

25. If you are interested in starting your own "Singing for the Brain" group, this link may help: https://www.alzheimers.org.uk/get-support/your-support-services/singing-for-the-brain.

26. Big Heath is an example of a 2021 UK rapper singer who has used rap and singing to overcome a stutter, and in the process achieved commercial success as a performer. See YouTube clip (2020) *Big Heath: Role Models (Official video)*. See also Wilson (2013) on the Stuttering Foundation website.

27. Menehan (2014).
28. For more on what music is for, Hesmondhalgh (2013) and Small (1996) are classic starting points. Hesmondhalgh's discussion of the function of aesthetic experience in modern life is grounded in his "complete theory of musical value" (16). This stresses the way in which music is the expression of both self-identity and collective identity. He critiques Bourdieu's view of high culture as intrinsically more valuable. He was also an early arguer of the relationship between culture, society, and power relations, and powerfully points out how inequality infects prevailing judgments of aesthetic worth in musical texts.
29. Francisco Núñez 2022.
30. Trecek-King 2012.
31. According to career statistics website Zippia, 82.8 percent of choral directors are white, 6.1 percent are of Hispanic descent or Latinx, and 5.1 percent are African American; 60 percent are over forty, 27 percent are thirty to forty, and 13 percent are twenty to thirty years old. In better news, women make up just over 50 percent of choral directors, according to NewMusicUSA.org (Siadat, 2020), though that number is skewed toward youth choirs and K–12 school directors.
32. This is according to the University of New Hampshire's Institute on Disability's 2018 *Annual Report on People with Disabilities in America*.
33. This is according to the UCLA Williams Institute School of Law.
34. Nina Simon's transforming work at the Museum of Santa Cruz shows how best practice integration of DEI work can lead directly to the re-engagement of audiences. Her organization created innovative exhibits that are grown organically from communities that would not previously have seen museums as relevant to them. See Simon (2016) and her 2016 TED Talk, on how to apply this model to other artistic practices. Her new nonprofit OF/BY/FOR ALL aims to embed change into the artistic and social practices of all kinds of arts organizations.
35. Tucker (1995): 326.
36. See Peretz, Cummings, and Dubé's (2007) fertile work on the genetics of tone deafness, for example.
37. Goodkin (2013) is especially eloquent on the curious distinction between being "a musician," being "musical," and "liking music."
38. Kat (2014).
39. In *Who Needs Classical Music*, Johnson (2002), for example, explicitly argues for the intrinsic meaning of "the music itself," and states, "Its claim to function as art derives from its peculiar concern with its own materials and their formal patterning, aside from any considerations about its audience or its social use." (3).
40. Ted Gioia's *The History of Jazz* (1997) is excellent on Duke Ellington's contribution to twentieth-century harmony, and the accomplished use of complex and dissonant musical materials by many jazz composers, improvisers, and performers. Likewise arranging and orchestration analysis books including Wright's *Inside the Score* (1982) goes through scores by Thad Jones and others, note by note, identifying all kinds of nuance.
41. Lucy Green's (2008) thinking on "inherent" and "delineated" musical meaning is one of the most coherent deep dives into how music is encoded and decoded, and so acquires meaning, both in artistic practice and in education.
42. There is a vast literature now on the aesthetics, analysis, and sociology of popular music, including 1980s subculture analysis (Hebdige, 1979) and 1990s post-structuralism and semiotic theory (Middleton, 1990; Shuker, 1994; Frith, 1996). All place the idea of "absolute" or "intrinsic" musical worth firmly in a social context, and further undermine any sense of the primacy of one particular musical style or approach.
43. For example, check out the Associated Board of the Royal Schools of Music's jazz grades.
44. Recent work by the UK-based "Equity, Diversity, and Inclusion in Music Studies" group is exposing how pathways into college-level music education exclude minority groups, and those who lack the

24　Transforming Choral Singing

classical-music-based keys to acceptance. https://www.edimusicstudies.com/?fbclid=IwAR0M_8ug48zKHRV53_6gcpGIKFzG_tGPLci_J4B216q3Y3z_u93dI_X2dsA.

45. Karin S. Hendricks in Talbot (2018) powerfully identifies issues of access and marginalization in music education: "The difficulty comes when a community of practice holds to rigid inflexible boundaries and does not readily honor the legitimacy of newcomers' skills and ideas and the boundary objects they bring with them" (68).

46. Roy Shuker (1994), writing before the advent of social media, already identifies the disempowering effect of the clear division between producers, mediators, and listeners in our commodified musical culture.

47. Grazia's 2013 study of nineteenth-century choral music, for example, includes oratorio choral-orchestral "masterworks" of Beethoven, Mendelssohn, Schumann, Bruckner, Brahms, Berlioz, Saint-Saëns, and Faure, still staples today.

48. Ethnomusicologist Mark Slobin's *Subcultural Sounds: Micromusics of the West* (1993) is an excellent start for the discussion of the more separated relationship between music and place, globalization, and the modern development of musical subcultures like K-pop and Bollywood, which has since burgeoned with the arrival of social media.

49. One such is the LA-based Outqueerapp community of fifteen non-binary and transgender musicians, that includes Anohni, previously Antony from Antony and the Johnsons, and Shea Diamond, who wrote the prize-winning "I Am America." https://www.outqueerapp.com/post/15-non-binary-transgender-musicians

50. Forbes (2001) is a wide-ranging survey on the breadth of repertoire being used by US high school choral directors, and their attitudes to its educational worth. In his 1998 PhD thesis, he concludes: "There is serious concern among directors regarding the perceived proliferation of choral programs that focus on the performance of popular music, much of which is in their estimation of poor quality and not well suited for the development of fundamental vocal skills." (154)

51. This recent Facebook post from a disgruntled choral director on the "I'm a Choral Director" Facebook Group (name, date, and time anonymized) sums up the frustration of many trained in a style that simply will not sit with many students: "I'm at a loss for words. And I'm sure I'm not the only one who has dealt with this. I'm at a new school teaching K–12 everything. For the longest time (like more than ten years) choir has been neglected by previous music teachers mostly focusing on band. I have kids saying, 'Why can't we sing in English,' 'Why can't we sing what's on the radio,' 'I don't like this,' and so on. I have been looking at two-part (that's where they are at) arrangements for popular music. I even chose 'Plaudit' by Victor Johnson (because I like it and I thought they would too, but it's 'not in English') and I can barely hear those singing in Part 2. Like I am probably only hearing two people in that part singing. I can hear Part 1 plain as day, but hardly Part 2 and it's pretty well balanced. My administration is very supportive and so is the community, but I am pulling teeth to get these kids to sing."

2
Defining Your Purpose

As choral directors, facilitating singing is important. It fulfills us and is central to who we are. We care about it passionately, or we would not do what we do. Let's call the reasons why we personally do direct choirs our personal purpose.

The focus of this chapter is related but slightly different. It is the larger purpose of the group you direct. Here I suggest that this larger purpose will be a unique articulation of the four principles from the previous chapter, specific to your particular choir. Defining your group's purpose could not be more crucial, because it will help you identify your goals. From those goals then emerges the music itself: what styles your choir should sing in; how you might teach in rehearsal; how you should lead as a conductor; where you should sing, who to, and so on. Your musical practices, then, follow on from your purpose, and are the means by which you achieve those goals.

Community Ecosystems

Your group may be in a sense independent, but it will also sit within a particular context, like a school, a college, or a community of faith. It may also be a community choir of another kind. Whatever its context, your group is embedded in what I am calling throughout this book a "community ecosystem." That community ecosystem is essentially a fertile and fluid network of relationships, which are energized and articulated through your musical and social practices. These relationships extend out from your group's activities in rings, from your artistic core via your closer community to your wider stakeholders. It is hard to cover all such relationships in a single diagram, but your community ecosystem might look something like the diagram below.

A choir's purpose can vary but it will always emerge from this network of relationships. A high school or college choir can have many purposes. It might function as the public face of their educational organization, for example. It could say things to wider stakeholders about what that school is good at, and what its values are. It could also create connection for its LGBTQIA+ youth, and provide them with a safe space or a tool with which to express themselves and the opportunity to find their voices. Meanwhile, a college choir might function primarily as a beacon of musical excellence. It could exist so that its singers can demonstrate particular skills and knowledge. Yet such groups are often tightly bonded communities too, perhaps rehearsing intensively for the goal of winning competitions, and this can also be their purpose. In a community of faith, perhaps a synagogue or

Transforming Choral Singing. Charles W. Beale, Oxford University Press. © Oxford University Press 2024.
DOI: 10.1093/oso/9780197657775.003.0002

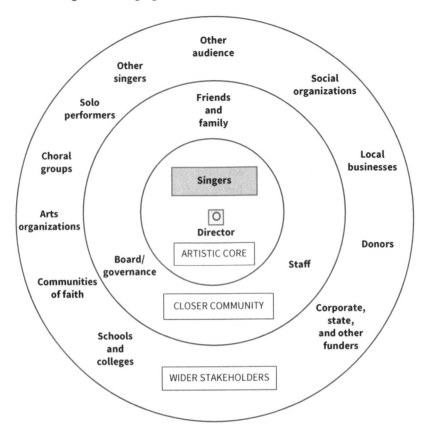

Figure 2.1 Community ecosystem.

Christian church, a choir can function by providing connection for its congregation. Sometimes, as with gospel choirs, faith communities and ethnic communities overlap. A choir's purpose can be saying something about who that faith community is to the wider world.

Whatever its configuration, your group's purpose will be complex, and will always relate to its community ecosystem. It is important to identify who your singers, your listeners, and the various communities and stakeholders that surround your choir are. Once you know where they come from, their skills, culture, and values, you can begin to define the relationship that your choir's musical work enables with them. What do you want to say *to* them, or express *about* them in your music-making? Are you stretching their artistic boundaries, for example, or bringing them the music they most relate to? Are you connecting them as a community, and if so how and in what way? Are you advocating for their lives, expressing their values, and telling their stories? Perhaps you are singing about an ideal world of some kind. If so, which stories are the ones to tell today, and which social issues are the most important to be advocating for right now? Answers to all of these questions will help you define your group's purpose, and so enable its musical and social impact.

Vision, Mission, and Values

In what follows, I use the term "mission" as shorthand, to point to three interrelated but distinct areas—vision, mission, and values. We often associate these terms primarily with corporate contexts, but they work just as well in the arts. All three are key to your choir's purpose. Let's take each in turn:

VISION   Your *vision* is your group's dream, aspiration, ultimate destination. It articulates the kind of new world your choir is singing about and trying to create. Your singing is bound to be about changing something, so think of your vision as the conditions or environment that are so changed that your work is no longer needed. You will need to achieve this new world through making an impact of some kind.

MISSION   Your *mission* is what drives you and your community every day to achieve your vision. It is the reason you exist, defines your core activity, and frames your everyday decision-making. As a choir, singing will almost certainly be part of your mission, because it is what Jim Collins calls your "output"—the means by which you achieve what you set out to do.

VALUES   Your *values* define the common set of beliefs that you use to guide your decision-making. As a choir, your values are expressed in two main ways—through your group's culture, language, and behavior, and through the music you create.

All three define your uniqueness, and a clear statement of each will help you articulate what your group is uniquely attempting to do within its community ecosystem. They will enable you to focus with clarity, define your goals, and assess whether you are being successful.

What follows is a series of six workshops. The first four cover your choir's vision, mission, and values, and the final two provide starting points for developing an artistic strategy that aligns with that mission.

All should be done collectively by your *key group*, who are the ten to fifteen leaders who will define the mission itself. This group is likely to include your artistic core: you as choral director, other artistic team members, and several singers. Depending on your context, it should also include a selection from your executive team, if you have one; administrators, school department heads, or music educator colleagues; your pastor and/or worship team; and a selection of volunteers, budget holders, donors, fundraisers, and senior managers. Audience or congregation members are also likely to be there.

Your key group will assess the initial data they find, and then look outward to consult people in the outer rings of your community ecosystem. They may return to them for more information and feedback a second, third, or fourth time, as they refine their

28 Transforming Choral Singing

core statements. Some of these wider stakeholders will only be involved early in the process, or later in it. Their perspectives will eventually contribute to what your group's mission is, what it stands for, and its future artistic strategy.

Before we dive in to the workshops, here are some pointers to help you tailor your process. First, you and your artistic team need to be part of your key group. Some managers or boards of nonprofit choirs see making art as merely a "program" of their organization, and may even decide what their mission is without consulting their choir, its leaders, or its singers at all. This is a huge mistake. It is unlikely that a company that manufactured cars or delivered health care would agree on its mission without consulting its car makers or doctors. You and your choir's singers embody and deliver your choir's mission and purpose, and are the most passionate about it. You know what goes on, what works, and what is possible. You are not the only contributors, but without you, there is no output.

Second, do not neglect outside perceptions. What we intend internally is clear to us, but outsiders can have a clearer view of our real impact, our community, and our brand. Their perspective can differ from ours in fascinating ways. Your key group needs to understand not only what *they* think you do, but also what *others* think you do too. We can become too immersed in the intimate detail of our singing, our own personal musical journey, or the politics of the individual singers in front of us. That said, outsider views can be informed by inaccurate or outdated information, but this makes them no less valuable.

Workshops

Workshop 1: The Memorable and the Meaningful (90 minutes)

What do you believe your choir's singing achieves in the world? If it makes listeners go, "Ah, that was lovely," or "That was musically ground-breaking," you have made a good start. But remember your social impact too. This workshop is designed to help you unearth *all* of your transforming work.

So how exactly *should* you define the full impact of your choir's singing? In all the following tasks, be specific, and focus on your uniqueness. This workshop can function as an ice-breaker, but it can also reveal valuable insights. Allow it to take up time, if it feels fruitful. Also allow space for emotions as well as facts. With one choir I worked with, this task made the group very tearful at one point, and at another very joyful. Such examples of strong emotion often reveal the reality of your impact, and the goals your group is passionate about.

1) **The memorable (30 minutes):** Divide into smaller groups of four to five people. Ask each member of that smaller group to think silently for two minutes. Then ask them each to share a story about a single moment in their time with the

choir that was especially *memorable*, meaning a moment they remember because it stood out. Stories can be funny, sad, compelling, or insightful, but they should always be personal. If possible and only with permission, write those stories down, or record the session.

2) **The meaningful (30 minutes):** The second task also involves the smaller groups thinking silently first. This time, each should share a story about an especially *meaningful* moment in their time with your choir in terms of the outside world, perhaps a moment where a change happened for an audience, or an experience went very deep for another individual or the whole group.

3) **General discussion (30 minutes):** All return to the plenary group. Share your best stories. Consider what these stories show about the impact of your group on its members and on the world. On a whiteboard or digital display, make a list of keywords and phrases describing that impact. Was connection also enabled in some way? Note that too.

Workshop 2: What Does Your Singing Do in the World? (90 minutes)

Figures 2.2 through 2.5 show a long list of common reasons why people sing. The reasons, in bullet points, are organized into four *clusters*, with numbered follow-up questions relating to each cluster. Prepare each cluster of reasons with its follow-up questions, on a separate slide or sheet of paper.

Divide into small groups of four to six people, at least one group per cluster. Each group has two initial activities, which together should take around forty-five minutes:

1) **Rate each reason:** First, go through your cluster of reasons. Each member should rate the value to them personally of each reason. Use a scale where 1 is "totally unimportant," and 5 is "life-changingly important."

2) **Decide which reasons are most important:** Go around the group, and say which reasons are the most important for each of you, and why.

3) **Discuss follow-up questions:** Now, in a further forty-five-minute plenary session, feed your reasons back to the whole group, and hear the reasons of others on the other clusters. As with "meaningful and memorable" in Workshop 1, collect them all, perhaps on a whiteboard or, if virtual, on a digital display that all can see. Is there consensus around what is important about what you do, and why you do it? If so, agree it. If not, keep talking, and begin to tease out complexity.

Discussion

I identified the following four clusters of reasons after discussions over many years with singers across several choirs. Few would agree with every reason, but most

30 Transforming Choral Singing

> **CLUSTER 1: SINGING ITSELF IS VALUABLE**
>
> - We sing because we love to sing.
> - Our ensemble exists to improve the singing skills of our members.
> - We sing because singing is important in the world.
>
> Follow-up questions:
>
> 1) Why do you personally love to sing in the group?
> 2) What skills do you enjoy most to learn in this group?
> 3) Identify the contribution you think that singing in your group makes to the world. How does your group uniquely make that contribution?

Figure 2.2

> **CLUSTER 2: THE ART OF SINGING IS VALUABLE**
>
> - We sing because we love this repertoire and this way of singing, and we want to celebrate and perpetuate it.
> - We sing because it is important to tell untold stories about our community's lives and experiences.
> - We sing to grow in our singing knowledge, and learn more about the art of singing.
> - We sing to feel empowered, and to show who we are inside to the outside world.
> - We sing because beauty of all kinds is important in the world.
>
> Follow-up questions:
>
> 1) What is special about this repertoire? What stories does it tell? Why is it important to sing it? How does the material you love relate to your life experience?
> 2) What is unique about the way your group sings? Perhaps its blend, placement, sound, approach to singing, or the voice?
> 3) How have you personally grown as a group in the last few years? How have you seen others grow? How has the whole group grown? What have you learned by being in the group?

Figure 2.3

CLUSTER 3: CONNECTION IS VALUABLE

- We sing to find new friends and maintain friendships with those who are most important to us.
- We sing to find our tribe, to be in a group of like-minded people, and to sing to others like us.
- We sing to grow, to heal ourselves, and potentially to heal others.
- We sing to engage, and to participate in our community.

Follow-up questions:

1) Who has met a new friend through the group, that has grown to be really important in your life? Who has had a lot of friendships in the group over the years? Any married couples or partnerships in the group? Share what has made those friendships special.

2) Who has met someone who unexpectedly helped them, or taught them something they didn't already know?

3) In life, we all have struggles as individuals—perhaps a bereavement or an addiction. Have there been times where singing with the group has helped you or others heal?

4) What, and perhaps who, inspires you to sing with the group? Who are the leaders that motivate you? Also identify other people, activities, or factors that engage you.

5) Do you enjoy the teamwork and bonding of being in a choir or chorus? Say more.

Figure 2.4

32 Transforming Choral Singing

CLUSTER 4: SOCIAL AND POLITICAL CHANGE IS NEEDED

- Singing makes us feel free, and likewise frees our listeners.
- We sing because we believe in something. Share how what you believe in is expressed uniquely in your group's activities.
- We sing to empower a less privileged group, and to create a strong community who can support each other with the basic necessities of life.
- We sing to fight for equal rights for a community. If so, who are they, and what brings them together?
- We sing to change hearts and minds about an issue. What is the issue?

Follow-up questions:

1) Why are the beliefs and values you expressed above important in your group? How do they express themselves in your group currently? How successful do you feel you are at expressing those values?

2) What groups and causes have you sung for in recent years? Identify who it would be important to sing to. Why?

3) What opportunities are there nearby to connect with new groups and demographics, who might be interested to join with you and enhance your mission?

4) Pinpoint the social change that you want brought about by singing.

Figure 2.5

would agree with more than one. Singers' reasons for singing can also change over time. Some begin with loving to sing for its own sake, and later find good friends and a social life. Others do the same, and then decide to sing in order to change the lives of others. Still more arrive lonely and needing community. They find it, and five years later want to improve their singing and get lessons. Others arrive as activists first and foremost, and then discover others with broader interests too.

After these first two workshops, you should be armed with a rich array of stories about your connection and impact, and be able to distill from them key reasons your choir exists, and the specific configuration of social and musical changes it aims to achieve. These will inform the first draft of your mission, vision, and values.

Defining Your Purpose   **33**

Workshop 3: Ends and Means, and Three Case Study Choirs (2 hours)

This workshop contains two tasks. In each, your group should first read the text, and then discuss what your group's vision, mission, and values might have in common with the characteristics outlined. The text is intended to provoke strong responses that will help you define your uniqueness. Answers will vary widely from choir to choir, and you may find characteristics here that you strongly align with, alongside others that you utterly reject.

1) **TASK 1: Ends and means (1 hour):** All silently read both the following two accounts of different choirs, A and B. Identify what your group's vision, mission, and values have in common with each of the two accounts given.

CHOIR A   Our music is an end in itself

Choir A sees their mission as grounded exclusively in their singing: their music is an end in itself. They see singers and choral directors as working in the world of making music. Their key achievements in both rehearsal and performance therefore relate only to music-making. "We sang this piece for the first time," they will say; or perhaps, "We are exponents of this particular way of singing, and we do it really well"; or "The audience really loved the Barber." They might define their vision, mission, and values something like this:

> *Our mission is to sing [this repertoire, jazz, classical music, gospel music, barbershop, a cappella, oratorio] in [these venues] in a group of [this number of singers] really well. Our values are that we believe there should be more of [this music] in the world, and we believe it should be sung [this way]. Our goal is to make ourselves feel good by singing it, and we hope our audience will enjoy it too. We uphold or plan to facilitate the growth of [a particular musical tradition]. Our vision is that others who don't know about [this tradition] should know about it, and enjoy it like we do.*

CHOIR B   Our music is a means to an end

Choir B see their music-making exclusively as the means by which they achieve other goals. Those goals are around people and relationships. It doesn't really matter exactly what they sing, as long as their music has impact because it "moves" people. Their artistic discussions tend to be less about music, vocal sound, and repertoire, and more about who they want to "move," and what their shows should be "about." They define their vision, mission, and values something like this:

Our mission is to use singing to [right the wrong of this issue, e.g., empowerment of older people, building bridges, reducing conflict, fighting for the rights of our community or a marginalized group]. Our vision is about a world free from [whatever this issue is] or a world that is socially equal, or where [this community, group of people] are more powerful, integrated, unified, or bonded. Our values are around [righting that wrong]. Singing is the perfect way to achieve this because the experience of singing can [empower, heal, celebrate, educate, cleanse the mind, bring people to a new spiritual place, allow space for reflection, create social change].

Discussion

Where does your own choir's mission sit in relation to these two? Most choirs will decide that theirs lies somewhere between the two accounts given here. Neither is perfect. In fact, the two are interdependent. You can't achieve social change as a choir unless you sound good, nor is any choir's singing entirely independent of connecting with people, and changing their perceptions and behavior in some way. Teasing out exactly what that looks like for you is the task.

All choirs grapple with both definitions, and lack of clarity around them often causes tension. It may sound familiar if I say that in many choirs, there is division between one set of singers that wants to simply "sing better," and another that are in it more for the social aspects, or for the cause that the group stands for. In my view, most choirs should examine their impact through both lenses.

Choir A's is an honorable if old-fashioned position. It assumes that there is no need to argue for the value of the music they sing. I beg to differ. In the 2020s, no one can take the value of their particular music for granted. All choirs need to feel a level of urgency about the work they do, and will do better work if they feel that urgency, advocate for that music, and focus on what they believe is important.

Also, groups like Choir A tend to feel that any community connection they generate is welcome extra positive energy, but is not a core reason why they exist. As a result, they sometimes see their work as having much less social impact than it actually has. They could add language to their mission to the effect that their work will also create community around some shared values. Their challenge is to identify what those hitherto ignored values are, and to articulate explicitly who they are in fact reaching out to, and whether they could broaden that reach.

Choir B's approach is also narrow. They see themselves solely as working toward a social or political goal, which they could be doing almost without singing. Their challenge is to remind themselves that their product is choral music, and the better (and more apt) their musical output is, the better they will be able to achieve that goal. Even if music-making is primarily the means rather than the end, their artistic values should be clearly articulated. They should add language about what music they sing and why. It should stress their values as they are expressed in their musical practices; for example, their singers, whatever barriers they face, need to sing well, show up to rehearsal, practice hard, and sing with precision, professionalism, and joy. How exactly those things are defined can vary enormously. But when their artistic engine runs faster and more efficiently, their social impact and ability to connect people will also deepen.

2) **TASK 2: Three cases (1 hour):** As before, all participants should silently read the following text, concerning three fictional choirs. This time, each of the three has some strengths, and each also has some issues that need to be addressed. The task is to identify what your own group has in common with each of the three choirs. It will probably have a little in common with each.

Choir 1: All about the music

The choral director LOVES a particular style of music and believes passionately in it. Although no one's perfect, she is good at her job, inspiring, musically competent, well organized, and good with people. The whole group trusts her, and the choir is known for singing that repertoire. They sound good, and the choir attracts good singers who want to sing in that style.

There are, however, not that many of them, nor is the audience for that music huge in their city. Their marketing team is struggling to come up with a new approach that will attract and inspire new audiences. Choir managers are concerned about widening their appeal. As they explore expanding their group and audience, the options that emerge are mainly around "reaching out" or changing what style of music is performed, to somehow broaden that appeal. The director, unaware of the social impact her work is having in creating community, is proud of the great musical work she feels they do. She is unwilling to change. There is conflict, she feels underappreciated, loses hope, and is eventually fired.

Choir 2: All about people

This choir aims to do impactful shows that make people laugh and cry. It attracts a large group of singers, and prides itself on doing "amazing" work in the community. Repertoire is chosen mainly by an elected group of members who like Madonna, Beyoncé, and Stephen Sondheim very much. The singers love this material too. They honestly believe they will bring people together into a community without boundaries, and they congratulate themselves that they have had some success. In the distant past, they had an important role, often in singing to mourn those who had died of HIV/ AIDS. But now modern treatments have made HIV/AIDS a more manageable disease. The singers continue to refer to this role because it means a lot to them, but for their listeners, this simply associates them with the past, like a Broadway show everyone saw in the '90s. They have an audience that extends out beyond their friends and family, but it is 60 to 70 percent based in people they know, who do indeed cry when they come to see their friends express themselves on stage.

Unfortunately, those outside the group will also tell you in private that they don't sound good at all. They don't have the heart to tell the group this. Their shows feel outdated, narrow, and self-indulgent, though the group are clearly enjoying themselves,

36 Transforming Choral Singing

and so feel that enjoyment to be infectious. Their suffering servant choral director knows the truth, but his job involves facilitating the group, so he does what he can; he shrugs his shoulders and grits his teeth. The group's lack of musical innovation and artistic craft will prevent them from ever having the deeper impact they want.

Choir 3: Gradual decline
This choir has been around for a long time. It is musically excellent though not outstanding, and initially had a large, dedicated audience. They feel they have a legacy to protect and are proud of their traditions. They sing the same core repertoire over and over. However, over time ticket sales have been gradually declining. Ninety percent of the choir and audience are over forty and mainly white. They see themselves as doing a good job, and are smart enough to be genuinely puzzled by what is happening to them. They have not yet hit a brick wall, but fear they will within a few years, as two-thirds of their concerts are not making money. They rely exclusively on a couple of rich donors, the PTA, and Christmas to keep themselves solvent.

Discussion
These examples are designed to provoke your thoughts, but they grow from the lived experience of my colleagues and me. Do you recognize any features of your own choir in the ones above? Do you perhaps see and hear resonances in your own audience's behavior or privately expressed feelings?

All three choirs require mission-based solutions. As before, one set of solutions is around the social impact that music-making has, and another is around the music-making itself.

Social practices: Let's take community ecosystem solutions first. Music-making is all about people, and here, principles of social justice apply around, for example, age, intergenerationality, and race. Case 2 is a great example of how choirs are groups, with group dynamics. Once a certain subgroup becomes established within a choir community, their ideas and social norms can become dominant. Even if that subgroup says the choir is welcoming, it can still be unconsciously excluding all kinds of people, and failing to move forward. Principles of equity require a proactive approach, so change is always ongoing.

Case 3 needs an intentional injection of younger people, which will take five to ten years to bring about. It also needs a cold, hard look at its attitudes toward race. In particular it needs to work out why non-white singers who like the repertoire it currently sings are not joining. Again, perhaps its initial welcome to singers is really only welcoming to one kind of person. Or only some feel engaged, so only people of a certain ethnicity or people of a certain age tend to end up in leadership roles. Choirs always generate belonging, but sometimes only certain people within a core group feel they truly belong. Social justice, then, remains important, and where this principle is consistently applied, your community ecosystem will continually refresh and re-energize.

Defining Your Purpose   37

Musical practices: Another set of solutions relates to music-making. We all love to perform, but however committed we are to changing the world or making it more equitable, it is no fun performing to empty halls, nor is it good business. To achieve our largest and most receptive audience, we need to program to ensure everyone in our community ecosystem can engage in what we do. If a choir sings a narrow repertoire that only one age group or cultural group knows and finds meaningful, then it will tend only to attract a narrow group of singers and audience members to its work. So if your group is to have the deepest impact and connect with the widest audience, it needs to define its musical purpose, and then sing the material that will impact the widest possible range of people. Stylistic openness leads to flexibility, and again can keep your group's artistic work fresh.

One message becomes clear overall. Your group's musical and social practices do not occur in a vacuum. Instead, they function within a community ecosystem, with its own networks of relationships and its own values. If the community that surrounds your choir finds your what you are singing about irrelevant or boring, your connection and impact will reduce. However, if your singing aligns with what people around you feel, and is memorable and meaningful to them musically and socially, you will connect with more singers and listeners, and your impact will deepen and widen.

Workshop 4: Creating Purpose: Your Choir's Vision, Mission, and Values (3 hours)

To create a first draft of your mission, vision, and values, convene a separate meeting after you have had time to process the results of the previous three workshops. Three activities follow. Do them in order, either in one long retreat lasting at least half a day, or over several occasions.

1) **Agree definitions of key terms:** Refer back to our earlier definitions of "vision," "mission," and "values," and review them with the group.
2) **Organize your content:** On three whiteboards or digital displays, create headings for each of the three concepts, and organize the content you created under those three headings.
3) **Generate language:** Now start work on the language itself, generating concise statements that gather and summarize your conclusions under each heading. Use precise language. These guidelines may help:
   a) **Vision:** To start on your vision, workshop your ideas by beginning a sentence with: "A world where [something happens] . . .," or "A world where [people act or feel in certain ways] . . . ." Start from the premise that you are aiming to create a changed world that is in some way different than the current one. Perhaps your new world may contain more or better artistic activity than before, or be a place where people behave differently toward

38   Transforming Choral Singing

each other in some way. Art can also be the means by which your vision is accomplished; whatever that world looks like, it will happen "through art." Paradoxically, some groups will therefore hardly mention art at all in their vision statements.

b) **Mission:** Your mission starts from what you do, often singing, so begin by simply describing it. For choirs, "We sing" is one way to start, though there are others. Next, say something qualitative in two to four words about how you uniquely deliver your output.

c) **Values:** Your values can seem a little opaque to begin with, but they underpin everything you do. Language around values can vary. Some organizations use single nouns like "kindness" or "reliability," and others use short descriptive phrases or statements. Try describing the most valuable features of your choir's culture. Next describe how those values are expressed. Focus on anything from how you greet each other on arrival, how you tell singers they did not make it into the choir, the repertoire you sing, the stories your art tells, or what you wear on stage.

Discussion

Do you already have a set of words that defines your choir's purpose? If not, creating some language will improve your focus. If you already have some, does it cover your social impact as well as your musical work? When was it last updated, and is it still relevant to today's more complex musical culture, and to your context economically, politically, post-COVID, and so on?

Vocabulary is all. At one stage, for example, my choir said its mission was to "sing fabulously." "Ab Fab" was a meme of the time, and in the word "fabulously," we tried to capture both the level of quality we were aiming for, and something about how entertaining, devil-may-care, and frankly gay we were. Words like "musical excellence" come up a lot in these statements, as does "best-in-class." Those aims were true for us, but those words didn't quite articulate our uniqueness. You also might want to define your musical purpose, perhaps as singing to preserve a certain repertoire, or to articulate the voice of certain group.

Suggestions and Tips

Refining your draft is the next part, and this is often harder than coming up with your initial language. This process can go on for many months, but you can also make progress in a few hours, over a couple of occasions. Whatever your time scale, go over and over these crucial statements. Below are some practical strategies and tips for refining what you already have:

1) **Schedule your wider consultations:** Plan time for consultation with stakeholders from your outer circle. Ask questions, and then listen hard. A neutral facilitator can help. After each consultation, return to your language, and modify it, adding what you learned.

Defining Your Purpose   39

2) **Refine your language over several iterations:** All creative processes benefit from returning to the task. So build iterations into your process, over a period of weeks or months, and set a deadline. A form of words should eventually coalesce that truly expresses your purpose. Eventually, there should be no lack of alignment on the main points within your key group. Where there are disagreements, discuss and resolve them.

3) **Consider scope:** Vision, mission, and values statements are only helpful if they can guide your everyday decision-making, so their scope is key. On the one hand, your statements need to be broad, so that if a new leadership takes over, your mission still applies. On the other, your statements will only be resonant if they express your specific uniqueness. For example, why might these mission statements be too broad?

We sing to change the world
Excellence in music

The first lacks a clear enough definition of what you are changing and why. If a gig comes up, your mission should enable you to say: "That's a great opportunity, but our mission relates to this community [or that repertoire]." Here, any gig might come in, and your mission wouldn't guide you. Likewise, the second lacks a specific repertoire focus, or any sense of what "excellence" means. When a donor suggests a particular piece to sing and offers to pay for it, your mission should enable you to say, "Many thanks for the offer, but a piece like this is not really what we do. How about this instead?"

Some other general qualities to aim for in your language:

- Be concise. Try saying your mission as a thirty-second elevator pitch.
- Mention exactly what you do.
- Be aspirational, but be realistic.

Workshop 5: Current Strengths and Weaknesses (2 hours)

These final two workshops begin the process of defining your artistic strategy, within which your group's musical work will sit. Where you are right now is the subject of Workshop 5. As you work from Workshop 5 to Workshop 6, you will begin to focus more on where you want to be in the future.

Again, consider carefully who should be involved. You may want to lead this workshop yourself, or ask others to facilitate the discussion, so you can participate. This could also be a closed session for artistic leaders only, and later findings can be shared more widely. Negativity and criticism around the artistic work can jaundice the process. It can be helpful to agree on honesty, authenticity, and mutual respect,

40 Transforming Choral Singing

an assumption of good intentions, and a constructive approach that lives in the solution.

1) **Video evaluation (30 minutes):** Choose at least one video of your group performing a single song, or a set lasting five to ten minutes. The whole workshop group should watch it together. Each member should note two kinds of observations: 1) anything they saw or heard that they thought was especially great or successful; and 2) anything they saw or heard that they felt needed improvement.

You can choose to leave this task there as fuel for later discussion, or discuss your observations then and there.

2) **Now, and in the future . . . (90 minutes):** Next, consider this set of questions one by one, which will require the group to be critical. They will help you distinguish between current strengths and weaknesses, and where you want to be in the future. Expect debate, and again keep discussion positive.

Group size: Are you currently a barbershop group of four, an a cappella group of ten plus a beatboxer, a community faith choir of sixty, or a massed chorus of three hundred? As that group, do you feel too small, too big, or just right?

Your singers now: Bearing in mind issues of data collection and privacy, it is vital to identify who your singers currently are. Likely categories are age, gender, ethnic mix, class, sexual orientation, voice part, and level of musicianship. Confidentiality is key. Be rigorously sensitive to the individuals concerned, and ensure they understand why the data is needed. Amongst your leadership team, ask yourselves who is *not* in your group, whom ideally you want more of. Also, there is the harder question of whom you have too many of. Are the voice parts balanced so you sound good? Is your group balanced and representative socially?

Next, imagine your ideal singers. What would be unique about them? What level of musicianship and vocal ability would they have? What personal qualities would be useful? What are their tastes and demographics? What sound do they make? Would they have a particular view of how the world should operate socially and politically? Who would you definitely exclude as "not a good fit," and why?

Audience: Who are your listeners currently, how many are there, and why do they come? What are their likely tastes, demographics, and political views? How does their worldview relate to those of your singers? Are you trying to convince your audience of something? Or are you assuming they are on the same page as you? To what extent are you hoping to be the voice of your community? Or are you reaching out to those beyond it? How successful are you currently at either of these goals?

Next, how big should your audience ideally be? What is the potential? Be realistic, but also be aspirational. What can you say about your audience's relationship with the music you sing? Why do they like it, or not like it, if that is the feedback? What do they care about? How much can they afford to pay for a ticket? If you have several shows in a year, do you get the same audience to each? What more do you need to know about them, to help you program, raise your ticket sales, and enable wider impact? Is there more than one kind of audience, or even several?

Sound: Is your group SSAA, SATB, TTBB, a variation of one of these conventional voicings, or something totally different? How is your sound currently? Identify the good, the bad, and the vocally ugly(!).

Next, what kind of vocal sound do you ideally envisage it making? Will you be aiming for a sweet, legato signature sound, a brasher and more belted tone, or perhaps a sound that is very authentic to your singers' speaking voices and musical level? Find and name some other choirs whose sound you aspire to. How flexible would you like your sound to be? Do you see yourselves as developing your singers' vocal skills at all, or do you simply accept where they are?

Venues: Think about location (city, rural, neighborhood), and the venue itself (church, theater, recording studio, on video). Where do you currently rehearse and perform, and why? Are you happy there? Is your venue the right size? Are the seats comfortable, and accessible to all? What about backstage and foyer areas? How is the sound? What about lighting and opportunities for media, projections, etc.? Do you sing unamplified or with a sound system? How important are the visual and theatrical aspects of your work? Is it expensive or reasonable? What is included, and what do you have to hire in? Does it feel full or half empty with your usual audience?

Next, look forward and assess your venue in relation to your mission. For example, if your mission is around homelessness, singing in a hall in an affluent area within an urban city might well get you a big audience of middle-class people, who believe in your cause and will donate more. Then again, if you want to "make a real difference," consider doing a partnership with the smaller, cheaper church in the less affluent area a few miles away, where the soup kitchen is. It might attract very different listeners, including some who themselves are experiencing homelessness.

Video: Since the COVID pandemic, many choirs are creating more video content, while some are conspicuously not. What about yours? What are the advantages and disadvantages, in terms of your connection and impact? What can you afford to do?

Next, how important could video be to your mission? How might that affect the length of a show, the amount of repertoire, how you rehearse, your costs, and your potential income? if your primary performances might be on video, this would also affect your workflow, the skills you need, how many singers you have, and how you present yourselves.

Repertoire choice: Is your repertoire currently high-art, low-art, from a specific choral tradition, or some kind of mixture? Perhaps you want to sing mainly in one style, but with occasional stylistic variety. Or do you aim to be truly eclectic? Whatever your aims, what has the reality been in the past few years?

42   Transforming Choral Singing

Next look forward. Consider the relationship between your mission and the songs you sing. Are you singing the right repertoire to connect best with the people who you say you want to sing to? In future, should you be singing all in one style more of the time, or become broader? What repertoire do you do really well, and what do your group find harder? What strengths can you build on, and what new skills do your singers or your conductor need?

Level of singing: We all want to be "good" and well prepared, and to sing with confidence, relaxation, and authority at our level. But what does "good" look like for you? Do you want to be good seven-year-olds, good amateurs, good semi-pros, or good professional singers? Does "good" mean standing still, or moving around to the music? What is distinctive about your choir's definition of musical excellence? And what are your future goals for improvement?

Absolute "no-no's": Now try a different way of asking the same questions: what would it be impossible for your choir to sing? Would it be impossible to sing a whole program of Christian music, for example? Should kids be excluded, as the material is adult in nature? Do we all agree that we can't stand show tunes?

Barriers to success: Identify any other barriers that currently prevent you from being successful. This will keep your goals realistic. Acknowledging those barriers explicitly may also help you to remove what is causing them.

End with a plenary discussion about what you have learned, focusing first on where you currently are, and second on the future.

Workshop 6: Future Artistic Strategy (3 hours)

You are now in a position to develop your artistic strategy. It will be future-focused, and should consist of a series of goals that will help define your priorities over the coming period of, say, three to five years. They might include developing a new audience or congregation, improving certain aspects of your singing, adding new capacity or resources, building budget, changing age-group, singing about new social issues, expanding or contracting your numbers, or singing a different repertoire in new places.

From these goals and priorities, a detailed, costed artistic plan with tasks and deadlines will later emerge. This is not that plan. However, your artistic strategy will guide you toward better operational decisions. For example, down the line you might have a chance to buy some new microphones, but also know you need workshops to develop new vocal skills. Where do you spend your money? If your artistic strategy gave you the three- to five-year goal of doing more video, buying the microphones makes more sense.

There is one task. Sketch out three possible options for your art, without critiquing each or making them practical. For this exercise, assume that once you have decided your artistic goals, they can be made to happen. There will be plenty of time and energy to work out the logistics, infrastructure, and budgets to get you there, and plenty of opportunities for compromise. This is your chance to dream.

The three options are as follows. In each case, size, art, and impact are the main considerations:

1) The "steady state" option: First, assume you will essentially continue "as you are." Sometimes this is the best option, or the only realistic one.

> SIZE: How would it feel to stay exactly as you are? What would you continue to do successfully, and what could you improve on? What is your minimum sustainable size?
>
> ART: What would your artistic work look like? Sketch out its quality, number of rehearsals, shows, type of programming, demand on members.
>
> IMPACT: What impact would be sufficient, to be sustainable and self-generating? Define that minimum impact both inside and outside the group.

2) The "next level" option: Now assume you grow gradually over five years to the next level.

> SIZE: How big (or small) would you grow? Why that big?
>
> ART: What would the new artistic work look like? Its quality, number of rehearsals, shows, type of programming, new demand on members, new styles.
>
> IMPACT: What would your shows contain that would be different from now? How would that grow your community ecosystem, create more impact, and fulfill the mission better? Define that impact both inside and outside the group.

3) The "dream big" option: Remember that resources are no object in this exercise. What would the group of your dreams be like?

> SIZE: What would be the perfect size? What would be too big or small, and why? How does that relate to your mission, vision, and values?
>
> ART: What would the quality of your perfect artistic work look like? Identify the number of rehearsals, programming, the sound, the demand on members, the quality of singers. Who would be newly connected?
>
> IMPACT: How would your shows be transformed? How would that create exponentially more impact, and fulfill your mission to the best that anyone could? Define the qualities of that transformed impact inside and outside the group.

Discussion

How does each of these three visions make you feel? Does your "big dream" plan fill you with excitement and perhaps anxiety? Or are you just thinking, "Well, that's never going to happen," and if so, why? Does your steady state plan already feel like a stretch to you, or are you ready to move forward? How far is your steady state from your dream? Are there aspects of your dream that you could do now, quite easily?

44 Transforming Choral Singing

What self-limiting assumptions do you have, that may be holding back your artistic potential?

Refer back to the initial exercise of Workshop 5, and your group's strengths and weaknesses. Why would you want to "steady state" at this point in your group's development? There can be good reasons for this, but take time to identify them and the assumptions that underlie them.

As an example of how these decisions might play out, here is a brief account of how artistic priorities changed over time with one of my own groups. When I first arrived, the most we could manage was "steady state." Even that took all our resources. Our main priority, we decided, was to convince our core but crumbling audience that we had changed, and that our shows were renewed and had artistic quality. We needed new, younger singers, and we also needed to remotivate our existing ones, by convincing them that rehearsal was fun and socially worthwhile, as well as a "serious" artistic endeavor.

As a result, in order purely to steady-state, we had to change! We planned a new season structure, and new programs and shows around different ways of articulating the message: "We've changed. Come and take a second look." Crucial to this were our *Big Gay Sing* singalong shows, which were a way of attracting back this core audience, who we knew appreciated show tunes and the latest pop music. We put the material in a singalong format, where we could emphasize that we were a quality operation, but also open, entertaining, and fun, and did not take ourselves too seriously. We changed the size of our venues, and sang in smaller ones, which gave us more budget flexibility.

Previously our "fun" and potentially more commercial shows were in June, a time of year when audiences were, we discovered, often lower in New York generally. So we moved them back to March, a time when more people were in the city, and we used them to grow our audience. We also did a series of less commercial and potentially riskier mission-based shows in our June slot, on the latest LGBTQIA+ themes of the time, including teen suicide, crystal meth addiction, and living with HIV. For more on the artistic specifics of both these programs, see Chapter 6.

Ten years later, we redid this exercise. By then it was time to dream big. Now better established and considered politically relevant, it was time to become known in the upper echelons of professional music in our city. We had grand ambitions to run our own venue. Now confident of our product, we prioritized collaborations, to raise our profile and to use our art to reach out to new communities that we had previously ignored. We sang at major international venues, backed pop celebrities, got ourselves on national TV, and sang in a couple of advertisements. We involved high-profile transgender composers and guest stars. We did fewer community gigs, became more expensive, and offered ourselves for paid performances at football games and other public events. In the following two to three years, we established a new high-quality a cappella group, to raise money and develop our profile in regional and national choral competitions. In both cases, our artistic priorities drove decision-making across budget, staffing, branding, marketing, and PR.

Defining Your Purpose   45

This chapter concludes with a reminder and a challenge. The reminder is that choral singing is in grave danger. We all love choral singing. Within our little bubble we see its potential, and congratulate ourselves on our success. In big picture terms, however, the significance of choral singing on the cultural map is shrinking fast. So many inward-looking and unfocused choirs are not being intentional. They continue to sing the same repertoire as before, in the same spaces, with the same sound, about the same things, and are surprised when fewer people come to hear them. Meanwhile, musical practice is adapting fast to new cultural norms, and the amount and level of singing outside choral singing remains buoyant, creative, and ever-expanding. As musical practices adapt in this way, our challenge is to be especially clear about our purpose, and then, without compromise, to have the courage to look outward to our community ecosystem, ask ourselves why we sing, change our goals, and use that new clarity to redefine what we do.

So far, then, we have established four principles that define a new way of looking at the function of choral singing. We have also established the importance of establishing a group's unique purpose, and have shown how your goals will define your musical and social practices as a choir. In the following seven chapters, we explore aspects of those musical and social practices: vocal sound; pulse, rhythm, and groove; improvising; programming, repertoire, and show design; teaching and learning in rehearsal; directing and leading a choral community; and the daily practice of equity and inclusion. In each case, we explore how a clear focus on connection, impact, social justice, and stylistic openness can reinvigorate and transform those practices. We begin that transformation with a look at vocal sound.

3
Vocal Sound

Painting

Imagine you are a painter. You have been forbidden from using red, orange, and yellow in your work, because historians teach that the best art ever, painted hundreds of years ago, did not use those colors. In addition, educators warn you that it is unsafe and less skillful to use red, orange, and yellow, and it can damage your paint brushes(!). Imagine if even today the mainstream convention in the best institutions of art education was to paint without red, orange, and yellow. Might many lose interest in painting, and see it as old, irrelevant, or somehow not for them? Might others feel excluded?

Yes, I know I am overusing an analogy to make a point, but this is not so far from where we find ourselves in choral singing. There are so many vocal colors available to all voices, and so many styles all around us. Yet many choral directors impose strict boundaries on the sounds their choirs may use, defining only certain sounds as beautiful, refined, or worthy of study.

Vocal sound is the core of our work. It is indeed the paint we use to create our musical canvases. The sound of many mainstream Western choirs is gorgeous, but it uses a well-established and limited range of vocal colors, and so only resonates deeply to certain people. In limiting what we do with our voices in this way, we exclude many talented and creative musicians from being choral singers, and we risk alienating listeners who find those ways of singing less familiar, expressive, and meaningful. Our impact diminishes.

This chapter starts from the premise that, if connection and impact are what define the best art, our goal should be to support choral singers in producing the widest possible range of vocal sound at every level of choral education. In doing so, our musical excellence improves, because our sound palette becomes wider and potentially more expressive. At the same time, we increase participation and engagement, and create social justice through singing in more styles and including more people more equitably in our choirs; thus our singing has more impact. We also become more stylistically open, so our repertoire becomes richer, and we offer all the amazing benefits of singing to the greatest number of people. In the end that makes our choral singing more impactful, and brings us all together.

To be clear, such stylistic openness does not require us to abandon previous insights about how to sing well or with artistry. Instead, it offers other insights that can sit alongside them. The goal here is not less vocal refinement, but a broader definition of what vocal refinement is.

Transforming Choral Singing. Charles W. Beale, Oxford University Press. © Oxford University Press 2024.
DOI: 10.1093/oso/9780197657775.003.0003

This chapter, then, is about the musical practices of the voice in choral singing. As before, it is not a comprehensive journey into stylistically open vocal sound, which would be a book in itself, but more of a proof of concept. The first section explores recent developments which are transforming the field of vocal sound in choral singing, and aims to get you excited by the possibilities these developments offer. The workshops that follow then give examples of strategies you can use yourself, to enable your choir to have fun exploring the widest possible range of color and resonance.

This opening section introduces examples of recent changes in vocal pedagogy. Two frameworks follow, drawn from the work of two established choral and vocal experts. These are followed by three longer examples of warm-ups in classical, musical theater, and pop styles. At the back is a brief Singer and Choir Appendix that lists examples of recorded solo vocal and choral performances from YouTube. Arranged by style, they offer examples of the range of possible vocal sounds, and enable more detailed follow-up and analysis.

In the rest of this book, I focus almost exclusively on musical theater, jazz, and pop styles, as they are my areas of specialization, and are by far the most common nonclassical styles. Non-Western styles are an important and insightful component of a stylistically open repertoire too. I do not cover them here, not because the music is of any less merit, but because of a personal lack of expertise, cultural knowledge, and space. The culture bearers of those styles should be the ones advising on how to explore those vocal sounds. We begin by developing a broader definition of refinement.

Refinement

When I was a twenty-year-old UK music undergrad in 1985, my parents gave me a famous recording of selections from *West Side Story* as a Christmas gift. It featured José Carreras and Kiri Te Kanawa, and was conducted by Bernstein himself.[1] I remember two parallel but contradictory feelings. First, there was an initial raw excitement at hearing a new, much anticipated album of a piece I loved. Second, there was an equally strong but inchoate feeling that vocally something was not quite right. With experience, I am now able to identify what was going on vocally and rhythmically, and this description will underpin my later argument. In what follows, I refer to two well-known songs on that album: "Something's Coming" and "Tonight."

Overall, the vocal sound in both these tracks could be described as operatic. Carreras is at his pingy best, and Kiri Te Kanawa's vocal characterization is full of her usual diva sparkle and youthful mischief. The tone of both is fulsome, in some ways gorgeous, with dark, low larynx fundamental tones and sweet but bright, resonant upper partials. Vibrato is continuous and wide. Consonants are long, while vowels are pure and Italian-sounding, and diction is subordinate to sound and legato. All would be entirely appropriate in Puccini, though to be fair, the occasional American-style "r" creeps in.

48 Transforming Choral Singing

In the more operatic moments of *West Side Story*, such as the climactic love duet, the experiment of using classical soloists works well.[2] As a composer, Bernstein knew his opera. Elsewhere, the musical result is vocally highly refined, but it contains refinements that blur expressive characteristics built into the score. For example, soft onsets prevent the rhythmic phrasing from being incisive. Opportunities to be expressive using broken-up, percussive New York street speech with Hispanic inflection disappear into the background. Instead, both singers foreground vocal refinements that smooth Bernstein's shorter jerky vocal gestures into longer, more generous operatic melodic lines.

Sound and articulation also affect rhythmic expressiveness and accuracy. As soon as unpredictable syncopation begins ("Something's coming, don't know when, but it's soon, catch the moon, one-handed catch"), rubato causes the smooth vocal lines to start to float ambiguously above the groove.[3] The pulse is not prioritized and becomes uncertain, as the singers rush, drag, or fail to lock in with the groove of the tight New York session orchestra. We return to such rhythmic issues in the next chapter.

How can such undoubtedly world-class singers, singing with exemplary refinement, fail to do justice to such an iconic piece as *West Side Story*? The answer is that classical music vocal techniques and taste choices were baked into their practice as singers.

Default Positions and Taste Choices

Classical music singing is vast. From choral singing to plain song, lieder, opera, oratorio, chamber singing, madrigals, and contemporary (classical) music, this is especially treacherous ground on which to generalize. Nevertheless, in comparison to vocal practice in contemporary pop music, or any period of jazz or musical theater, we can point to what I am calling here a single set of stylistic *default positions* characteristic of common practice classical music. These vocal default positions are taught today by vocal teachers using words such as "legit" and sometimes "bel canto." Around those default positions, there is of course wiggle room for individuality. Singers and choral directors then make what one of my teachers calls *taste choices*, which enable them to make their performances unique and more specific to their time. Knowing what these default positions and possible taste choices are is key to knowing how to sing in any style.

We can drill down to near infinite levels of nuance and detail singer by singer and performance by performance. Overall, though, these default positions and taste choices have formed the basis of what we now call classical vocal teaching. Current exponents might include Chapman (2006), Bunch (2009), and Vennard (1968), all of whom have contributed honorably to this tradition, and are commonplace on current choral curricula. Such default positions and available taste choices influenced composers, listeners, and teachers, and a powerful global artistic community ecosystem has emerged around them, which supports and nurtures their use.

Looking at the major vocal and choral textbooks of today, few make any serious attempt at teaching non-classical styles. A major choral textbook like Philips (2004), for example, deals with the classical repertoire of all of choral singing post-1900 in two pages (326), discusses "non-traditional choirs" in three pages (360), and "popular music presentations" in twenty pages (220). Instead, where the voice is concerned, vocal teachers and choral directors have tended to pass down the hallowed classical practices that they were themselves taught by their professors. In these practices, the white European vocal sound of the eighteenth and nineteenth centuries is somehow intrinsically more beautiful, superior in itself.[4] The goals of choral singing teaching at the time ostensibly included the development of the individual singer's skills. However, teachers only developed vocal individuality through making taste choices within this single tried and tested set of default vocal practices.

Legato, Fold Mass, Diction, and Vibrato

To illustrate my argument, what follows is a deeper dive into four more specific example areas of vocal practice: legato, fold mass, diction, and vibrato. Much of this will be obvious to the specialist reader, I know, but bear with me. In these four areas, they were defined something like this:

1) **Legato:** It was seen as vitally important to be able to create a smooth and even flow of sound through a single vowel or a sequence of them—a legato. The perfect smooth flow of air across the vocal folds was defined as especially desirable. Sustaining that flow was seen as helping to generate perfect fold closure and consistent resonance. Some teachers described consonants as "floating" on top of that flow. Soft onsets were not just the default position but, in some approaches, obligatory. They were seen as facilitating the most beautiful sound from the very moment the breath meets the folds, because they helped the singer avoid a click or bump when a vocal sound begins, or a new word starts.

2) **Fold Mass:** Fold mass is the control of the density of the true vocal folds. It can change a singer's sound from a "thick fold" (sometimes "belt") sound, common in speech, to a "thin fold" sweeter one, which is the default in much but not all classical singing. As with legato, it was seen as vitally important for singers to create this thin-fold "singerly" sound. It tends to be sweeter and rounder, and is considered beautiful. Again, soft onsets are implicated in helping reduce the likelihood of a harsher, more belt-like sound.

3) **Diction:** Most of us are familiar with the continuum between the "pure" vowel use of conventional classical singing, and vowel use common in day-to-day conversation. The five pure vowels were definitely seen as the default position. Depending on the language being sung, classical singers sometimes used diphthongs and vowel modification too. Consonants had a similar default position. To generalize, consonants were often enunciated with exaggerated clarity,

50   Transforming Choral Singing

and less often left lighter, as you would speak them. This was in part because singing was generally unamplified before the 1920s. The older unamplified vocal styles of opera, classical, and church music were characterized by longer (and hence more present) consonants, with bright and evident sibilants, and conventionally they demanded more physical energy in those consonants than would be used in quieter, conversational speech.

4) **Vibrato:** Vibrato was generally considered intrinsic to producing a good vocal sound. Its default position was "on" most of or all the time, and "fast." A straight tone voice without vibrato was heard by teachers and listeners as lacking certain qualities of relaxation and ease in the voice, and this relaxation and ease became both a taste choice and a technical goal. As a result, most singers would work hard to create a rich, wide, and fast vibrato, that became integral to their sound.

To summarize, a core legato, thinner fold mass, soft onsets, pure vowel use, enunciated consonants, and a mainly continuous vibrato became the default positions of both vocal practice and vocal pedagogy. Over time these default positions stopped developing in a healthy way. Instead, they became academicized, a set of unchanging conventions seen as intrinsically valuable for *all* solo and choral singers. There was debate, but at base vocal pedagogy was conceived around a single conception of the vocal mechanism. A single set of conventionally "good" vocal sounds was the ideal to be aimed for.

New Tools, New Taste Choices

The science of the voice has changed hugely in the past thirty to forty years. Recent research has helped us reconceive exactly how we use air flow to activate the vocal folds, and how we use the various resonators to amplify and attenuate the core sound.

Previously, voice teachers often identified vocal sounds through metaphor. We would learn, for example, about the "mask," about "squillo," or perhaps about laser beams of sound appearing from between our eyes. These metaphorical ideas were based on the expert knowledge of the time, much of it grounded in the European high art classical norms of nineteenth century voice teaching. The language used did delineate the quality of the sound to some extent, but exactly how to do it remained vague. It helped singers learn what they were supposed to feel emotionally or imagine. All the same, many learners were left unempowered about exactly what to do and feel physically. As teachers, we lacked concrete tools.

From the 1960s, Vennard and others began to base their pedagogy in science.[5] Now, thanks to advances in digital analysis[6] and technology, we can be even more precise. An operatic soprano can reach for a resonant top B-flat with "squillo," and use MRI video scanning to see what exactly is going on in her vocal tract to create it. If you've never seen the full vocal mechanism moving in real time, check out the fascinating YouTube channel *Singing in the MRI*, by Tyler Ross,[7] where he sings the same short phrases using different vocal sounds. Likewise, a spectrometer in an iPhone app can now show any singer exactly how changes in the use of a specific part of the vocal mechanism can modify the formant and its harmonics. Singers and choral directors can download the app, sing into their phones, add twang or raise their larynxes, and watch the graph of their sound instantaneously change as they sing.

Turning to pedagogy, this means we choral directors and vocal educators can at last reliably identify the specific parts of the mechanism over which a singer should have control. We can explain a specific muscular activation around, say, the larynx, soft palate, or aryepiglottic sphincter with some precision. We can point to the part being used, and enable our singers to make the sound themselves and proprioceptively experience the physical sensation that relates to that use. They can also relate that sensation to their acoustic perception of the sound. We can record it, and show them the result aurally and visually. We can even teach young children to control those same parts of the mechanism in isolation, and the best vocal teachers are already out there in schools and colleges doing just that.[8]

My point is that educators and choral directors now have the concrete tools to change the vocal sound of their singers and students, to access different stylistic results. We can build color, dynamics, expressiveness, and stylistic choice more reliably into performances in a much wider range of ways. We can maintain refinement and nuance while remaining stylistically open, with all the benefits for connection and impact that will bring.

Let's look again at our four example areas of vocal practice, and see how these new developments have changed them:

1) **Legato:** Within every style, it is still important to be able to create a legato, and all singers need this vocal tool regardless of the style they want to sing in. However, there are now a much wider range of taste choices to be made. In some stylistic contexts, a core smoothness of flow is useful, while in others, we have the tools to break up that flow, and create the wide range of articulations needed in jazz, pop, and musical theater. In jazz singing, for example, stops and starts, longs and shorts, and bright and dark timbres are an absolute priority in every phrase.

   The use of hard onsets is another interesting example of a change in default position in recent years affecting legato. Hard (or glottal) onsets are no longer universally seen as bad vocal practice or unsafe technique. They are after all normal in everyday speech, starting English words like "I" and "each." They too are an essential vocal tool in musical theater, where variety in attack is a key expressive device. Singers now need to understand the glottal onset in its production and resultant behaviors, and should be able to use it safely and in moderation. Doing a glottal onset is also implicated in making a resultant thick fold sound easily and safely. One choir that uses the glottal onset to great expressive effect is the London-based Capital Children's Choir. Listen for the subtle but percussive onset on their "oo-oh-oh" in their YouTube video "Shake It Out: Choral Tribute to Florence and the Machine."[9]

2) **Fold Mass:** We now understand that the ability to control fold mass is a useful tool for all singers. Good singers will access different fold masses to various extents in all styles, and add different resonance to them. Belting and other kinds of thick-fold singing used to be considered vocally risky and unhealthy, even though it has been common on Broadway stages and elsewhere since the early twentieth century, and in indigenous music long before. Now musical theater and pop vocal teachers like Tom Burke and Jeremy Powell in New York, and Ann-Marie Speed in London, know how to teach it well. Like a lack of legato and glottal onsets, belt used to be considered bad practice, but now it is a standard vocal quality in many popular styles, and one that all can safely master to some degree. Belt is now a default position of its own, and within belt, there are now a range of taste choices for individuals to make, based on the period of the song and the instrument of the individual singer.

   To add further complexity, styles overlap. Many musical theater singers have of course had classical training. Indeed, in some musical theater, moments of singerly sweet sound and thinner fold mass are entirely appropriate, and provide welcome expressive contrast. I think of Kelli O'Hara singing "So in Love" from *Kiss Me Kate* (again on YouTube[10]). Likewise, some classical and opera teachers now recognize where belt qualities might appear in their work.

3) **Diction:** In all styles, pure vowels are sometimes needed. Equally, diphthongs appear in all styles to some extent, and vowel modification is also useful in most styles. But we now recognize more of a continuum between the "pure" vowel use of conventional classical singing and the conversational vowel use of day-to-day conversation. Singers can sit at different places on that continuum depending on the style, the piece, and whether or not their singing is amplified.

   Jazz, popular music, and some musical theater are more likely to need conversational diction and articulation, and that is now the default position in these styles, when a microphone is used. Indeed, try using long British-style received pronunciation consonants and pure classical vowels on a pop song with your choir, both for entertainment value and as a pedagogical exercise. It can sound hilarious! Meanwhile, classical singing is more likely to involve those pure vowels and extended consonants, even though, as with legato and fold mass, conversational vowels can appear in all styles.

   Some vowels change from style to style and language to language too. Singing the verb "do," for example, the pure classical "oo" sound that Peter Pears might use in a Britten song is likely to be spacious, dark, and "rectangular." In a piece of Lambert, Hendricks, and Ross jazz or a Beach Boys song, we might hear a brighter, narrower, and more attenuated "oo" (almost a French "ü") with a higher, more forward tongue. As taste choices have broadened, so have stylistic openness, vocal practice, and pedagogy. We can and should teach both kinds of "oo."

Consonants operate similarly. In jazz, for example, some consonants, like the hard "t" in "cat," are sometimes essentially silent. Jazz, pop, and some musical theater also require American English, which has its own characteristics, including, for example, the distinctive "r" (as in car), the voicing of "t" (as in city) and the dropped "/j/" after certain consonants (as in "tune" or "news"). Because earlier musical theater was unamplified, conventions of classical consonant singing applied more there. However, in more recent musical theater, largely amplified using microphones, sung consonants are similarly shorter, and contain expressive characteristics and an intimacy more common in the way we speak to each other. Now that microphones are the norm, professional vocal coaches even teach singers how to sound unamplified on classical and early musical theater repertoire, while actually using a microphone.

4) **Vibrato:** Like legato, vibrato is still an important option, a key skill for all singers. It strengthens the muscles that help with thinning the folds and can add a desirable warmth and resonance to all kinds of singing. Looking across styles, classical singing does involve vibrato more often. Right away, though, we come again to the various taste choices, which become more complex and varied. First, flexibility in vibrato has become much more important. Since the early 1980s, in early music and certain sorts of church music, straight-tone classical singing is sometimes the taste choice norm. The sound of the Choir of King's College as opposed to that of the Vienna Boys Choir springs to mind, as does the sound of early music soprano Emma Kirkby, sometimes free of vibrato particularly in her younger days. In eighteenth, nineteenth, and some twentieth century classical music, however, deeper and wider vibrato remains common. Even within classical music, then, there is a breadth of taste choice.

In musical theater, vibrato is less universal. As with diction, this can vary hugely from, say, Rogers and Hammerstein to contemporary Broadway styles (*Rent, Next to Normal, Hadestown*), and from amplified to unamplified contexts. Also, of course, there is the phenomenon of the actor-singer. Judi Dench on "Send in the Clowns" is a fascinating example of that approach. She communicates the resignation of that song brilliantly, using speech voice much of the way, and hardly any vibrato at all. Moving to jazz and the R&B rock/pop tradition, vibrato here is definitely turned on and off more, sometimes in coordinated ways within a single vocal gesture. Jazz singers sometimes assume a default position of straight tone, and add vibrato specifically toward the end of long notes, for especially expressive moments. The various sub-styles and tempos of jazz and gospel music often require different speeds and depths of vibrato.

Finally, choral singing is a special case where vibrato is concerned. In any style, straight tone can be especially helpful in a group context to clarify tuning.

It enables certain chords to ring. However, an entire choir singing with vibrato can be rich and beguiling too. Many choral directors will know the frustration of working with a choral singer taught by a rigidly pro-vibrato teacher, because they will sometimes find it nearly impossible to turn their vibrato off! In my experience, such singers are also more likely to protest that to do so would "ruin their voices." For us in choral singing, being able to vary vibrato is crucial to tuning and choral blend regardless of style. Again, stylistic openness and flexibility in teaching vibrato are the most sensible starting points.

Bringing these ideas together, this recent transforming work in vocal pedagogy has enabled a deeper understanding of what singers are doing, both within each style, and equally importantly, *across* styles. So when a musical theater and a classical singer create what they each call a resonant sound, we understand better what each does. Both kinds of resonance can be found at different levels of refinement, from *good* amateur resonance to *world class*. Vocal technique will be different in some ways, but the same in others, and we are now able to map those differences and similarities onto a single set of vocal tools. Vocal pedagogy is now a single set of tools that can be used to facilitate a *range* of styles at a *range* of refinement levels.

New Goals

We need a new set of goals, that will turn old thinking on its head. First, rather than recreating an accepted concept of "good singing," the main goal of any vocal teacher or director should be to use this new range of tools to enable a singer to have the deepest ability in their home style. If gospel music is what they have sung since they were a child, they love Billie Holiday, or they are expert at karaoke pop singing of '80s rock anthems, that should be the starting point. We can broaden from there. Teachers and choral directors should draw out the natural voice of their singers, to develop their vocal "mother tongue." Better singing in non-classical styles becomes a possibility for all, and this is good for choral singing as a whole.

Second, in line with our principle of social justice, we as teachers should be enabling all singers to make vocal choices appropriate to their culture and identity. We are no longer upholders of a single tradition, but facilitators of singing across all traditions. Our primary role becomes to empower all singers to sing with skill and flexibility, and so to help singers from a wider range of musical, social, and ethnic backgrounds to feel comfortable in our choral groups. The Stellenbosch University Choir in South Africa is a great example of a multiracial group that holds and celebrates many singing cultures in its individual singers, but can nevertheless create stunning choral blend, and draw on huge variety of resonance and style options.[11]

Third, choral educators should make it their goal to enable all their singers to vocally code switch when the repertoire demands it. The full diversity of vocal sounds should be explored, celebrated, and studied in depth by all vocal students at every level. Pop singers should be familiar with classical conventions, classical singers with pop conventions, and so on around all styles. Most may never sing in other styles quite as well as they sing music that aligns with their own cultural experience. Nevertheless, the range of stylistically open vocal color they learn will always be useful, they will learn to stand in the shoes of other singers, and the human connection and insight that singing the music of others brings is hugely beneficial for the individuals concerned and for society.

Finally, there is an urgent need to make these new pedagogical tools available to all student choral directors, and to update the vocal skills of existing ones. Otherwise, the same narrow practices will continue to be passed to the next generation. Alongside these new vocal skills, they also need a wider stylistic experience, so they can aptly choose when these sounds, gestures, and colors should be used. They too need to be stylistic chameleons, with a specialist knowledge in at least one style, which need not be classical music, and a working knowledge of how the voice is used in many others. Once all these tools are in place, choral directors will no longer be upholders of a single choral tradition, but instead become facilitators of singing in its broadest sense. Only then can equity and inclusion become a real possibility in the musical *and* social practices of choral singing.

Workshops: Two Frameworks, Three Warm-Ups

The rest of this chapter is more specific and practical. The focus is warm-ups. We turn first to two well-established frameworks for structuring them. Over the years, I have organized my choral warm-ups in many different ways, but these two have emerged for me as the most successful. At times, I use one, sometimes the other, and as you'll in this section, they work well in combination. Three longer warm-up workshops follow, which demonstrate how you can use those frameworks to actively facilitate stylistic openness in your singers' vocal sound.

Framework 1: Body, Breath, Sound, Pitch, Diction

My first framework is distilled from the work of the James Jordan.[12] He identifies five main areas for warm-ups, which form a logical sequence:

a) **Body:** As a singer, your body is your instrument, so start by getting the body and mind ready for singing. Your singers arrive for practice after a day using their bodies in other ways, so preparing the body first is crucial.

b) **Breath:** Once the body is prepared, we can focus on the breath, the basis of our singing.

c) **Sound:** Once aware of the breath, we can begin to make a sound, gradually involving all five vowels: ee (b<u>ee</u>) e (g<u>e</u>t) ah (f<u>a</u>ther) o (box) oo (food),

56 Transforming Choral Singing

but exploring a range of other timbres and dynamic levels too. Don't forget diphthongs.

d) **Pitch:** Once we have explored a range of sound, we can explore a range of pitch on that sound, and also introduce the ear (intervals, solfège etc.).

e) **Diction:** Once we have a range of sound and pitch, we can introduce the extra complexity of whole words: how to sing them with clarity and meaning, in ways that create the best articulation (smooth or broken up) within the vocal line.

In every choral warm-up, I aim to do at least one exercise in each of these five areas, and usually follow the logic of this order. Notice that this list is stylistically neutral. I often add a sixth area: rhythm, which is always beneficial but particularly useful in groove-based styles. I cover rhythm separately in the next chapter.

Framework 2: The Estill Figures

The second framework is derived from the model of the voice developed by Jo Estill.[13] For space, I have modified and simplified it slightly. It consists here of twelve areas of the vocal mechanism that she identifies in her "figures." Each enables control of a particular part of the vocal mechanism to create different sounds. In later rehearsal, we can apply these figures in combination, to produce a wide range of vocal color.

When I first discovered the Estill model, right away I found it fantastically useful for unlocking a flexibility of sound in my singers. Feedback was that when we used these tools, our dynamics and diction instantly improved, and our performances had more character and authenticity. I should add that this is by no means intended as a comprehensive guide to using the Estill model, nor an advertisement for it. All systems have their limitations, and since the Estill model was originally published, others have since debated, developed, and critiqued it in healthy research-based conversation.[14] Nevertheless, it is great to observe the useful concepts and vocabulary she birthed becoming more commonplace. Crucially, Estill's work is also stylistically neutral, and indeed her research was some of the first to investigate how the voice worked across styles.

In each rehearsal, I focus on only a handful of these twelve areas. Over time, I cover them all, appropriate to the music being sung. For space, there are simplifications in what follows.

a) **Fold mass:** Awareness of fold mass enables singers to make distinctions, for example, between what I call here "singerly" voice (*thin* folds) with "belt" voice (*thick* folds) used in speech. The singer gains control of the intrinsic vocal quality, maintains better fold closure, and develops a range of core timbres. Also explore what she terms stiff and slack folds.

Vocal Sound   57

b) **Onsets and offsets:** Onsets and offsets are created as the breath and the folds meet, and so relate to fold mass. Awareness of *hard*, *soft*, and breathy onsets and offsets can improve articulation and awareness of tone quality. As discussed earlier, all kinds of onsets and offsets occur in all styles of speech and singing, including glottal starts and stops. Also explore aspirate and smooth onsets.

c) **Larynx position:** Larynx position has many functions, and two important ones are pitch and color. The larynx moves up and down as pitch changes, and you can also consciously change larynx position on any given pitch to create a range of color in your sound. All larynx positions are useful in all styles. Initially explore *high*, *mid*, and *low* larynx.

d) **The false folds:** Above the true vocal folds in your larynx lie your false vocal folds. They can *retract* to create a sense of space in the sound, and a feeling of ease. We experience that sense of space when we cry, and also when we laugh. The false folds can also *constrict*, narrowing the vocal tract. Constriction tends to happen when we are nervous or tense.

e) **Head, neck, and torso:** The head, neck, and torso are implicated in creating an engaged yet flexible structure within which the whole vocal mechanism can operate. Warm-ups engage head, neck, and torso in *anchoring* with different levels of effort. This allows the breath and vocal mechanism to work without tension, important in all kinds of singing. Explore a range of levels of anchoring and relaxation.

f) **Lips:** The lips have a number of roles, above all making the whole vocal tract longer by *protruding* on an "oo." Also explore issues around *mid* and *spread* lips. To maintain stylistic neutrality and reduce work, keep lip movements understated.

g) **Jaw:** Jaw position is key, and a tense or wrongly placed jaw can also affect the sound indirectly, via the larynx, the tongue, and the lips. Explore *forward*, *mid*, *back*, and *drop* jaw. A tense jaw can also affect larynx position.

h) **Soft palate:** The soft palate or velum can be *raised*, *lowered*, or in *mid* position. It is implicated in timbre and resonance changes, and in forming some vowels (for example, the French "ü" mentioned earlier). Some classical vocal teachers insist on certain soft palate positions more rigidly than others. Extra brightness and even nasality can be a useful taste choice, depending on style, language, and context.

i) **Tongue:** Tongue position and a lack of tongue tension are key to easeful tone and making resonant and understandable vowels. Explore *high*, *mid*, and *low* tongue positions. At the back, the tongue connects with the larynx, and can be implicated in making the sound unintentionally dark and "hooty."

j) **Aryepiglottic phincter (AES):** Up and behind your nose, the AES is actually the narrowing of a tight space created by the lowering of the epiglottis and the lifting of the arytenoids, directly above the larynx. Explore making the AES space *narrower* or *wider* to create a brightness in the tone and a forward attack

58   Transforming Choral Singing

in the resonance. My singers know the AES affectionately as their "twanger," though other areas of the vocal mechanism are also engaged for a full twang.

k) **Cricoid cartilage:** Your cricoid cartilage *tilts* forward in certain sorts of "yells." It is especially useful in belting, often found in musical theater and some dramatic and high classical singing.

l) **Thyroid cartilage:** *Tilting* your thyroid cartilage is closely related to thin fold singing, and functions in the creation of lighter, sweeter sounds.

The central insight of Jo Estill's model is that when a singer can engage these twelve areas of the vocal mechanism in combination, they have the tools to create a vast array of vocal possibilities, that includes the most common vocal qualities we hear across most musical styles. These qualities include what Estill called "speech," "falsetto," "sob," "twang," "opera," and "belt." "Twang," for example, can be created, Estill says, by engaging five specific areas of the vocal mechanism: a thinner fold mass, a mid to high larynx position, a mid velum, a high tongue position, and a narrowing of the AES. The result is brassy and bright, key to some pop and R&B styles, and core to country music. Alongside Jordan's five areas, Estill's areas of the vocal mechanism enable the possibility of stylistic openness for all singers, from beginners up.

Three Warm-Up Workshops

To conclude this chapter, here are three example warm-up workshops, each in a different style: classical, musical theater, and pop. All three workshops apply *both* frameworks. In each case, my starting points are:

a) Each warm-up takes no more than twenty minutes.
b) Every warm-up covers the five Jordan areas of body, breath, sound, pitch, and diction. I like to add rhythm to all warm-ups, so groove skills are also built week by week.
c) Every warm-up enables the singer to engage a minimum of two to three Estill areas of the vocal mechanism.

For clarity, the five Jordan areas are given in order as headings below, while the Estill areas appear as part of the activities under each heading.

The music used in these warm-ups is: Morten Lauridsen's "Sure on this Shining Night," Irving Berlin's "No Business Like Show Business," and Queen's "We Are the Champions." Each requires a markedly different vocal sound, a primary color, if you like. All require years of training to achieve professionally with real nuance and refinement. All are also technically achievable by amateur choirs, given the right tools. Each is hopefully familiar. At the time of writing, good performances of all three can be found on YouTube, Spotify, and other free music services.

Workshop 1: Classical—"Sure on this Shining Night" (Morten Lauridsen)

Figure 3.1 "Sure on this Shining Night," measures 6–15. © Copyright 2005 by Songs of Peer, Ltd. All Rights Reserved. International Copyright Secured.

BODY

1) **Head Rolls:** Begin with slow head rolls from side to side, to establish flexibility and ease in relationship between head and neck.
2) **Shiver:** Shiver as if cold, to engage HEAD AND NECK muscles.
3) **Floating:** Finally establish an effort-free feeling of floating "up and forward" in the head-neck relationship. Feel the rest of the body, and especially the shoulders, drop into place.

BREATH

1) **Long breaths:** Aim for long breaths with sustained airflow, and become aware of resting breathing in and out.
2) **Feel the space:** Take a deeper breath in, and then hold it in with an open throat. Do not close the FALSE VOCAL FOLDS. Then release, feeling the space, making no air noise, and noticing how air will simply flow out without effort.

SOUND

1) **Siren:** Begin from a siren (Say the word "sing," and hold the "ng"). Keep the tongue in mid-to-high position, and engage the SOFT PALATE to create the "ng" sound.
2) **Glissando:** Gently and quietly slide up and down your whole pitch range on your "ng," starting and ending on the lowest pitch. Your sound should be so quiet that only you can hear it.

60 Transforming Choral Singing

3) **Siren to vowel:** On a comfortable mid-range straight tone pitch, move smoothly from "ng" to all five vowels, again quietly: *ng-ee, ng-eh, ng-ah, ng-oh, ng-oo*

4) **Singerly sound:** Aim for a pure, unbreathy, sweet, light, "singerly" sound with THIN FOLDS. Repeat, taking a deeper breath.

5) **Add vibrato:** Next, repeat, adding a light vibrato, and make the vowel longer. Listen for vowel blend, reminding singers to keep the TONGUE forward. Focus especially on creating space on an "ee" vowel by retracting the FALSE FOLDS.

6) **Raise larynx:** With your finger, find your Adam's apple, if you have one. It is the protruding tip of your THYROID CARTILAGE, which sits in the front of your larynx. Explore raising your LARYNX by swallowing, and lowering it by yawning. Feel the Adam's apple move.

7) **Lower larynx:** Lower your larynx as far as you comfortably can, and make a dark "Yogi bear" sound, as you say "hi" to your neighbor. Now sing "ng-ah" and "ng-ee" again with low larynx. Hear how much darker and richer the sound has become. This may be too dark for the Lauridsen, but some darkness will sound good here.

8) **Dark sound:** Agree on a group level of darkness in the sound, and use it throughout the rest of the warm-up.

PITCH

1) **"Ah-ee":** The diphthong "ah-ee" (in "shine" and "night") is a key sound in "Sure on this Shining Night." Sing the word "shine" on a comfortable pitch. Aim to sing on "ah" with a hint of "ee" and then move to the "ee" just before the "n." Note the TONGUE position.

2) **"Ah-ee" down a scale:** Now sing "ah-ee" down a major scale 5-4-3-2-1. Use a SOFT ONSET on the "ah," so that the breath and the phonation start at the same time. Explore a hard onset too, and feel and hear the difference.

3) **Repeat across whole range:** Finally, starting at a high but comfortable pitch, sing down a series of 5-4-3-2-1 scales on "ah-ee." Go down in half steps, across the whole range of the voice. Aim for long legato lines. Check low larynx position. Is the sound still at the level of darkness you agreed?

ARTICULATION AND DICTION

1) **Consonants:** Focus on the two consonants in "Shine"—"sh" and "nn." Sing "shine," lengthening both consonants ridiculously. Introduce the idea that clarity can be as much about the length of consonants as how loud they are.

2) **Shorten and lengthen:** Repeat, shortening them to the point where they are virtually inaudible. Repeat, lengthening the consonants again to normal speech length.

3) **The whole word:** Now work on "shine" as a whole, more aware of its complexity. Where is the TONGUE on "nn"? Finally, repeat, agreeing on the longer but still natural-sounding length of consonants the choir will use. Repeat, using "shining," lengthening all the sounds—sh, ah, ee, nn, ee, ng.

Go straight into the opening phrase of the piece, and perhaps rehearse it. If time, listen to the exemplary *Vox Humana* performance on YouTube,[15] or any number of other university-based choirs.

Workshop 2: Musical Theater—"No Business Like Show Business" (Berlin)

Figure 3.2 "No Business Like Show Business," from the stage production *Annie Get Your Gun*. Words and music by Irving Berlin, © Copyright 1946 by Irving Berlin. Copyright renewed. This arrangement © Copyright 2023 by the Estate of Irving Berlin. International Copyright Secured. All Rights Reserved. *Reprinted by permission of Hal Leonard LLC.*

BODY

(Vary the key according to your singers)

1) **Roll down, roll up:** Bend down, extending the arms. Make the head, neck, and shoulders as floppy as you can. Bend the knees if necessary, and sway from side to side. Return to the upright position, unrolling upward slowly from the hips. Breath in and become aware of your TORSO engaging naturally.
2) **Wiggle your ears:** Wiggle your ears, and engage HEAD AND NECK, as if straining to hear a person whispering behind you.
3) **Chest stretches:** Focusing on shoulders and upper TORSO, join your hands behind your back, and stretch, sticking the chest forward and shoulders back.

62 Transforming Choral Singing

Hold for five seconds on maximum effort, then relax. Try the opposite stretch, arms by your side, this time pushing the shoulders forward and chest in. Alternate. Find your comfortable position, with open shoulders dropped into their natural sockets.

4) **Arm Swings:** Walk around the room and swing your arms. Aim for ease through your whole body, while still engaging your torso.

BREATH

1) **Torso anchor:** Holding that easeful position, take a slow, deeper breath in, while pushing down slightly with the hands and arms toward the floor. Your palms should face downward. Again feel the TORSO anchor, this time with a little more effort. Let the breath flow in and out but hold the torso engaged nevertheless. Hold the breath out and get used to that feeling. Then relax and feel the air rush in.

2) **Quick in-breath:** Repeat, but this time, after holding, take a quick in-breath on the conductor's downbeat.

3) **Retract and breath in:** Aim to breathe in silently, without a gasping sound, by retracting the FALSE FOLDS. Insert the gasp, feeling the slight dryness in the throat as you constrict. Remove the gasp by retracting again, and hold the feeling of space while saying "eye."

SOUND

1) **"Ng-ee":** As in Workshop 1, on a comfortable mid-range straight tone pitch, move seamlessly from "ng" to all five vowels, again quietly: *ng-ee, ng-eh, ng-ah, ng-oh, ng-oo*

2) **Thick folds:** Repeat, but this time, aim for a speech-like, almost ugly sound with THICK FOLDS. Repeat, taking a deeper breath. Introduce the "belt" concept as a controlled yell.

3) **Hard onset:** Say "I" quietly, as you would in normal speech, in two different ways: first as in "eye," and again as in "in." Note the HARD ONSET, or glottal click, where the folds briefly hold airflow up, creating a small build up of air pressure below the folds, and then release. Note the heavier "speech" level FOLD MASS the hard onset can lead to.

4) **Controlled yell:** Change to "ay" (as in "day"). Now repeat "ay" up higher in a controlled yell that glissandos down in pitch. Check that the glottal click is clear, but not explosive.

5) **Controlled yell with engaged torso:** Repeat, but this time add the breath more strongly by engaging the TORSO. Try with a slow in-breath, and then a quick one.

PITCH

1) **Three times with glissando:** Sing "ay" with thick folds and a hard ONSET three times, each on a slightly higher pitch, still glissandoing down on each vowel.

2) **Awareness of air:** Repeat, and note how little air you need to sing with heavier FOLD MASS. There is little need to consciously manage the air. Pushing air from below can adversely affect the action of the folds. Let the body manage how much air it needs to make the sound you intend. Try breathing out first before doing this exercise, noting how even a small amount of breath can last a while on this sound.

3) **Extend glissando:** Focus on pitch in two exercises. Play a pitch on the piano that is high but not uncomfortable. First, extend your hard ONSET "ay" by sustaining the sound on that pitch for two seconds. Then glissando all the way to the lowest point in the range over five and later ten seconds. Aim to keep the sound consistent without vibrato.

4) **Keep pitch consistent:** Second, taking care to engage TORSO and keeping breath light, sing "ay" as before. This time, keep the pitch consistent rather than glissandoing down, on a straight tone for five seconds. Repeat for ten seconds. The sound will not be "pretty" or sweet-sounding, but should be very bright and clear, able to carry a long way.

5) **Add vibrato:** Continue to engage the TORSO, feeling a lift as you anchor HEAD AND NECK too. Sing "ay" as before. You should be able to sustain your sound for a considerable time. Repeat, but now introduce vibrato. Practice turning vibrato on and off. Return to the "ng" exercise from earlier to cool off for five to ten seconds.

ARTICULATION AND DICTION

1) **Speech voice speaking:** To the rhythm of the song, in speech voice, say, "There's no business like show business like no business I know, Everything about it is appealing." Repeat to "bah."

2) **Finger pointing:** Repeat. This time point the rhythm in the air with your finger as you speak, for even more emphasis on each "bah," as if adding weight to every syllable. Notice how clear the rhythm becomes in your sound.

3) **The rhythm to "bah":** Now sing the phrase to "bah" but with pitch. Ignore any need you may feel for a legato phrase. Instead sing each syllable as though it were separate from all the others, with finger pointing. Engage THICK FOLDS, speech voice. Replace "bah" with the words.

4) **Light and shade:** Now add more light and shade. Add accents and vibrato as per the classic performances, on "THERE'S," "NO," "SHOW" and "KNOW." Leave other syllables in this phrase unstressed. Create rhythmic contrast by

64   Transforming Choral Singing

stressing (pointing with your finger) on every syllable on "Ev-ery-thing-a-bout-it-is-a-ppeal-ing." Try using THICK FOLDS on the shorter eighth-note syllables to add clarity, and then switch to THIN FOLDS on longer notes like ap-PEAL-ING," as in Warm-up 1 above.

5) **Compare sounds:** Finally, let's compare styles. Add a little legato back. Repeat the opening phrase ("There's no . . ."), but this time as if it were a smoothly classical legato phrase, Lauridsen-style. Note how much less exciting the line has become. Discuss exactly how much legato you feel the eventual performance needs. It will need some, but the rhythm is more in the foreground in the style. Finally, slightly lengthen the consonants "Z" and "SS" on "business" and "SH" on "show."

Go straight into the song rehearsal. If time, listen to Ethel Merman's classic version, or the more recent one by Nathan Lane.

Workshop 3: Pop—"We Are the Champions" (Queen)

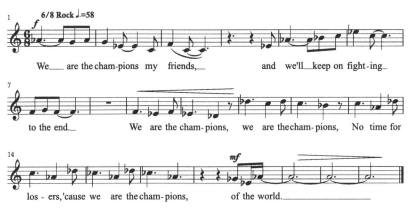

Figure 3.3 "We Are the Champions." Words and music by Freddie Mercury, Copyright © 1977 Queen Music Ltd. Copyright renewed. This arrangement Copyright © 2023 Queen Music Ltd. All rights administered by Sony Music Publishing (US) LLC, 424 Church Street, Suite 1200, Nashville, TN 37219. International Copyright Secured. All Rights Reserved. *Reprinted by permission of Hal Leonard LLC.*

(vary the key according to your singers)

BODY

1) **Tapping:** To build energy and alertness physically and mentally, use two fingers on each hand to tap lightly on your face, neck, and shoulders. Tap fast and with energy, gradually covering your whole body. Build to five to ten seconds of especially intense tapping using both hands on your torso, legs, and arms.

Vocal Sound **65**

2) **Tingling:** After a crescendo of tapping, stop suddenly on cue, and stand still in silence. Feel your whole body tingle for ten seconds. Your eyes should be wide open, and you should be feeling mentally alert.

3) **Shoulder rolls:** Roll both shoulders in slow circles forward, and then backward. Roll one forward and the other backward as a mental exercise.

4) **Free dancing:** For groove, next use your whole body to dance to a recording of your favorite pop song, or perhaps the one you are about to work on. If no sound is available, ask singers to imagine they are in a club and dance to their favorite song in silence, as it plays in their heads.

5) **Stop and start dancing:** Stand still, then on cue dance at any pulse for five seconds. Repeat, this time dancing for a ten- or perhaps fifteen-second burst. Physical ease is the goal here, rather than the slickest moves. Practice stopping on cue. For fun, freeze in place on cue, aiming for the most striking pose.

BREATH

1) **Hold air out, then let it rush in:** Breath out all air first. Hold all air out on an open throat (FALSE VOCAL FOLDS retracted). Feel the tension build. When the director claps, allow your body to breath in, and enjoy the release of tension as air rushes into your lungs. Then breathe normally for a few seconds.

2) **Breathy "h":** Say "ha" and extend the breathiness of the ONSET into the "ah" sound. You should quickly run out of air. Do the same, but this time, say "ah" to a speech-style vocal sound with thicker FOLD MASS. Note how the air lasts longer, without you having to manage it consciously.

SOUND

1) **High Larynx:** Raise your LARYNX as far as you comfortably can, and make a light, childlike sound, as you say "hi" to your neighbor, like a five-year-old.

2) **Light sound:** Agree on a group level of lightness in the sound, and use it throughout the rest of the warm-up.

3) **Chipmunk:** Narrow your AES by crying like a baby to "waaah." Laugh a shrill laugh like a witch, to "hehehe." Sing "Happy Birthday" like a chipmunk (as in Alvin and the Chipmunks). Feel your AES squeeze and your LARYNX rise, to make the sound younger, brighter, and more present.

4) **A song as a chipmunk:** Now, starting on a high but comfortable pitch, sing "Weeeeeee . . ." on a long piercing note like a chipmunk, witch, or baby. Next, sing the whole of "We Are the Champions" chipmunk style, changing every vowel to your piercing "ee": "We eer thee cheeempee-eens, mee freeends."

66   Transforming Choral Singing

5) **Bright but retracted:** Now change back to normal vowels, adding more space by retracting the FALSE VOCAL FOLDS. Notice how much brighter your "normal" voice now sounds.

6) **Vary your chipmunk:** Next, explore singing chipmunk style at perhaps 5 out of 10, adding back only 50 percent of your normal voice. How was it? Try 25 percent and 75 percent too. Decide on a level of brightness, treating Freddie Mercury's bright sound as your guide. Keep retracting the FALSE VOCAL FOLDS.

PITCH

1) **Sing a phrase:** Sing the whole phrase "We Are the Champions." Stay aware of your vowels, of FALSE FOLD retraction, and AES.

2) **Repeat down a tone, again and again:** Repeat the phrase down a tone (a US whole step). Continue down in tones across the whole range of the voice, aiming to hold on to the brightness as the pitch goes down.

ARTICULATION AND DICTION

1) **Bright sound on the phrase:** In your new younger, brighter high LARYNX pop voice, sing "We are the champions, my friends." Try a short glissando or bend into the note on "We" in the first phrase. This is not lazy singing. It originates from the blues and is part of the style, a taste choice.

2) **Dead on pitch and glissando onset:** Practice coming in dead on the pitch, and then repeat with the glissando, starting around a whole step below the note. The slide is made more attractive because it happens on a "w," creating a soft ONSET. Start at a medium pitch, and use the phrase as a vocalese, going steadily higher. Check everyone singing does the slide consistently.

3) **"S" and "z":** Now work on the "s" in "champions, my friends." The "s" is an effective "z." Note the forward TONGUE position. Practice making it short and conversational here, as the microphone technique of the original allows for shorter consonants to be heard clearly. Practice the elision of "nzmy" in this phrase slowly as a separate item. Note that you can keep the pitch, air and line going throughout, as all are voiced sounds.

Continue into the song. If time, listen to the vocally incomparable Freddie Mercury.

Conclusion

How were you taught as a singer or as a choral conductor? Were you lucky enough to have stylistically broad training, or did you learn from the same repertoire as generations before you? Was the goal of your teachers to collaborate with you, and enable you to sing the repertoire you wanted to sing, and use the vocal colors appropriate to that repertoire? Or did you come across some "my-way-or-the-highway," top-down conservatory-style pedagogy?

Now think about your practice as a choral director. To what extent do you feel comfortable teaching vocal resonances common in musical theater or pop music styles? Do you ask your singers to use "belt" or "twang"? Were these sounds part of your college training? And do your singers present as encultured only in classical music, or do you get great singers in other styles too, and then have to somehow train their voices to blend in? What about your BIPOC singers? Are their vocal sounds different from those of your white singers, or are they experienced in classical vocal technique? What assumptions might you be making about their voices, their level of training, and whether their vocal sound would "fit" in your group?

This was never going to be a complete picture, but I hope these workshops indicate the value of inclusion and stylistic openness in thinking about vocal pedagogy. It is obviously a stretch to argue that simply by changing your singers' larynx positions, you will enable your choir to connect better with audiences and widen its impact. Changes to your choir's vocal sound alone may make little difference. Yet a more inclusive and flexible vocal pedagogy that takes account of range of valid and safe approaches will certainly enable the many singers out there with pop, jazz, gospel, musical theater, and other non-Western backgrounds to feel comfortable singing in your group. If those from black and brown neighborhoods feel their traditions of vocal technique and resonance production, classical or not, are useful and valuable in the group, then that too is an excellent basis on which to build new community. These approaches to the voice can be done safely, and are being taught across the world in schools and colleges on many courses outside choral singing. They also overlap with classical vocal technique, and will widen the palette of sound your choir can make, regardless of what styles it chooses to sing. Jump in, the water is warm!

Notes

1. *West Side Story: Highlights* (1985 Studio Recording, Deutsche Grammophon).
2. https://www.youtube.com/watch?v=74UmUhAsMgM
3. Carerras's rhythmic issues are most evident in this famous rehearsal video, available on YouTube here: https://www.youtube.com/watch?v=UoKZlcidbms&t=69s
4. There is not space here to explore this argument against white supremacy in classical music in full. Perhaps the most devastating critique of the intrinsic superiority of white classical music default positions is Phillip Ewell's "Music Theory's White Racial Frame: Confronting Racism and Sexism

68 Transforming Choral Singing

in American Music Theory" (2019–20). While he himself does not apply his work specifically to choral music, he traces a clear relationship between the concept and history of white supremacy and the fact that so many of the "great" composers are eighteenth and nineteenth century white European men. He also demonstrates shows how "music theory" is treated as an absolute term with very closed boundaries, and reflects in its definitions of "rhythm," "melody," and "harmony" an exclusive concern with this racially skewed repertoire, and with its values, culture and communities. In doing so, he argues "music theory" systematically ignores and excludes all other styles, and by implication other cultures, ethnicities, and often genders too.

5. For example, Vennard (1968: 197–202) uses what he calls "sonograms" of Maria Callas, Joan Sutherland, and others in his discussion of the control of classical vibrato.
6. Estill (1997).
7. Ross (2017).
8. Gitika Partington is one such vocal coach, who has worked extensively in London schools.
9. https://www.youtube.com/watch?v=Gj-ntawOBw4
10. https://www.youtube.com/watch?v=kRzrHCLlHdI
11. At the time of writing, "Baba Yetu" and "Some Nights" are two great examples of the range of their vocal color, both available on YouTube.
12. James Jordan, *Evoking Sound: Fundamentals of Choral Conducting* (2009).
13. Estill (1997), and Klimek, McDonald, Obert, and Steinhauer (2005).
14. https://www.estillvoice.com/symposium/
15. https://www.youtube.com/watch?v=LF7cxke__hU

4

Pulse, Rhythm, and Groove

A third-year undergraduate classical piano student arrives in the studio for their first one-to-one jazz piano lesson at a major London conservatory. They ask if it is okay to warm up for thirty seconds. I agree, and the student launches into the opening flourishes of the last movement of the Tchaikovsky Piano Concerto. It is impressively precise and authoritative. My inner voice is saying, "Hmm, this is a much better pianist than me technically. I wonder if I am the right teacher for this student." Then we start work.

I begin by lightly tapping four beats in a bar at around 80 beats per minute. I ask them to clap on the first beat of the bar, and then on the "and" of 2. They find the "and" of 2 tricky, and do a vague approximation. Next, I try the same in swing, along with "Surrey with a Fringe on Top," a relaxed medium tempo Miles Davis track from 1956. It's worse.

Rhythm is a central element in all music, and a key skill in every style, but different styles demand different approaches to rhythm, and musical trainings differ in their emphases. In classical music pedagogy, we love our solfège and our Bach chorales, but as this story shows, the skills of pulse, rhythm, and groove are often not taught as systematically, or given the same prominence as those of melody and harmony. So my starting point here is that rhythm and groove skills are vital to all good choral singing, and indeed to all music-making. They should be a more prominent feature within the education of both choral singers and choral directors. These skills open the door to more authentic and confident performances of all musical styles, but they will help especially with groove-based ones.

In the first half of this chapter, I use my jazz education experience to identify these skills, and discuss what a renewed focus on rhythm and groove might look like in choral singing, and across music education as a whole. The second half consists of three sets of rhythm workshops, designed specifically for choirs. Covering the main concepts at beginner level, each contains simple groove-based activities that you can integrate into your warm-ups and rehearsals, and adapt to suit many vocal groups and kinds of material. We begin with a section about rhythm and groove in general.

Groove, Musical Style, and Connection

Groove-based music is a feature of all styles, and has its origins in group rhythm and dance. It is an especially essential feature in styles historically rooted in the music of the African Diaspora, which includes jazz, R&B and almost all current popular

Transforming Choral Singing. Charles W. Beale, Oxford University Press. © Oxford University Press 2024.
DOI: 10.1093/oso/9780197657775.003.0004

music, not forgetting of course salsa, samba, bossa nova, and rhythmic traditions of Central and South America and the West Indies. But what exactly is a groove?

In musical terms, a groove consists of a series of rhythmic patterns organized in polyphonic layers, that go round and round. Some patterns have melodic or harmonic content and are called riffs (in classical music ostinatos). Others are unpitched rhythmic patterns, and some are basslines. In groove-based music, instrumentalists and singers use these rhythmic patterns and riffs to create complex contrapuntal textures, and many add subtle but significant improvised embellishments to those riffs as they play. Some leave big silences while others fill the texture. Some may contribute to the groove in sixteenth notes, while others use eighths. Some may be primarily on the beat, and others off. Rhythmic counterpoints create tension and release, but overall, the groove itself has a unity. In a classic Isley Brothers song like "It's Your Thing," for example, or a Fela Kuti song like "Teacher Don't Teach Me Nonsense," the groove repeats for long periods with joy and insistence, and its musical gestures are specifically designed to be compelling and easy to move your body to.

The whole groove is a gestalt, the combined effect of all the patterns. It stays constant, and spirals in satisfying circles like a kaleidoscope, continually returning to where it started. As it repeats around a central pulse, the groove settles, grows, and deepens. In contemporary club-based dance music, grooves build layer by layer into long, intense magnetic forms that draw dancers and listeners in, climax over several minutes, and then drop back to nothing. In pop songs, shorter "verse-bridge-chorus" structures may break the melodic and harmonic form up into shorter chunks, but an underlying groove is often maintained throughout a song, and textural embellishments signal where the form changes. Returning to my theme of musical refinement as present in all kinds of styles, the way the contrapuntal patterns within a groove interlock can be incredibly refined. Studio musicians can work on precise nuances within rhythmic textures for weeks on a simple three-minute song, and it takes years of experience for drummers, percussionists, and other rhythm section players to play and create grooves well.

Let's turn immediately to the voice in a groove-based context. Even if it is pitched, the rhythmic role of a vocal sound increases when it appears in a groove. Position, duration, weight, density, and sonority all become more prominent. A vocal attack takes on added significance in a groove, as does articulation and offset. Even the exact timbre of stressed and unstressed individual syllables within a sung word become highly expressive. The vocal parts of lyrical pop melodies of course contain legato lines, but may also include percussive sounds, including clicks, grunts, and added syllables. The opening line of the first verse of Michael Jackson's *Billie Jean* ("Ah-she was more like a beauty queen") is one of the simplest and best-known examples of this.[1,2] Such rhythmic detail is what gives these songs character, and is incidentally often omitted in commercial choral arrangements, because it is hard to notate and even harder to explain to a classical singer.

Grooves appear in all styles. For example, jazz is primarily a groove-based style, as is contemporary pop music, and both were originally designed to be explicitly danced to. However, jazz began to leave the dance floor and developed as a virtuoso art form in its own right with bebop in the late 1930s and 1940s, and now we generally tap our toes to jazz rather than dance with our whole bodies. Groove is nevertheless always its key feature, and complex melody, harmony, and above all improvisation is common in most but not all jazz. Likewise, some pop music works best in clubs where dancing and dating are the norm, while other groove-based pop forms are designed for listening to without moving to that extent.

The musical content and vocal styling of musical theater is also often groove-based and grounded in popular styles. However, it contains little or no vocal improvisation, and instead prioritizes telling a dramatic story. That said, from "Tea for Two" to "Don't Stop the Beat," musical theater performance often involves dancing and singing to grooves.

There is also groove-based classical music. Ravel's *Bolero* is one example. Groove is an important component in the sarabandes of Bach suites, the minuets of Mozart and Haydn, and the waltzes of Strauss.[3] In this art music, the groove is more stylized, and is rarely constant for long periods, as it would be in music whose main function was dance. We are not supposed to dance to classical music anymore, but as with some pop music above, where there is a groove, we feel like we could.

When we hear a groove, our impulse is to embody it by moving our bodies along with the musical gestures. Not everyone finds this easy. In my work in schools, I found many children who moved naturally, kinesthetic learners who had to be actively told to sit still. I return to this in musical learning styles in Chapter 7. By contrast, in every country where I have worked with classical piano teachers, or with adults in classical choirs, I found they needed to be *told* to move, or at least be given permission and then gently encouraged back into it. Something about mainstream classical music education teaches us that rhythmic movement in listeners and players is to be discouraged. As adults, we learn to control ourselves, so we don't necessarily need to move around the room as we listen. In our heads, we still imagine the dance, and say we "feel the beat," and grooves are powerful musical experiences that move us physically and emotionally. They can change our mood, tell us a story, and bring us to a very different psychological space.

Finally, back to connection and impact. Remember my great niece Sreya's bouncing to "Baby Shark" in Chapter 1? As well as being proof that human beings of all ages will respond to a groove by moving their bodies, that story is also a great example of connection through moving together. From Broadway choruses and African American hip-hop dance to classical ballet dancers and Javanese gamelan musicians, human beings connect when they move to grooves together in time. That togetherness through physical movement is key. Connected by creating analogues of the musical gestures with their bodies, they can also become connected in the way they feel and think. As anyone who has ever gone clubbing will tell you, grooves have great power to connect people.

Feeling the Beat by Externalizing the Pulse

Feeling the beat is the most basic concept in rhythm skills, and not always clearly understood. When I tap the beat on my thigh with my hand, I "feel the beat" in two ways. First, I am feeling the beat inside, and enacting it externally in my body. Second, I physically feel the percussive effect of my hand on my thigh. This external feeling is sent back to my brain by my nervous system. What I feel externally reinforces my inner perception of where the beat is.[4]

So we learn to feel a beat not only by knowing and then feeling how many beats there are in a bar, but also by enacting the pulse through our limbs, and then feeling it back from them. We gradually internalize that second process, until the physical reality of the pulse in our bodies is no longer necessary. Nevertheless, that feedback mechanism to our brain from our body, and to our body from our brain, is very musically satisfying, when the two align. It is also a crucial learning tool. We are only later able to internalize the pulse once we have externalized it. Learning is reinforced by watching others do the same, and copying what we see. In short, we learn a rhythm by doing it, listening to it, and watching it. If rhythms are not externalized in this way, as seems to happen more in classical music contexts, our rhythm skills suffer.

Our voices work in the same way. In jazz with scat singing and in South Indian Carnatic music's complex vocalized systems of rhythmic training,[5] for example, we use our voices to externalize rhythmic events, which are often not written down. Even if we don't move our whole bodies, we singers use our breath, our mouths, and tongues to learn rhythmic accuracy, flexibility, and nuance. As vocalists, we get our rhythmic feedback by feeling the rhythms through the nerves in our tongues, mouths, and vocal mechanism. In both learning and performing a vocal groove, then, it is again more educationally effective and more musically satisfying for singers to externalize the rhythm using their voices and bodies. Singers "do" the groove, by putting it in their voices, and literally feeling it there; by preventing singers from moving their bodies, we are directly inhibiting their rhythmic learning. As a side note, moving the whole body while singing has other benefits for the voice too. For example, it can reduce physical tension, and add ease to the diaphragm, tongue, jaw, and many parts of the vocal mechanism.

Through externalizing the pulse in the body, a choir also becomes tighter because it can *see* the pulse as well as hear it. As long as the eyes of singers are not buried in the sheet music, they will breathe more together, move more together, and sing more together, creating deeper rhythmic connection.

Continuing the theme of connection, listeners to groove-based choral music also feel compelled to move to it, and sometimes clap and sing along too. A groove enables (and I would argue encourages) active participation in the musical community of a performance. Musicians and listeners appreciate the music in a different way, because they move with it together, and are emotionally moved by it. Through groove-based audience participation, audience members are more than silent, evaluative listeners. Groove-based movement draws everyone in, and blurs the distinction between performer and listener. I clap, move, or sing to the beat. So do you, so does the choir; and we all feel more connected as result. Impact widens.

Groove in Music Education

Most music educators grew up with groove-based music, even when classically trained. Many love it, and we are all encultured in it at some level. However, even though singers and choral directors may have been listening and moving to groove-based styles all their lives, many feel they lack the skills to teach it. Often this is because they have not focused on it, or "done" it enough as learners. Ethnicity and cultural background are also a component here. Certainly grooved-based music takes on special significance in many BIPOC communities, from some African American grooves through to salsa, samba, and bossa nova. As with classical music for white folks, the skills flow naturally from the musical culture. Nevertheless, we should be wary of making assumptions about a relationship between skin color, culture, and exposure to groove or groove skills. In our internet-based world, musical culture may still be local and individualized, but groove is now a global phenomenon.

Outside the choral field, musical theater, jazz, and rock educators have defined excellent strategies for developing rhythm skills in recent years, all the way from beginner to post-graduate levels. I include some of them below. As I noted above, however, these skills are rarely taught to mainstream choral directors, educators, and singers. This neglect is bad for our musicianship in general, and from the social justice perspective, it also erects barriers of musical and social exclusion, that adversely affect both choral singing and choral education. Singers whose home musical culture is grounded in groove can find mainstream choral practice less expressive, because its musical practices involve less dance-based bodily movement.

Singers from musical traditions grounded in groove can also find the rhythmic conventions of classical music limiting. Often the rhythm skills of their fellow singers are markedly less advanced than their own, because of their cultural experience, and this prevents them from connecting with them. To be clear, I am not suggesting that that musicians trained in classical music are somehow poorer musicians. The music they tend to play is organized differently, and does not demand the specific skills of rhythm and groove to the same level.

Rhythmic Education for All

Where does this complex mix of rhythmic experience leave us as choral directors and educators? Following our four principles, I now believe we need a stylistically open approach to musical pedagogy across all of music education, and one that brings all stylistic voices to the table regardless of ethnicity and musical background. At the center of this more equitable approach should be some kind of "solfège" of rhythm, a regular rhythmic practice for choral musicians in all styles, that proactively builds rhythmic musicianship and sense of groove into all music education, regardless of culture and ethnicity.

More specifically within choral music education, we need a more systematic approach to pulse, rhythm, and groove, that restores equity by celebrating and empowering those directors and singers whose home musical style is a popular music of some kind. These directors and singers are often but not always from BIPOC backgrounds, and may come from cultural traditions more grounded in the informal learning styles associated with jazz and popular music. They often have great talent, skill, and experience to offer but can avoid mainstream choral singing, do poorly in auditions, and become marginalized.[6] The curriculum as it usually appears in high schools and colleges privileges those skilled in certain styles and ways of making music, and few train or test rhythm and groove skills systematically.

More research needs to be done in this area, but it is my experience (having worked in both classical and popular music) and that of my colleagues that this is a key reason why the cycle of privilege, whiteness, and classical music exceptionalism continues, both within choral music and choral music education. BIPOC singers and conductors who come up through their local church and cross over into R&B are often highly skilled in rhythm and groove, know how to use their voices in complex ways, and can lead choirs toward performances that have powerful connection and impact potential. They are nevertheless much less likely to get the minimum master's degrees necessary to become pro choral directors and vocal teachers, because the music education system does not value those musical skills and give them credit.

My own view is that a step change is required for both students and choral professors, so that rhythm and groove skills are integrated into choral pedagogy at every level, and given the same prominence as Kodaly and the rest. This would be key to opening up the field to a wider range of repertoire within choral singing, and also enable singers from a wider range of ethnic backgrounds to take part, succeed, and feel comfortable. In short, we should all be able to feel and perform the standard grooves of popular music, jazz, and musical theater that have been a growing part of Western musical culture since ragtime in the 1890s. All are of course deeply infused with the rhythmic traditions of African American and Latinx people, whose musical cultures are thousands of years old. Big picture, these musical practices are as emotionally rich, varied, and structurally complex as Western classical music, and deserve the same respect. People from those communities are undoubtedly the most suitable to be teaching them. My humble hope is that the warm-ups and exercises I present below will at least make a start.

As choral directors, we need to admit that these are areas of our musical practices that need updating and improving. I have been to many choral performances of pop songs, where the pulse was erratic and the groove and style of rhythmic communication did not engage the audience in wanting to dance, either literally or metaphorically. Two possible explanations emerge for this. Either the choir and director mistakenly thought they were doing a fine job, or they were setting lower standards, and not taking the artistry of popular styles seriously. Stage one of all learning, then, is to recognize what it is you do not know.

As we have seen, it is much harder to improve someone's sense of rhythm, if they do not externalize it. So an initial solution is to enable more physical freedom and movement for choirs. both on stage and in rehearsal. This movement can sometimes be choreographed, and at others left up to individual singers. It needn't be for every song, nor need it be a free for all. I develop this line of thinking further under learning styles in Chapter 7.

Workshops

Before we dive into the workshops themselves, some starting point questions about your own practice. First, what training specifically on rhythm did you have yourself as a choral director? Are there areas in your own rhythm skill where you are particularly strong, and others where you could do with a refresh? How comfortable do you feel dancing, or even moving to music as you conduct? Were you even taught to direct standing absolutely still? Second, are you aware of rhythmic habits your choir has, or aspects of rhythm your group is strong at, or finds hard? If so, how much time do you spend in an average rehearsal focused on rhythm, and developing the rhythmic style of the piece you are rehearsing? How many choral warm-ups specifically targeting rhythm and pulse do you use regularly?

What follows are three sets of practical rhythm workshops to get you and your group started. They cover pulse, then rhythmic feel and musical character, and finally groove and locking in.

A. Pulse

The first stage of rhythm skill is to re-establish that fundamental connection between the pulse and the body. One initial skill is for a choir to feel a group sense of pulse. Once that pulse is physicalized, grounded in the bodies of the singers, a choir's tendency to rush or drag is diminished. A stronger and more assertive sense of pulse in a choir can also free up the conductor. Once they can set a consistent tempo, a group can then gradually learn the skill of staying at that tempo autonomously. They can feel a groove themselves, and keep it constant regardless of emotional intensity or dynamic change. Strong articulation of the pulse will also help your group's articulation, its diction, and its sense of forward motion in the music.

What exactly is a pulse? Grooves and rhythms are sound events, but the pulse is a framework that sits behind the sound of the music, and divides the musical space

76 Transforming Choral Singing

into regular and satisfying periods of time. The pulse holds it all together, and is simultaneously expressed by the various rhythmic layers. We begin with three short choir-based workshops on pulse that build on each other. They reinforce clapping with the voice, and vice versa. Use them separately in rehearsal, or as part of a warm-up.

Workshop 1: Clap, Then Sing on Different Beats of the Bar (15 minutes)

1) **Define four sections:** Divide your choir into four sections—if you have an SSAA, SATB, or TTBB group, then divide by voice part.

2) **Speak and clap:** Ask everyone to say "1, 2, 3, 4" round and round, at a speed you conduct. I find 80 beats per minute works well initially. Then all clap on all four beats as well, with voice and clap as a single gesture. Finally, only clap, omitting the voices. Continue to think the numbers. Don't clap too loud.

3) **Interdependence:** Now ask each section to clap on a different beat of the bar, to create a group pulse. For example, "1 [soprano], 2 [alto], 3 [tenor], 4 [bass]." Continue round and round for at least forty-five seconds. Did it rush or drag? Discuss. Repeat, saying the numbers. Note how dependent we are on others for our sense of the pulse. If you rush, I also become unclear about where my beat comes. We all need to feel the pulse together, as a team. We bond when we do.

4) **Question and answer:** Introduce beat 2 as being the answer to a question, set on beat 1. Try stomping on beat 1, then clapping on beat 2. Likewise, beat 4 can be seen as the "answer" to beat 3. Now try stomping on beats 1 and 3, and clapping on beats 2 and 4, round and round. Seen in this way, you should find that beats 2 and 4 rush and drag less.

5) **Thinking the pulse:** Still clapping on beats 2 and 4, replace your full stomp on beats 1 and 3 with a silent nod. Once that is secure, omit the nod too, imagining beats 1 and 3 silently before each clap. Consciously try not to move. Define your clap preparation (both hands open pre-clapping) as a silent rhythmic event, on 1 and 3. Repeat, but this time also breathe in on 1 and 3.

6) **Vary tempos:** Repeat this exercise at different tempos. Select two pieces from your choral repertoire in 4/4, fast and slow. Repeat the exercise as you sing them. Do you find your body gets tense at faster speeds? Check singers stay relaxed when the tempo is quicker, perhaps by moving the hands less far between claps, or by clapping less strongly. Physical ease is key to a regular pulse.

7) **Apply to your repertoire:** Finally, sing a whole piece of groove-based repertoire, where the pulse needs to stay consistent for a long period. Allow movement so singers feel the groove in their bodies throughout. Focus above all on consistent pulse. Repeat, without moving and discuss. What did the workshop teach you about your group's rhythmic strengths? Where is there more to learn?

Pulse, Rhythm, and Groove 77

Workshop 2: Placing Sounds on the Pulse: Knowing by Doing (15 minutes)

1) **Interdependence again:** Repeat the exercise at Workshop 1, 3) in the previous section. This time, when the conductor shouts "NOW," or signals with their hands, everyone move forward a beat. So those clapping on 1 move to 2, 2 moves to 3, 3 to 4, and 4 to 1. Repeat until everyone has clapped on all four beats.

2) **Where in the bar is easy and hard?** Discuss the previous exercise. Ask singers which beats of the bar they felt more confident at, and which they found harder. How did clapping on, say, beat 4 feel? We all have areas of the bar where we feel more comfortable, and others where placement comes less naturally. We learn by doing. Practice placing claps on the beats that you find less easy.

3) **Games:** If this is too easy, here are some variations:
   Add off-beats: Add off-beats (eighth notes, quavers) as possibilities, i.e., the "ands" of 1, 2, 3, and 4. Next, direct each voice part to clap on one of the eight subdivisions, or on 2. Typical patterns might include:
   i. Clap on the "ands" of all four beats
   ii. Clap on 1 and the "and" of 2; or on 3, and the "and" of 4
   iii. Clap on 1 and the "and" of 2, or on the "and" of 3, and 1
   Singers choose two off-beats: Play a game where individual group members can raise a hand, and choose two places in a 4/4 bar for the whole group to clap, i.e., 1 and the "and" of 3; or the "and" of 2, and 4. You count them in, and then all clap only in those places, while silently feeling the pulse the rest of the time. Try this in 3/4 too.

4) **Focus on a set point in the bar:** Now sing a song from your repertoire, where a particular vocal part has to come in on a set point in the bar—say, the third beat. All clap on that beat when the part comes in. Then practice that part. Next find an upbeat entry, and rehearse that in the same way. Try singing a song, while all clap in unison on a set point in the bar throughout. Do some rhythms recur a lot in that piece?

5) **Placing your breathing:** Next, the role of breathing. If your voice part has to come in on the third beat, where do you breathe? Often, you breathe on 2, or the "and" of 2, depending on the tempo. Practice all breathing together on 2 and then clap on 3, as if you are all going to come in on 3 together—1, [breath], [clap], 4.

Workshop 3: Keeping in Time at Slower and Faster Tempos (15 minutes)

1) **Medium tempo:** Find a medium tempo but legato song, for example, Ola Gjeilo's "New Year's Carol" in 12/8. Ask singers to listen to the piano part and

externalize beats 1, 2, 3, and 4 in their bodies, by nodding the head, tapping a foot, or even conducting. They should feel in their body the length of time between each beat.

2) **Say the words to deepen the sense of the tempo:** Repeat, but this time, say the words in time to the music. Externalize the beat as a group, watch and listen carefully to each other, and make sure your version of the pulse is grounded in that of the group. Prioritize the pulse more than the melody as you sing, so the pulse is really clear.

3) **Explore internalizing this:** Repeat, but this time stay still, so the only way the pulse is realized is in the voice. Was this harder? Did you move a little anyway? Stress the importance of listening, when the pulse is no longer in the body. Aim for a feeling of forward motion and lightness in the pulse, alongside a sense that the pulse is clearly articulated in the line.

4) **Over and under-sing the pulse:** Try OVER-singing the pulse, i.e., using stress or onset to make it too strong and evident in the line, to the detriment of the melody. Also try making your performance SUPER-legato, i.e., keeping the pulse too far in the background. Where is that sweet spot in between, that best suits this piece?

5) **Now vary tempos, and repeat:** Repeat these exercises on a piece with a very slow tempo. For example, Lauridsen's "Sure on this Shining Night," or Whitacre's "Lux aurumque." Try feeling every eighth note in your body to ground the pulse. Repeat over something very fast, perhaps singing the main melody from Offenbach's "Can Can," or Rimsky-Korsakov's "Flight of the Bumblebee." This time feel every half-note. What happens to your body when the space between beats gets longer, or shorter? Aim for bodily ease at all tempos.

B. Rhythmic Feel and Musical Character

A pulse is something that we feel. It is relatively abstract. In this next section, we focus instead on simple, concrete rhythms, initially clapping and later with the voice. We begin with subdivision, and how that can vary in different styles.

Workshop 4: Swing and Straight Eighths (30 minutes)

Musical character can be revealed in music in a number of ways, and *subdivision* is definitely one of them. Musicians in all styles learn to subdivide the pulse differently depending on the context. In classical music, some examples of that are the French dance styles of the early Baroque era, where *notes inégales* are common. In jazz and some pop music, we often come across a similar difference between two ways of subdividing a beat, or what we call "feel." Two common feels are "straight eighths" and "swing." We work in straight eighths most of the time in classical music, so here we begin with five exercises that focus on swing.

Pulse, Rhythm, and Groove **79**

1) **Basic swing:** In a four-beat bar, begin by defining a straight eighths pulse by saying:

One-an-two-an-three-an-four-an

round and round. Place the "an" subdivision exactly half-way between each beat. No need to add the "d," as it can disrupt the rhythmic flow. The "an" is the off-beat.

2) **Swing subdivision as "weight":** Next, emphasize the off-beat slightly, by adding "weight" to it:

One-AN-two-AN-three-AN-four-AN

You can also achieve the same effect by subtracting from the weight of the on-beat.

3) **Swing subdivision as triplet:** Practice changing the position of the off-beat. In straight eighths, the "an" off-beats fall exactly half-way between the on-beats. In "swing" or "swing eighths," some educators begin by saying that off-beats fall on the third triplet of each downbeat. Begin by making a triplet feel:

One-an-a-two-an-a-three-an-a-four-an-a

Round and round. Then omit the "an," place the "a" as before, and say:

One-a-two-a-three-a-four-a

Add weight to the "a" as with the straight eighths "an" above.
Repeat, moving the "a" closer to that half-way point. In different kinds of swing and at different speeds, the triplet feel can become more or less pronounced. Often the "a" is relaxed, and positioned closer in reality to the half-way point of straight eighths than you might think.

4) **Practice to some recorded swing feels:** To demonstrate, try using the syllables above to speak the feel along to some classic swing music examples of your choice. Recorded examples at medium and slow tempos include the Miles Davis Quintet's "Surrey with the Fringe on Top," from *Steamin'* (1956), and Mark Murphy's "Li'l Darlin'," from *Rah* (1962).

5) **Alternate swing and straight eighths:** Alternate the two feels, doing four measures of straight eighths:

One-AN-two-AN-three-AN-four-AN
followed by four swing eighths:
One-a-two-a-three-a-four-a

80 Transforming Choral Singing

Apply this to a song you sing in swing. Have half the group say "One-a-two-a-three-a-four-a" round and round, while the other half sing the song. Switch. Finally, try singing a song that is normally sung in straight eighths in swing. And likewise, sing a swing song, in straight eighths. Discuss how it made the song sound and feel different.

6) **Stress on the backbeat:** In swing feel, try saying "One-a-TWO-a-three-a-FOUR-a." Click your fingers on beats 2 and 4, and add weight to "two" and "four" in your voice. This is the "backbeat," a characteristic of many grooves in jazz and pop, and key to "swing" as a feel. Now find a pop song where there is a backbeat. Divide the group in half, so all parts appear in both halves. One half sing the song, while the other half clap on 2 and 4, and say the pulse "1, 2, 3, 4." Switch. Next, all sing the song, and feel the backbeat in our bodies. Walk or dance around the room, singing the song and clapping the backbeat. On drum kit, the backbeat on 2 and 4 is often taken by the snare drum. For singers, this is represented in classic swing by a click of the fingers on beats 2 and 4.

Workshop 5: "Centerpiece": Long and Short, Stressed and Unstressed (15 minutes)

Having established swing and straight eighths as separate feels, this workshop applies both in the context of real musical material.

1) **Sing a simple melody:** First listen to Lambert, Hendricks, and Ross singing the first line from "Centerpiece" (or a similar simple tune of your choice). Learn the four-bar phrase by ear (without a score!):

> *The more I'm with you, pretty baby*
> *the more I feel my love increase.*
> Repeat until singers are comfortable.

2) **Long and short:** Now sing the phrase to these scat syllables:

> *ba-do ba-do ba-do do doooo-bup*
> *ba-do ba-do ba-do do-baaaah*

Listen to the final note in the first phrase, the "bup." Is it long or short? In both jazz and pop, a staccato can sound a little heavier or more relaxed than its lighter Mozart equivalent. Imitate the length on the recording here. Accents also come in two forms. They can either be longer like a classical music accent (in which case the "v" shape is on its side), or very short, in which case the "v" appears vertically. Sing it again, trying a longer and then a shorter accent.

Pulse, Rhythm, and Groove **81**

3) **Stressed and Unstressed:** I have placed all the on-beats on the syllable "do," and all the off-beats on "ba" or "bup." Next, try adding vocal resonance and rhythmic weight to the "ba" on the off-beat every time:

BA-do BA-do BA-do do doooo-bup
BA-do BA-do BA-do do-BAAAAH

How does it feel when you disrupt the legato line and the pulse by adding more sound on the "BA" off-beat? Also try unstressing the "do," to the point where it becomes very soft, almost inaudible. Regulate both the stress and the unstress to make them more subtle, but keep some extra weight on the off-beat.

4) **Sing the line again:** Now sing the line again with the lyric, again stressing the off-beats, by adding extra vocal resonance and weight to the syllables in capitals:

THE more I'M with YOU, pretty babY
THE more I feel MY love incREASE.

Feel how the new rhythmic inflection makes the melodic line swing expressively against the pulse. Finally listen again to the Lambert, Hendricks, and Ross original. Hear how their version uses the same principles, but is more nuanced and subtle than ours. The off-beat syllables feel somehow fatter and slower, as though the regular 4/4 pulse has been distorted. The line swings.

Workshop 6: Clapping Patterns for Choirs (20 minutes)

Finally, here is a workshop focusing on common clapping patterns that appear in some choral jazz, pop, and gospel music. I offer three activities, at different levels:

1) **Simple clapping on the backbeat:** It is almost inevitable that choirs have to clap on beats 2 and 4 while singing. Review workshops above on finding beats 2 and 4, and avoiding rushing and dragging. Practice turning the clapping on and off while singing.

2) **"Single Ladies":** Next, two slightly harder examples of more complex rhythms that my groups have had fun clapping while singing the songs concerned. Here is the two-part clapping pattern to Beyoncé's "Single Ladies," divided by part as follows: Try this along with a recording of the song. Identify any physical tension for part 2 in the off-beat 2nd bar. Also try it at different tempos. Discuss what is easier and harder.

3) **"America":** Next is something even more complex. Repeat the exercise, with this clapping pattern from Bernstein's *West Side Story*: Divide into two groups, one taking the accented lower part (simpler), and the other the upper one (harder).

82 Transforming Choral Singing

Figure 4.1 Clapping pattern of Beyoncé's "Single Ladies."

Figure 4.2 Clapping pattern from Bernstein's *West Side Story*.

C. Groove and Locking In
Workshop 7: Locking In (15 minutes)
If you listen to a James Brown or Duke Ellington groove, the main feature will be the sound of bass, drums, chords, and melody, all what we call "locked in." Everyone in the group, including the singers, will be feeling the subdivisions in the same places. There is counterpoint between the different rhythmic elements, and they all come together into a precise but rhythmically easeful groove that "swings." Listening, and externalizing the pulse as per the workshops above, are key.

1) **Try locking in:** Find a song in several parts, including a bass line, melody, and chordal elements, each with their own rhythmic and melodic gestures. A piece of Renaissance or Baroque counterpoint can also work well here. Stand in a circle as you sing, perhaps mixed up in parts if confident. Did you lock in? Discuss and repeat, both for rhythmic accuracy, and for a relaxed feeling of groove and rhythmic momentum.
2) **Short sounds only:** Repeat, but this time all sing on a short vocal sound. "Ba" can work well. Even if a note is long, only sing a short sound. What did you notice about your role in keeping the pulse going? And the role of others? Were there places where the groove became inconsistent without the long notes? Were you all feeling the pulse at the same speed? Repeat. Express each subdivision of the pulse clearly in your own part, as that will help others do the same. How much weight should the subdivisions have in the style?
3) **Locking in with live band accompaniment or backing track:** Try singing a piece that needs band accompaniment. Sing it a cappella to the band first, so the band can hear the exact tempo and feel you are using. Then sing it with your band. Discuss with band and singers where the tempo and feel felt natural, and where it felt less comfortable.

Pulse, Rhythm, and Groove **83**

Workshop 8: Putting the Groove in Your Body (20 minutes)
Externalizing the groove by tapping toes and swaying hips enables everyone to lock in better. Once enabled to move, however, some choir members will tend to move more than others. This next workshop is designed to establish consistency.

1) **Sing a groove-based song and move:** Sing sixteen bars of a song with a groove from your repertoire, to get it back into your head. Suggest your choir moves their bodies as they sing. They can express the meaning with their hands, move their hips to the groove, and use their faces.

Alternatively, play a recording of it, loudly enough for them to move to.

2) **Sing the song but consciously stand still:** Sing again, but this time do not move at all. Discuss. Does the groove feel natural? Do they feel compelled to move in time to the music? If so, how much should they move? Repeat again. Allow singers to make their own choices as to the level of movement.

3) **Sing the song, and exaggerate the movement:** Repeat again, moving as before. This time, when the conductor claps once, turn the movement up by 200 to 300 percent. Make your moves insanely exaggerated. Have fun, go crazy. When they clap again, go back to normal. Repeat, but this time, on the clap reduce the movement, so it is really understated.

4) **Face each other, watch and discuss:** Divide the group in half, and ask both halves to turn and face inward, so singers can see each other. Suggest this time that when the music/singing starts, one half sings and moves, while the others observe. Repeat the other way around.

   Using non-judgmental questioning, ask the observers about what they saw. Was energy generally high enough for you to feel like you wanted to dance? Who in the group was standing out because they were moving more than the others? And who was standing out because they were moving less? Come to a group consensus, as to what a good level of physical energy looks like in your group. Try it out.

Suggestions and Tips

In-breaths as rhythmic events: Discuss the effect of a relaxed and easy in-breath before an entry, as opposed to a tense one. Try doing a silent one with open throat, a feeling of space and retracted false vocal folds. Then try a noisy in-breath, where they are constricted. Which is going to be vocally better for the vocal entry that follows it? Which is also going to be more rhythmically precise? Which is noisier? Finally, practice a slow, relaxed, and retracted in-breath, and then a fast and relaxed one. Note that placing a vocal sound at a given point in the bar requires bodily ease.

Foldback and live instrumentalists: When a choir is working with instrumental accompaniment, foldback speakers are vital, so that we can all hear the pulse clearly and lock in. When I hear choirs singing over grooves, one very common issue is that the singers can't hear the drums, bass, and piano clearly enough to lock in with them. Another is that the conductor can't hear all the parts, or is more concerned with projecting the vocal line and its phrasing than with projecting the groove itself. We are all the conductor in that sense, and we all need to hear and feel the subdivisions in the same places.

Working with backing tracks: Ideally, practice with the backing track early in the rehearsal period. If you have the technology, don't be afraid of digitally editing the backing track to slow it down slightly or speed it up, so that it fits with your choir's sense of how it goes. Where you rehearse with a live accompanist, who can be more flexible, singers have the new task of locking in with a recording, whose groove feels different. This can sometimes mean relearning the tempo, feeling the phrasing in a different place, and rethinking where to breathe.

A note on clapping in gospel music: We often see spectacular gospel choir performances, where clapping patterns of various sorts are integrated into the music seamlessly and add energy. The temptation is to dive in and try it oneself. Be cautious. Done badly, such patterns can look and sound inaccurate, and can be disrespectful to gospel musicians and the African American church. That said, the skill of clapping while singing is absolutely one that can be practiced. If the expectation is that it will be done, but it will be done well, it is entirely possible to get a whole choir clapping on beats 2 and 4 or doing more complex clapping patterns. The key is diligent and repeated practice of the exercises above as intrinsic to the sound and groove of the song, not an exotic add-on. Careful practice clapping and singing at slow and fast tempos can also help, possibly with step-touching too, as per the workshops above.

Managing movement in your choir: In spite of Workshop 6 above, some individuals will get carried away, and make their movement so big that they will stand out. Some lack self-awareness; some find physical self-control difficult. Here a one-to-one conversation may be more successful. Agree that during a performance, if you give a signal (perhaps with eye contact), they tone it down a little. Likewise, agree a signal that encourages other individuals to be more rhythmically demonstrative.

Notes

1. Three good starting points on the circular musicology of rhythm and groove are: Middleton (1990: 279–284), on riffing and what he calls "musematic repetition"; Chernoff (1979) on formal

structure in African music; and Samuel A. Floyd Jr. in Walser (1999: 404ff), on the "dialogical, conversational character of black music" and call-response.

2. https://www.youtube.com/watch?v=Zi_XLOBDo_Y
3. *Tafelmusik* is an early music ensemble that for me best encapsulates the potential and the rhythmic concept of locked-in groove in Baroque music. One example is their 2014 performance of the Gavotte and Tamburino from Handel's Dances from *Alcina* (https://www.youtube.com/watch?v=tNxBIMXovdo), and later their more radical but rhythmically insightful 2016 exploration of the music of Bach, Telemann, and Handel through the groove-based lens of classical Arabic music (https://www.youtube.com/watch?v=HHLyc6D8dh8).
4. This process is known by neuroscientists as proprioception.
5. For more on Konnakol, the rhythmic foundation of South Indian Carnatic music, one starting point is the Shankar Mahadevan Academy website here: https://www.shankarmahadevanacademy.com/
6. In general music education, Elpus amd Abril's (2011) demographic study shows how "white students were significantly overrepresented in music programs across the United States," while Bond's 2017 review of literature around culturally responsive education in music education indicates the breadth of research in this area. Lundquist and Sims (1996) were seminal in advocating for "culturally congruent teaching" (330). See also Hamilton's (2021) discussion of "Culturally Responsive Pedagogy," and Hess's (2019) concept of "Activist Music Education" and her (2013) observation of the need for Canadian elementary school educators to introduce "multiple musical epistemologies, creating space for students to own the means of cultural production." Specifically in the field of choral directing itself, Shana Oshiro (2020) likewise bemoans the lack of BIPOC students in "top tier" choral conducting, and contrasts the privilege of her mainly white contemporary with her own journey into choral conducting: "Not having moved through the same circles in my own community which happened to be predominantly Black, I can't help but wonder whether there would be more BIPOC top-tier choral conductors if there were more BIPOC students in top tier high schools like his."

5
Improvising

Vocal improvisation can strike a very special kind of fear into the hearts of some mainstream choral directors, many of whom have honorably gone down the classical and recreative path. My hunch is that even now, some of you are thinking, "At last! I love improvising," while others are already considering turning the page to the next chapter.

But wait! Improvising and embellishing are intrinsic to many popular styles, and appear in classical music too, more than you might have been taught in college. Bach, Mozart, Brahms, and Liszt were all master improvisers. Also, vocal improvisation can in itself be huge fun, and learning to improvise connects your singers with styles originating in BIPOC communities.

There is more. Speaking as a music educator, I have seen how starting with a really simple improvising activity can substantially benefit your choir in all kinds of ways. A thirty-second free vocal warm-up can facilitate vocal flexibility, reduce all kinds of body tension, and facilitate a freedom and relaxation that will positively effect everything later in the rehearsal. It can improve motivation, concentration, expressiveness, pitch range, tuning, and vocal character. Try adding a surprise improvisation game into your rehearsal two-thirds of the way through, when minds are beginning to wander. Improvisation also involves that crucial singer skill of trusting your ear and having the courage to launch your sound confidently into the void. Group improvisation is also all about listening and ensemble skills, and can help develop "in the moment" flexibility in your singers, especially when there is no "song" to recreate correctly.

The skills and performance practices of improvising dropped out of classical music curricula one hundred years ago, and it would help us play classical music, and indeed music of all kinds, better if we brought them back into the mainstream. Finally, improvising and embellishing are an everyday occurrence in the musical practices of everyone else, from rank amateurs to seasoned professionals in pop and jazz, from Bobby McFerrin to Billie Holiday. Classical singers are at a musical disadvantage if they lack skills and vocal confidence in this area.

I am not naive enough to imagine that somehow, we can change the paradigm in choral singing overnight. Yet just as everyone can sing, everyone can improvise at some level. My hope is that these workshops will reduce your level of fear somewhat, and introduce a new element of creativity and childlike joy to your warm-ups and rehearsals. The more ambitious can go on to open up improvised sections in the pieces they perform.

Transforming Choral Singing. Charles W. Beale, Oxford University Press. © Oxford University Press 2024.
DOI: 10.1093/oso/9780197657775.003.0005

Something Fixed, Something Free

There is a misconception that creativity somehow happens spontaneously, as if from nowhere. In fact, of course, we all need to know what we are being creative ON. There is always something fixed and something free in music-making.

Like singing from the part, the best creativity comes from solid preparation of core "fixed" material. Repetition of simple improvisation strategies builds your singers' confidence and flexibility, just as practicing a fixed arrangement does. Looked at this way, the distance between improvisation and recreative performance is much less that you might think. All kinds of performance require some in-the-moment decision-making, even if there is no creation of new melody or rhythm. There is always some freedom there for the choir director or individual singer. They control exactly how long a note goes on for, how far it swells, whether to embellish in some small way, and what the exact tempo is in the moment. A good way of thinking about improvising, then, is to see it as building on the small decisions that we already take in the moment, by taking slightly bigger ones that involve rhythm, melody, and form. For singers, there is also the skill of following those in the moment decisions when they are taken by the director.

Improvisation in rehearsal can also help solve specific choral issues. When, say, the altos are blasting away at their part but taking no notice of the tenors, a quick improvisation task can enable a new awareness of them. Likewise, all of us have singers in our groups whom we wish would sing out more. Getting your basses to improvise a quick low bass line while pretending to be Muppets can suddenly add rhythmic incisiveness to your choir's low end, and empowers your basses to be present in the sound. It can also make them more present as human beings too, and help a section to sing in a tighter unison with better teamwork.

Playing improvisation games gets your singers' eyes and ears up out of the page and into the reality of the sound the group is actually making. It can get your higher singers used to a new vocal freedom. Your aural learners who find reading and memorizing harder, and are perhaps more "in the body," will shine and become leaders. So too will your more spontaneous thinkers. Those with particular kinds of visual disabilities can make full contributions as equals. Even if your singers have no intention of becoming solo improvisers, and are not especially accomplished at it, the group can still benefit, fun can be had, and new styles can be explored.

Much depends on what is communicated about improvisation from the podium by the choral director. If they are themselves comfortable improvising, and there is a sense of spontaneity and freedom in their directing, singers are more likely to feel free to take risks themselves. An inexperienced director can achieve fabulous results, if they signal "this going to be fun" in their face and body language, and jump in with physical and emotional energy. All teaching is in that sense a confidence trick. If you believe it is possible, your singers will believe it too. By contrast, glum signals that "improvising is this really hard thing that only specialists can do, but we are going to try it," can be an immediate buzzkill, and an impediment to learning. It is also vital to create a safer space where failure is welcomed as a learning opportunity. Positively reinforce vocal mistakes as increasing self-awareness, rather than frowning upon them, at least until the performance nears.

What follows in this slightly shorter chapter are six improvisation workshops for you to try. An easy place to start is to do one or two short group improvisations in warm-ups and rehearsals, so this is the focus initially here. The first four are fun, unthreatening, and intended to be for absolute beginners. Individual elements can be used as thirty-second vocal warm-ups. The final two are longer, and relate to a specific groove-based song. While still being accessible, they offer something more substantial for your group, and are an example of how you can explore improvising in performance.

Before we dive into the workshops, here are some questions to reflect on, around your own experience of improvising as a choral director. First, what styles of classical music are you already involved in, that include elements of improvisation? What about Baroque music, with its melodic ornamentation and freely improvised continuo playing? Or the free improvisation of the 1950s and '60s? Second, do you personally enjoy jazz and pop music? Do you perhaps sing karaoke, or listen to Nat 'King' Cole over a cocktail—or did you play in a rock band in your mis-spent youth? Do you have experience with styles from outside Europe and the US, like Carnatic music from India, African drumming, or Brazilian samba? Third, in your own current conducting and directing of choirs, what parts of the performance do you like to be the same every time, and what parts do you like to leave to the moment? If you take some decisions in the moment that make every performance different, as most good conductors do, you are already improvising.

Workshops

Workshop 1: Question and Answer (15 minutes)

Stand in a circle facing inward. Repeat the following two-bar funk groove, and listen to it. Your pianist can embellish freely if they like.

Figure 5.1 Two-bar funk groove.

1) **Clap and step touch:** You or the pianist play the groove round and round. All clap on beats 2 and 4, and step touch in time with the music.
2) **Create a repeating two-bar space:** Ask the group to say "1, 2, 3, 4, 2, 2, 3, 4," making the 1 louder. Clap on the 1 of every other bar. Now omit all the other numbers, creating a musical space to improvise in that is two bars long.
3) **Improvise a two-bar clapped rhythm in the space:** This time, ask each person in turn to clap their own two-bar rhythm in the gap. All clap on the 1 of every other bar as before, to indicate the beginning of a new improvisation.
4) **Improvise a two-bar vocal rhythm, and later melody, in the space:** Next, instead of clapping a rhythm, each person uses their speech voice to make up a two-bar rhythm in the gap. Use the syllables "bah" or "bup," as if clapping. Restrict rhythms initially to speech voice or to one pitch. Then a second time, allow them optionally to add extra pitch, to make a short melody. Some may hold back, so gradually encourage exploration and confidence.

Workshop 2: Boom Chack (15 minutes)

1) **Stomp and clap:** All sit down on a chair, ideally in a circle or semi-circle. First establish two sounds: i) stomp on the floor with both feet (or say "boom"); ii) clap (or say "chack").
2) **Learn the "boom chack" pattern:** All clap and stomp this rhythm, and then leave a one-bar gap:

Figure 5.2

Go round and round until comfortable. Then *say* it without using your body, pretending to sound like a drum kit. Finally, say it and stomp/clap at the same time. Now you are ready to play the "boom chack" name game.

3) **The "boom chack" name game**

   i) **Pairs:** Divide into pairs, one "inner" and one "outer." Then all face each other in two circles, with the outer person of your pair facing into the circle and the inner one facing out. Ideally, pairs do not know each other's names. The game is to discover and then say the name of your partner while listening *and* simultaneously saying your own name. Here is all the musical material at once (taught in stages below):

Figure 5.3

ii) **Say and clap the boom chack:** For practice, initially both singers in a pair say and clap the first bar. Call this the "boom chack." When comfortable, say and clap the "boom chack," and then leave the second bar empty. Go round and round. The second bar is the space where you and your partner will say your own name.

iii) **Now rehearse your names:** Next, in bar 2, you both simultaneously say your *own* name first, and then your *partner's*, like this:

> Boom Chack buh Boom Boom Chack
> My name's [Char-lie], Your name's [Sa-rah]

While you are saying your own name, the game is that you have to listen carefully for the name of your partner, and then immediately say it. You also both have to fit each name into the two-eighth-note space allotted.

iv) **Repeat, this time with your partner's name first:** Now you do the "boom chack" again, but this time you both say your partner's name first, so it sounds like this:

> Boom Chack buh Boom Boom Chack
> Your name's [Sa-rah] My name's [Char-lie]

Now rehearse the whole four-bar pattern with your partner, by adding the two parts above together:

> Boom Chack buh Boom Boom Chack
> My name's [Charlie], Your name's [Sa-rah]
> Boom Chack buh Boom Boom Chack
> Your name's [Sa-rah] My name's [Charlie]

Repeat until secure.

Improvising **91**

v) **Explain the listening part:** Once the game starts, the inner circle will move around counter-clockwise after each four bar pattern has happened twice. This means that each person will get a new partner. As with improvising in a group, you can only discover your new partner's name by listening to it in the first half of the "boom chack," *while you say your own*!

vi) **The real game:** Now comes the real game. All stand. The pulse keeps going throughout. First perform bars 1–4 twice with your partner. Then all those on the *inner* circle take one step to the left, so they are facing a new person. Then all perform parts 1–4 twice again, with your new partner. Repeat until tired, or you have learned everyone's names.

vii) **Try walking around the room randomly:** A fun variation of this game is to play it in an open space, with singers simply walking around the room, stepping in time to the beat. They start with a partner, then walk around, and then stop in front of their new partner, and repeat the full routine.

4) "Boom chack" with body percussion improvising

Now that we understand the routine, we can replace the naming part with real improvising: first just rhythm, and then pitch too.

All sit in chairs in one circle, or semicircle, facing inward. Add one more sound for an extra creative challenge—a "slap" on the thigh with both hands. This makes three sounds in all (clap, slap, and stomp).

i) **Introduce stomp, slap, and clap:** Ask for a volunteer to start it off. All do the boom chack together, leaving a one bar gap as before. This time, instead of putting names in the gap, we are going to use our three sounds: stomp, slap, and clap. Practice them all together.

ii) **Improvise one-bar rhythms in bars 2 and 4:** Next play the "boom chack" game as before. This time, in bar 2, one person improvises a one-bar rhythm using their "body drum kit" of those three sounds. Then comes a "boom chack" from everyone, and in the next gap, the next person in the circle improvises in the same way. Continue until all have improvised a one-bar rhythm using three sounds.

iii) **"Boom chack" with vocal percussion improvising:** Repeat, but now improvisations can contain only unpitched vocal percussion sounds. If a couple of pitched ones appear, that's fine. Sometimes it can be fun to do both body percussion and voice together.

iv) **"Boom chack" with vocal melody improvising:** Repeat, but as confidence increases, improvisations can contain vocal rhythms or melodies. It is a cappella, so any key will do. If there is a shyness from some initially, the instruction to improvise a vocal rhythm but add a longer sound at some point can help start a melody off.

Workshop 3: Riffing (20 minutes)

Divide the group into smaller groups of three to five people. Stand each smaller group in a circle facing inward in different parts of the room.

1) **Clap and move:** The pianist plays the piano part round and round as before in Workshop 1 throughout the exercise. To warm up, all move to the music and possibly clap on 2 and 4.

2) **Each group member invents and sings one riff:** Give the instruction: "Your small group's task is to spontaneously come up with one riff (a repeating melodic pattern) that you all sing together. To do this, listen to the piano part, and wait. When an idea occurs to you as an individual singer, sing it and repeat it. It can simply be a rhythm on one note, or a whole phrase. You may initially end up with two to three ideas from individuals, who all repeat them simultaneously in your small group.

3) **Choose one riff and learn it in your small group:** Keep singing your riffs individually round and round until one seems the strongest. Then connect by memorizing that one, and singing it together. Keep going until all small groups are singing one riff each. Sometimes it takes two or three rounds of the exercise for all the groups to come up with an idea confidently, and sing them simultaneously with each other.

4) **Sing riffs together a cappella:** Once the patterns are going, cut out the piano part, so they sing the patterns alone. Enjoy the improvised polyphony.

5) **Discuss and sing each other's riffs:** Next, to practice by ear skills, listen to each other's riffs and then all sing them. Which was the most fun to sing, and why? How well did the riffs fit together as a whole texture?

6) **Repeat on other grooves:** Repeat with new two-bar and later four-bar riffing patterns on grooves from other jazz or pop songs you are working on.

7) **Make one riff or texture the basis of a whole song:** It can be useful to record this workshop as you go. Then, when one good riff appears, you can capture and later teach it. Once you have several, form a piece, which you can perform in a concert.

8) **Devise an improvised riffing performance:** In front of an audience, create a performance in the moment that consists only of the groups' repeating patterns, or layers them together.

9) **Add a riffing section to your performance of a song:** Add impact by inserting your choir's improvised choral riffing into one of the jazz or pop songs you are performing. Find a section that repeats over a two-bar chord progression and repeat it round and round. Then see what happens if your choir riffs in the moment. This is always a crowd pleaser!

Workshop 4: Making Up Chords (15 minutes)

This warm-up/improvising workshop aims to show how a choir can "compose" interesting chords in the moment, by making the simplest choices of individual pitch. Listening is another skill here, as is the skill of becoming present in a texture, by deciding on a note and then singing it right away.

1) **Choose a note:** Everyone in the group is asked to silently think of a note, but not sing it. The conductor chooses a vowel. Then, on the conductor's cue, all sing their notes together quietly, creating a random atonal chord. Initially the skill is to hear and then hold your own note, undistracted by others that may not fit with it. Encourage everyone to be equally present in the texture, so that no one sticks out. Breathe when you need to.

2) **Repeat and vary:** Repeat two to three times, asking everyone to choose a different note each time. Encourage deeper listening, by discussing which sounded good and why. Ask everyone to sing a high note, then a low note, then a loud note, and so on.

3) **Choose a note, then move to a unison:** Singers choose their note, and hold it as before. This time, on cue all glissando over five, ten, or even thirty seconds fanlike to a unison, so all are on the same note. Hold that note. Listen for tuning, resonance, and blend.

4) **Repeat, going in and out:** Repeat as 2) above, but this time, once on the unison, fan out on cue to another different note, creating a new group chord. Then go back to a new unison. Repeat, making each chord as different as possible.

5) **Move to a new vowel:** Fan out to the same chord as last time, so singers have to remember the pitch they last chose. With each new chord, the conductor moves the group to a new vowel on each new chord.

6) **Move to a new dynamic:** With each new chord, move to a new dynamic as directed, i.e., forte on an "ah" high up; pianissimo on a hum; a dark "oo"; "a bright 'ah.'"

7) **Move to a new pitch range:** With each new chord, use a new prompt to move singers to a new pitch range, i.e., "all sing high"; "all sing low"; "all sing in an extreme pitch"; "all sing where you feel comfortable"; "sing your most beautiful note."

8) **Follow the accompanist:** Accompanist plays a chord, and singers choose a different note that they feel fits with that chord each time.

9) **Come in at different times:** Rather than all starting together, this time the conductor may cue individual singers or small groups to come in at different times. Or individual singers can choose when to come in on their note. Singers can reinforce a pitch that is already going on; sing in a higher or lower

space in the chord, which is empty of pitches; sing to the extremes of their voice, or sing in a comfortable mid-range.

10) **Add decays:** This time, all initially come on a pitch. Then each singer decays gradually on that pitch, and chooses their own moment to *stop* singing too. After a pause, each singer can choose to come back in on another one. Continue until conductor cue, or decay to silence. Also, try this one in groups of three to five singers, where each group comes in, decays, and goes to silence together.

The final longer workshop is in two halves, which I am calling Workshops 5a and 5b. Both together take a total of 90 minutes. It is based around part of a famous Clarence Williams song, "The Bucket's Got a Hole in It." Workshop 5a is made up of a series of nine exercises in total and finishes with a set of small group improvisations. It encompasses learning the rhythm, melody, and harmony of a song, all by ear, and then improvising on it. Workshop 5b adds two more activities, and leads to a final performance, which could be in front of an audience. I have successfully completed the whole workshop several times in exactly this format with a group of forty adult amateur singers, none of whom had improvised before.

Workshop 5a: The Bucket's Got a Hole in It (45–60 minutes)

The workshop begins with the group learning a simple song in every aspect by ear. Later, singers improvise on it, in a large group, in small groups and finally as soloists,

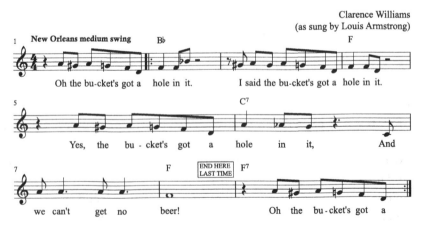

Figure 5.4 "My Bucket's Got a Hole in it." Words and music by Clarence Williams, Copyright © 1933 UNIVERSAL MUSIC CORP. Copyright Renewed. This arrangement Copyright © 2023 UNIVERSAL MUSIC CORP. All Rights Reserved. Used by Permission. *Reprinted by permission of Hal Leonard LLC.*

Improvising **95**

if they like. If you can, listen to the recording of Louis Armstrong singing it before you start.[1] Note that the workshop uses Armstrong's lyric, 'The bucket ...' throughout

1) **Learn the lyrics and melody:** Say the lyrics, and memorize them. Focus on the beginning of each line: "Oh"; "I said"; "Yes." Next sing the melody to your singers, chunking it into four two-bar pieces until they have it. Add the melody. For the purposes of the workshop, the song goes round and round in eight-bar segments (so after "beer," go straight back to "Oh, the bucket"). The original song has more verses to it. Authenticity is critical, so check out the early jazz swing phrasing of the Louis Armstrong version again.

2) **Add a bass line:** Sing the four-note bass line round and round to "ah": B-flat, F, C, F. If you know roman numerals or solfège, identify as IV, I, V, I, or *fa-do-so-do*. Divide the group in half, and have half sing the melody, while the other half sings the bass line to whole note (semibreve) "ahs." Swap, so all sing both parts.

3) **Improvised harmony on a single chord:** Next try this this preparatory exercise on one chord. The idea is to give just enough musical information, so the singers can find the harmony by ear for themselves. Initially play the chord of B-flat in bar 1, and ask all members to sing B-flat. Now roll the chord continuously, and ask all group members to sing another note that they feel fits with the chord. They can try a note above B-flat (and are likely to hit D), or one below (likely to hit F). Make clear there are no wrong notes here, and if they no longer feel the note they are singing fits, they can change it. Ask the group to sing their single improvised chord above your piano chord and hold it to "Ah." Next, repeat over the same chord, this time asking them to choose a different note. First all choose a higher one. Then, all choose a lower one. Show that most of the notes they have sung will tend to be in an arpeggio (B-flat, D, F). All sing up the arpeggio they just found.

4) **Improvised harmony on all four chords, using long "ahs":** Review the bass line to get it back in the singers' ears. Announce that this time, they will hear the chord sequence round and round. All sing a loud confident "ah" throughout, and they should initially find and hold a first note over the B-flat chord as before. This time, when they hear the chord change, move by step up or down to another note that fits. They can also stay put if they feel that fits too. Play the chord sequence round and round, and all sing "ah" on and on. No one is allowed to stop singing, and all mistakes are good. If the note you choose does not feel like it fits, change to another one.

5) **Improvised harmony with rhythmic change:** Next, add rhythmic variety to the "ahs." Teach one of these two rhythms to the group by ear, and ask them to sing improvised harmony over the sequence as before, singing the rhythm.

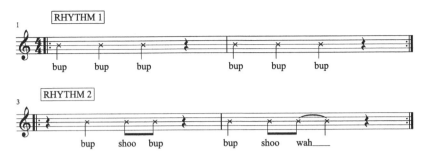

Figure 5.5

If confident, divide into parts: some sing the rhythm, some the bass line from 2) above, and some the melody.

6) **Improvised harmony, with arpeggio:** Next, still playing the groove round and round, singers are instructed simply to "sing arpeggios" up and down to a steady rhythm. Start with the instruction to keep singing steady half notes on harmony notes of their choice. Repeat, but this time use quarter notes. Repeat, with the option of eighth-note arpeggios too. Finally, allow the singers to choose their own rate of change, and modify the rhythm as they go. For example, they could begin with quarter notes, but then do a couple of bars of longer half notes, followed by a more intense run of eighth notes.

7) **Improvised melody with scales:** Review the long "ahs" from 4) above, to get the sequence back into the ears of your singers. This time, singers can only sing stepwise scales. Initially, restrict the scales to continual quarter notes, spinning an endless melody. Breathe where you like. The choral sound will initially be a cacophony, but it will gradually coalesce around the harmony. Persist, ensuring the piano continues to play the sequence and groove round and round each time.

8) **Gradually vary the rhythm:** Next, repeat, but ask the group to sing only eighth notes continuously to do-ba-do-ba-do, again trusting that their ears will draw them to the right pitches. Suggest a) they sing high stepwise scales in eighth notes, then b) low scales in in eighth notes, then c) use their full vocal range.
   Repeat, but allow a choice of either half, quarter or eighth notes, but no gaps. Finally, allow gaps as well. So effectively they can sing anything they want, but using three possible strategies that you have practiced with them: arpeggios in any rhythm, scales in any rhythm, and rests. Again, allow all responses as correct, and all are singing at once.

9) **Small group improvisations:** Stand the whole group in a circle facing inward. Then divide them into groups of five, so in a circle of, say, thirty people, you have six groups of five. The groups should stand next to each other in a line, but all face into the circle. Suggest that everyone in each small group should try improvising all at once in a group of five, for, say, four bars.

Some singers will feel some fear, so emphasize that no individuals will be heard, that we are all covered by each other, and that we will all receive a round of applause after each go. Play the piano groove, and go around the circle, bringing in each small group in turn. All the individuals in Group 1 sing simultaneously for four bars, and are applauded by the rest, then Group 2 and so on. Give each group two to three tries without stopping, if possible, so there is a chance to experience the improvising several times and become more comfortable with it.

A Note about Applause

At some point, I teach the whole group to applaud each other after solos, as in a jazz club, so that effort, risk-taking and "having a go" always feels generously rewarded, and all are included. We workshop polite applause, warm applause, and ecstatic applause, and decide which we would want to receive from everyone else in the group. Ensure the mood in the group is celebratory and exploratory, as these singers will feel they are taking risks. There really is no such thing as a bad choice in this exercise. Your singers' warm applause for each other is also a great example of creating the respectful social space I propose in Chapter 9.

Workshop 5b: The Bucket's Got a Hole in It 2 (30 minutes)

Assuming that this is on a separate occasion, warm up by singing the song. Review and reinforce previous activities 1–9 as needed. Introduce the idea that the group will perform the song in a show.

10) **Add optional solo improvisations:** After an initial round of small group improvisations (9 in Workshop 5a), offer the option of a solo improvisation. If any individual singer would like to, they can step forward into the circle or put their hand up. A few will, and others will initially be more tentative, but will want to have a go later. Give the soloists a chance one by one in a continuous musical flow, again with generous applause after each. Finally, ask if anyone feels ready for a longer improvisation alone, perhaps accompanied by a group backing on "Ah." If so, they can begin to improvise and continue to sing until they feel like stopping.

11) **All walk around improvising, or singing any part:** On cue, during whole group improvising, ask the entire group to walk around the room in time to the groove as they sing. Instruct singers to find their own comfort level. Less confident singers can simply sing the melody, the bass line, or any backing

they like from earlier. You will feel the sound become more confident as the walking leads to an increase of air in the sound and some loss of inhibition. Explore quiet and loud, high and low pitch with the whole group, while still improvising. After they have been going a few minutes, encourage more risk-taking.

12) **A workshop performance:** Do a workshop performance right away. Alternatively, over several rehearsals, do several. Each can contain a number of elements in a range of orders, depending on the level of your group and what they have enjoyed doing. The form of a typical performance might look like this:

i) Melody, all unison
ii) Melody with bass line
iii) Melody with bass line and "ahs"
iv) Group solos in groups of five
v) Individual solos
vi) Recap of the melody louder
vii) All improvise a cappella, as piano drops out, and walk around the room
viii) Continue a cappella, singing higher and louder, then gradually diminuendo to pianissimo and low pitch. Melody pianissimo a third time; singers return to places in the circle.
ix) A final rousing round of the melody with backings.

Note

1. https://www.youtube.com/watch?v=ddM2EomCYow

6

Programming, Repertoire, and Show Design

Like vocal sound, programming is a core skill for choral directors. It is what we do. Creativity is key to programming, but often creativity is not taught explicitly in choral programs, so this chapter opens with three models of creative practice, that you can use as tools to support your programming work. Later, I demonstrate how those models might be implemented via a detailed examination of programming and designing two contrasting shows that I and my creative teams wrote for my groups in the past ten years: *Big Gay Sing* and *Accentuate the Positive*. Special thanks is due to Jeff Lettiere and Jason Cannon, who were my main co-collaborators in designing and programming those shows.

Big Gay Sing was a fun singalong show that focused on connection through pop music, jazz, and musical theater. Our first one was in 2009, and it became a yearly fixture in our season from then on, because it proved so successful with audiences. *Accentuate the Positive* was a show for a particular moment in time about living with HIV/AIDS, and we produced it in June 2011. Here, I break down the very different programming processes of both, lay out strategies used, and go through a selection of our repertoire and design choices one by one, along with the rationales that underlie them. To be clear, the goal is not to encourage you to program the same pieces as we did, but to explain the creative practice we used and the journeys we went on to reach our eventual decisions.

The chapter finishes with two longer practical workshops, that offer you the chance to apply those same programming strategies to your own choir's work. One should help your group generate a flood of new show concepts, while the other asks you to identify your own programming clichés, and offers a range of ways to create a different flow in a given set, that will challenge your current habits.

As ever, our focus is on programs and repertoire choices that facilitate connection, impact, stylistic openness, and social justice. The premise is that the most successful programs tell musical stories that facilitate change in singers and audiences. The chapter is in two parts, and follows the structure of previous ones by moving from theory to practice.

A. Programming as Creative Practice

Programming is a creative process. It is about having ideas. How strange it is, then, that we as choral directors are rarely trained directly in developing ideas, or

Transforming Choral Singing. Charles W. Beale, Oxford University Press. © Oxford University Press 2024.
DOI: 10.1093/oso/9780197657775.003.0006

evaluating and molding them once we have them, nor are we often given even the most common tools that others use to facilitate creative flow. Instead, our field tends to focus on recreating existing work, visiting websites to find the right arrangements and compositions, and putting them together in concert order. So we begin with three ways to think about your programming as creative practice.[1]

Approach 1: Impulse, Medium, and Form

Creativity advocate and arts educator Malcolm Ross (1978)[2] identifies a really great approach to creativity of all kinds, that I initially discovered at teacher training college, when I was learning to teach children to compose. In what follows, I show how I have use it in adapted form, in my programming.

Ross uses five key terms, in italics here: *impulse, direction, energy, medium,* and *reciprocal form*. For Ross, the creative process begins from what he calls an *impulse*, a feeling inside or an energy of some kind. For me, it's a feeling of, "Wouldn't it be great to do a show about [x]," or "I love this song, and I can really hear my group singing it." So an impulse is like a vector that goes from A to B with energy "a," and might be represented as follows:

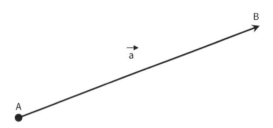

Figure 6.1 Like a vector, a choral program's impulse needs direction and energy.

Below are four diagrams inspired by his work that I have devised to represent good and bad creative processes in designing choral programs. I wonder if you can recognize any past programs of yours in what follows.

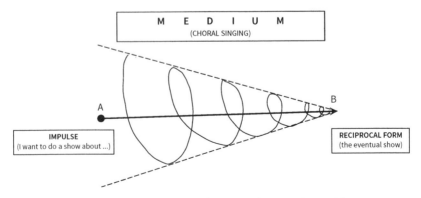

Figure 6.2 The ideal choral program's journey from impulse to reciprocal form.

Programming, Repertoire, and Show Design   101

As we make decisions, our impulse begins to take on energy and direction. Good decisions pull the impulse back *toward* the straight line in the center, which is the path to the currently unformed show we desire. Bad decisions pull the impulse *away* from the arrow in the center, and therefore away from the show we intend, which he calls the "reciprocal form." The ideal journey of our impulse follows the direction of the arrow in a spiral, and our decision-making ideally pulls us closer and closer to it. Of course, we don't know what that eventual direction is when we start. In words attributed to Picasso: "I begin with an idea and then it becomes something else."[3] The spiral represents the tension between decisions that take us closer to our ideal program, and decisions that take us further away from it.

Figures 6.3–6.5 then indicate how creative processes can fail in different ways. In Figure 6.3, the energy of our impulse is very strong, but our sense of direction is not strong enough to pull our process toward the center. Instead, bad decisions spin us off in a new direction, and our program never reaches an eventual coherent form.

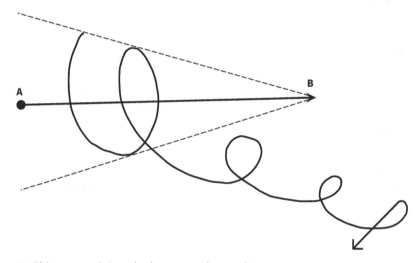

Figure 6.3 This program's impulse has energy but no direction.

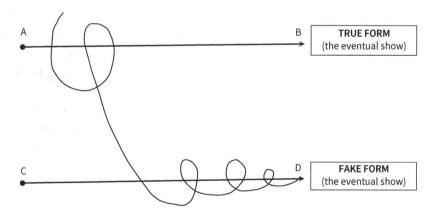

Figure 6.4 This program is coherent, but refocuses around a new impulse.

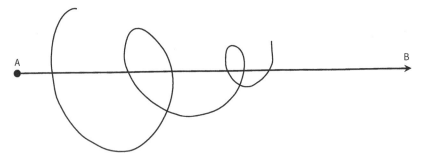

Figure 6.5 This program's impulse has direction but no energy.

Now think back over past programs that you have devised, successful and less successful too. Do the more successful ones have an eventual form? Did some of your less successful ones have good initial impulses, but lose direction at a certain point? Work out why, and see if there is a pattern there.

Approach 2: Open and Closed Mode

When we start to program, it is important to stay mentally in what creativity expert (and one-time Monty Python comedian and writer) John Cleese calls "open mode."[4] Open mode is a special place the brain goes to, that involves being open to all possibilities. In open mode, you are more childlike, allow play, and accept all ideas, however absurd. As ideas float up from your subconscious, you identify the ones that are useful, and allow them to pull the show toward its eventual form. Others will pull the show away from it, and you reject those. One of the jobs of a choral conductor is to facilitate open mode in our singers, and sometimes our managers too.

"Closed mode," by contrast, is where we are in most of our artistic practice, implementing a plan and dealing with logistics and operations. Decisions have been taken, and they become givens that become increasingly hard to unpick. We are no longer choosing. Knowing when you are in open mode and when to close the creative phase down is crucial. There are always pressures to go into closed mode too soon, and a recurring theme in this chapter is to be practical but to allow yourself the possibility of open mode throughout, even up to the day of the show.

In your program design process, do you consciously allow times of brainstorming, where openness, risk-taking and childlike fun are the goal? What kind of creativity is your choir known for? Also, do you stay in open mode for long enough? What pressures do you have in your context to close your programming down and become inflexible too soon?

Approach 3: Iterative Design

I have found one other model of the creative process especially useful: iterative design. Its origins are in industrial design rather than the performing arts, but it still has insights we can learn from.[5] It involves five stages:

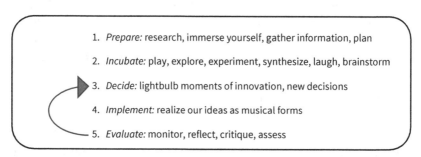

Figure 6.6

The process of iteration means that after we evaluate, we return in cycles to Stage 3 (indicated by the arrow), where we make new decisions that reflect our evaluation, and repeat 3–5 again, differently than the previous time. With each iteration, our product improves, so it is always useful to keep iterating. Below, I show how I might put together a ninety-minute choral show using these five stages. Adapt it to suit your own context.

Stage 1: Prepare and Research Widely

I tend to have at least three and sometimes six to nine show ideas going in my head at any one time. Ideally, I start to prepare each show roughly eighteen months ahead. At times, I work with a team, a singer group who helped me develop themes and made song suggestions. You could include your students, your congregation, or your community members. A show concept would be introduced for initial song suggestions, and team members would post songs on a closed Facebook page that I moderated. Later, we would sift, share opinions, follow up on hunches, consult others, search for new fertile but unexplored areas, look through old lists, archives, or folders, and make new ones. A great song can inflect the show theme at this point, and vice versa—the whole process is like moldable, like putty. Facilitate lively debates with all kinds of people at this point, and watch for the interaction between your own personal tastes, expertise, and experience, and those of your team members. Stay open yourself, and respond to it. Also expect them to do the same.

Stage 2: Incubate

It is unwise to share half-formed concepts too widely until they are sufficiently solid, as they can lose energy and direction (see Figure 6.3). I would incubate a fragile, moldable show design with a smaller group of trusted advisors. Volunteer or paid, this group might include a *staging director*, with whom I could bounce ideas back and forth; an *assistant music director*, a trusted ally and second opinion; a *composer/arranger*; a *production manager*, who deals with logistics, and says things like, "I love the idea of those risers but we don't have the budget"; a *choreographer*; and a *costume designer*. Audiences, after all, absorb 80 percent of their data through their eyes. Again, adapt your team to suit your resources and context, but if possible cover these roles.

Here are some tips, some adapted from Cleese, for running Stage 2 incubation (often called a brainstorming session):[6]

Set aside a length of time, over several sessions: You will need longer than thirty minutes but usually no more than three hours. It takes time to get into the right frame of mind, and it is hard to be continually creative for too long. Allow no distractions. Turn phones off.

Give yourselves a deadline and stick to it: All creative processes benefit from limitations, so agree to complete your program by a due date, perhaps after several sessions, and stick to it.

Agree openness and authenticity: Start a session with introductions and ground rules around openness and authenticity. Discussion should be relaxed, expansive, less purposeful, contemplative, childlike, and inclined to laughter. All contributions are valuable, however silly, extreme, or illogical. No person should feel less important, and everyone should contribute.

Return gently but persistently to the creative problem: If you stay truly open, you will find yourselves in a range of conceptual spaces unrelated to the problem, and may become disheartened. This is useful, and not inefficient, so don't give up. Instead, gently move on with persistence.

Allow bad ideas: To reach your reciprocal form, you need to feel what the wrong direction of your arrow is. So bad ideas and periods of feeling you are in the wrong creative place are fine, even essential, and having them means your process is going well. Stay in the feeling of failure, so you learn. A decision that "We are definitely NOT doing that," means you have a clear direction where to try next, which is great news.

Use positive language: If an idea comes up that you want to challenge, be constructive nevertheless. Ask the person to amplify their idea, and positively reinforce their contribution for its own sake. Emphasize fun, play, and honesty. Try language like, "So in your scenario, what if [a] or [b] happens?"

"Yes, and . . ." thinking: In improvisational comedy, there is a convention known as "Yes, and . . .," by which you should always accept what is already proposed by the players in a scene, and build on it. So if someone says, "Oh, look there's an elephant over there," your response should be to go with it and add something, rather than say, "Oh no, there isn't!," which could immediately close the group creative process down.

Trust your subconscious: Let programming ideas bubble from your subconscious to the surface intuitively. Sometimes my best ones come outside the meeting, while in the shower or driving. Capture them, as they are like gold dust, and you may forget them. Take notes in the moment, use voice memos on your phone, or write them down on a notepad.

It can seem like nothing is happening, and that's good: Feeling like nothing is happening or you are getting nowhere is part of the process. You are being productive even so, waiting for the next idea. You may find it better to talk about something else for a minute or two. With some groups, periods of silence are helpful.

Group size: Truly creative sessions facilitate individual voices, so I tend to work in smaller groups of no more than five or six. Varying group sizes can also be good. Sometimes a pair works well. Also try setting the same task to two different groups, and then bring them together. Try a return to small group work after a pause, to allow deeper exploration. Mix it up.

Flow: When in your flow, you are completely present, effortlessly focused on the task in hand. Your goals feel clear and motivate you in themselves. Time feels like it is standing still, the work is easy, and you feel in control of the task. Action and awareness merge, and you cease to be aware of your own thought processes. The difficulty of a task affects the potential for flow, so tasks should be hard enough to stimulate, but not too hard to be successful.[7]

Stages 3–5: Decide, Implement, Evaluate

Now you are ready to finalize a concept and choose a first list of music. We go, at least in part, into closed mode, and iteration begins. A first set of songs or arrangements is chosen and gets feedback, and further decision-making signals that the process continues. This can often be the point to declare a show concept and commit to it, so that marketing, PR, and logistics can begin.

After Iteration 1, a messy cycle of decision-making, implementing, and evaluating begins, while all the details of a show gradually form. Creative changes continue, and activities at this stage might include:

Cut or edit a whole section: Be disciplined about your form, and stay true to your vision, but don't be afraid to cut a whole section that no longer seems to fit. In the words attributed to Coco Chanel, "Before you leave the house, look in the mirror

106 Transforming Choral Singing

and take one thing off."[8] Something else may emerge to fill that space, or an existing section may need to expand to fill the space.

Add or edit a song: Leave a space for "something new that has yet to arrive," and have a cheap and fast arranger standing by. A new song can come out, that feels utterly right for the moment, as happened for us when "Born This Way" came out in January 2011. We had it arranged, and sang it less than two months later in our mid-March show. Also, a particular song can be a great choice, but there may be just those few bars that have never quite worked. If necessary, cut or rewrite them, with permission of course.

Leave a decision for later: Choosing the right moment for an artistic decision is a key skill here. Often logistics, a production schedule, or a printing deadline will lead to pressure to decide. But you may need to wait for an insight to reveal itself, or check that a concept really is going to land as you intended, by trying it out in rehearsal before finally choosing it. Consciously leaving a decision for later can be smart, rather than a procrastination.

For a choral director, rehearsal remains an intensely creative time, when open mode remains incredibly useful. We are building the plane while flying it. We are teaching the material, which demands clarity and precision, but simultaneously evaluating, sifting, trying new sound ideas out on the voices of the singers, and making fresh decisions in the moment. New insights about the show's shape, impact, and flow will continue to emerge, and final edits will always need to be made in the light of the lived experience of rehearsal and performance.

When you find a creative solution, implement it quickly and decisively. I've added songs and speeches on show day, and indeed cut them in response to events. Situations I have dealt with include; a riot near the concert hall on show day; a guest star with a sudden cold; a bomb in a local subway station; the show running unavoidably long, and needing cutting in the moment.

Staying flexible is key. Some of the most profound and impactful moments in our work were a direct response to world events. One that had huge impact was when we sang the song "Light" from *Next to Normal* on national TV, in direct response to the bombing of the "Pulse" nightclub in Orlando. This was a terrible tragedy in which scores of LGBTQIA+ people died. Only twenty-four hours later, we sang in Times Square on national TV to honor the victims. By being flexible and well prepared, we were able to catch a wave of emotion and ride it in real time, expressing the grief, anger, and shock of our community. The video went viral, was viewed by several million people, and I got highly emotional emails from people in New Zealand and elsewhere across the world.

Another was our show two months after Trump's election, where we invited our sister choir from Mexico City, Coro Gai Ciudad de México, to perform with us. Two massed LGBTQIA+ choruses from New York and Mexico stood together in international solidarity, against building walls of division and hate. Above all, when both situations arose, we had the creative flexibility to make new choices in the moment. In both cases, the flexibility of our artistic result led directly to more stylistically open singing, brought people together in community, and actively facilitated social justice. We learned new repertoire from our Mexican counterparts, we drew together new communities around our cause, and we raised awareness of the bombing in ways that helped people empathize with our community's feelings of shock and horror.

Finally, a note about finding repertoire. Try starting from what you want your message or impact to be. Then find the material to suit that purpose. I find many published arrangements disappointing in their homogeneity of texture and vocal approach, particularly in the popular realm. Often, they are designed to fit into predetermined categories of pedagogical level, range, or length, and publishers do not encourage arrangers to strive persistently for authenticity, or to be original and make them their own. You don't have to start only from available arrangements and compositions. Indeed it can sometimes be cheaper, quicker, and more innovative to commission a local independent composer to write something, or get an arranger to devise a song exactly as you want it. Those people are out there, and are perhaps one or two degrees of separation from you, but they may not be in your immediate network as a choral musician. Even one piece of genuinely innovative or custom arranged work can lift an entire program, if well placed.

Some questions to conclude: How many iterations of a given program do you personally go through? How much research do you do when planning your programs? Do you have separate incubation and implementation phases? Do you work alone, or with a team?

B. Two Example Shows: *Big Gay Sing* and *Accentuate the Positive*

Next is an account of how we applied these approaches in two example shows: *Big Gay Sing* and *Accentuate the Positive*. Both were innovative choral performances in their own terms, but in totally different ways. All four principles from Chapter 1 were evident in both shows, but *Big Gay Sing*'s explicit focus was to create impact more through connection and bonding, while that of *Accentuate the Positive* was on raising awareness of a social issue, and articulating the joys and traumas of a community ecosystem.[9] Both involved collaborative leadership, and both grew out of my personal experience as a musician and gay man, so your own context will of course lead you to entirely different programs.

Big Gay Sing

Big Gay Sing grew out of two initial goals. The first was to regrow the finances of our group after an extremely fallow period of ticket sales before my arrival. The second was to convince our core New York gay man audience that we had artistically changed. We had a reputation for being "worthy" and supporting the just cause of the LGBTQIA+ community, but we were no longer seen as innovating artistically. We felt "important" to ourselves and to our core donors, but in reality, we were like the Broadway show that everyone had already seen. We needed to become more approachable, sing better, but above all attract younger singers and be more fun to watch. We had to reconnect with our audience, and engage with them where they were. Below is an account of the major decisions that shaped the show.

50/50 balance of singalong to set-piece: We still wanted to produce a quality choral product. So we programmed 50 percent well sung set-pieces and 50 percent singalong material. The singalong elements were chosen because they were already well known, simpler in their arrangements, often mainly one or two parts with brief, more chorally complex openings and final gestures. This allowed our rehearsals to focus on a smaller number of entertaining and chorally spectacular set pieces.

Be interactive always: To connect even more, we innovated by being interactive in many different ways throughout the programming and rehearsal process. We involved the audience as singers, and as speakers, soloists, dancers, participants, etc. We invited audience members on stage, and took our singers out into the audience to sing with them. We also gave a questionnaire to our audience online about songs to include, and posted dance routines for them to learn. We put creativity into audience interaction song by song, even if it was only "Stand up, sit down," "Wave your light here," "clap on 2 and 4 on the chorus" etc. We invited our audience to come to our *Big Gay Sing* shows in costumes appropriate to the theme, as, say, monsters or TV characters, and we also found sponsors who would give them party hats, goody bags, and pom-poms. We started an online "Big Gay Idol" singing competition. Here, entrants sang a thirty-second audition extract of a chosen song a cappella on YouTube, and posted their video to our "Big Gay Idol" channel by a certain date. The winners got to be soloists and sang the song in full with a 300-strong chorus on stage. We did absolutely anything that would create connection.

Turn up the volume: We especially wanted to connect with our core gay audience, but not in too obvious a way. So this show, we decided, should be BIG. It was spectacular and visually exciting, with choreography, gender-fluidity and costuming, even if the singing took a back seat some of the time. We planned a very specific emotional response from our community ecosystem. It should look and sound so gay that audience eyes would be rolling. They should, we decided, be cringing in slight embarrassment, while at the same time laughing in knowing recognition at their own community. Instead of one torch song, we did three. Instead of one drag Tina

Turner on stage, we had five. We were simultaneously celebrating our "gay," and also pushing boundaries by subverting it.

Exploit the obvious and the clichés: Our song choice strategies were unconventional in their familiarity. Previously, we would often do a couple of songs in our *Big Gay Sing* that were obvious, perhaps too easy, old hat, clichéd, or "over." Here, we had many more, as those clichés were exactly the ones we needed. Our goal was not to move forward the art form, but simply to sing songs that our subculturally savvy audience knew, liked, and identified with. We were creating belonging.

Research what songs people really know: Research was needed at incubation stage before we commissioned arrangements, to discover the songs and even sections within them that our audience actually knew. Did they really know the bridge of "Somewhere over the Rainbow," for example, or the lyric to Madonna's "Vogue"? If those we focus-grouped did not know the words to the bridge of a song or verse 2, we cut that part, or got the choir to sing it instead. We even tried out some of the arrangements with people on the street, asking them to sing along in the chosen key until they could no longer remember how the song went. It transpired that singalong success depended a lot on how old they were, and what songs they had dated to. Likewise, we found out that our younger New York audience members needed us to be really contemporary, and sing songs in the current charts. Even six months old, the latest pop songs and Broadway shows were passé. Interestingly, my new audience in San Diego seems a little less concerned with the contemporary. Past shows that have been especially successful have been uniquely Southern Californian, in their focus on specific mainstream pop styles of the past, for example Motown, '80s rock, or the music of the Temptations.

Keep musical flow going to maintain engagement: Big band directors and DJs know the importance of keeping a musical flow going. It ensures that dancers stay out on the dance floor, and in this case, flow also kept audience members singing along. Once an audience stops singing, it is harder to restart them. In that sense, we were creating longer continuous singalong forms out of short one- to two-minute items. To keep the audience singing, short transitions were key, and we kept tempos rising, so tension built. We avoided long introductions, musically complex key and tempo changes, and other long periods of instrumental music. Again our innovation in choral terms was to focus on the listener, keep the musical material direct and simple, and get straight into the song.

Choose keys carefully: My earlier background as a church musician proved useful, in that we arranged songs in "congregational," audience-friendly keys and tessituras, rather than in the keys that suited our ensemble best. This was low for tenors at times, so other choral elements other than the melody would often sit above a baritone melody. With an SATB group, we learned as a general rule that if your altos are comfortable on the melody, so will your audience be.

Break down your fourth wall: Think about ways to break down the invisible barrier between choir and audience. Often, a host was key, to explain the concept, get the audience singing at the start, be "on their side," and do their own party piece(s).

They would banter with the conductor, chat with audience members from the stage, and connect audience and stage, relaxing us all. Choral shows are always about great singing, so we sometimes engaged a vocally accomplished guest star, who could sing at professional level in whatever style the show was about.

Add a moment of activism: We would always program a moment of activist seriousness, around an LGBTQIA+ advocacy issue, with a song attached. In a program of generally lighter, more familiar material, the audience needed that, as did we. It was all the more touching as a contrast in a generally lighter show.

Add a moment of quality, possibly classical, choral singing: This was a stylistically open show, but it was nevertheless good for our brand and a useful contrast to really nail at least one piece of conventional but accessible choral singing in the program. One year we did an especially fun segue straight out of Orff's "O Fortuna" from *Carmina Burana* into Michael Jackson's "Thriller." While being innovative in your focus on connection, you can also have impact in this kind of show with some well-chosen mainstream but accessible choral repertoire.

Add choreography: Visual interest is all, so for these shows, we often get singers to do some choreography, or "choralography" as we call it, which is mainly step-touching, and other movement from the waist up. We also have a dance team, made up of singers who would leave the risers and do more extensive routines. We found that a small amount of really tight movement is often more effective than too much that is less confident. Some songs need none at all, and some can be enhanced with two or three short, powerful moves. Some singers will be good movers, and others will just do their best. We put confident movers in the front row, and section dance captains rehearsed the moves, focusing on hands, face, arms, and shoulders.

Project the words: We projected all singalong words clearly and in large font on a screen above and behind the audience. We found printed words worked less well, causing audiences to look down a lot, so we used PowerPoint, taking care about font size and how much text to put on one slide. Punctuation and sections with "La-la-la" and so on can be hard to read, and put audience singers off their stride. We also varied the colors of projected words, and kept listeners looking up by adding pictures and captions.

Night-out concert dress: We aimed for singers to wear what they would wear on a fun night out with friends. Often a colorful T-shirt, jeans, and sneakers was a singer-friendly, gender-flexible basis, and we would then add items in line with the theme that year. Sometimes uniformity was good, and at others, we encouraged individuality. A combination can be good—for example, "anything as long as it is black or white."

A party atmosphere: We booked a DJ and put them on stage before it started, playing familiar dance music, show tunes, and material the audience knew. Many were singing along before we even got on stage! As audience members came in, we aimed for an animated party buzz to the audience chat, rather than hushed, respectful whispering. Stage and audience lighting was as for a pop gig.

Programming, Repertoire, and Show Design **111**

Singers and "celebrities" in the foyer: We placed singers in the foyer and audience, welcoming people in costume. They were briefed to say, for example, "Hi, I'm [x]; I am a tenor and [something personal about themselves]." This helped listeners feel they "knew" at least one singer in an impersonal sea of faces. We also had a "step and repeat" in the foyer, where listeners could pay to have their photos taken with a drag "Cher" or "Madonna" in front of our logo. This raised money, and we got audience members to post our pictures on social media, again widening our impact.

Add a community connection: We often invited our local firemen, a gay volleyball team, or cheerleading team to appear on stage with us. They would add color and help spread the word, and we would sing to them for one song. We thanked them, found songs that fit around what they did, and it all reflected on the welcoming tone of our brand.

Offer a licensed bar: A performance venue with a bar really helps, especially if it can be open before the show starts, so the audience can drink as the evening progresses. Get your venue to put on more staff than normal if possible. If your audience drinks more than most, the venue will make money and ask you back.

Choose the day of the week carefully: We used to avoid doing concerts on Friday and Saturday nights, because we wanted to avoid clashing with other events. In our new guise, we actively programmed our *Big Gay Sing* on Friday and Saturday nights, because we found audiences wanted a party then, and had the right expectations.

How can you adapt these concepts to your context? Some questions follow.

Do you already do this kind of collaborative, informal, community-based singalong choral show with your choir? If not, what might be the impact if you did? What might you lose? How would your audience change? If so, how does it differ from the model I lay out above? Also, how could you make your concerts more interactive? What songs would create belonging in your context? What should you and your singers wear, in order to look approachable and fun, rather than "high art" and distant? Who are the other ensembles and organizations nearby that you could celebrate by singing to or about them? How could you use your singers and venue to create opportunities for social media posts? How could audience members join in with you, or interact in some way? What elements of lighting, costume, dance, and movement could you include, to add visual interest? What should your choral set-pieces be? If you wanted to add one moment in a concert where you highlighted an issue of relevance to your community, what would be the issue? And what song could you sing that would bring people together?

Accentuate the Positive

Accentuate the Positive was a very different show concept, stylistically open but laser focused on educating people about a social issue. It was also artistically innovative through its stylistic juxtapositions, the surprises in the arrangements, the band choice, and in combining choral singing with semi-staged narrative.

112 Transforming Choral Singing

Timing is all in social change, and *Accentuate the Positive* was first presented in June 2011. New York had been an epicenter of the HIV epidemic since it began in the mid-1980s. Before my arrival, my group had lost 150 members to the disease over twenty years, and this left a lasting scar on our community and organizational culture. Remembrance and grief were key emotions in the singing, and looking at past programs, one notices that we had sung a *lot* of ballads(!). Previously, our main artistic goal had become to make the bottom lip of our audience quiver with sadness, and to leave them feeling hopeful, yet determined. A frequently heard meme was that we had to get them to the "happy-sad" place, where we smile through tears because "at least we have each other." As with *Big Gay Sing*, I felt it was time to change our aesthetic, establish a wider emotional range, sing from the place of "victim" less often, and instead celebrate the strength, vibrancy, and wisdom of our community as it faced its own pandemic.

Time had also gone by in the real world. Anti-retrovirals were improving the life-expectancy of HIV positive people, and the HIV positive were no longer primarily in gay male communities. It was time for our group of mainly gay men to look outward, and sing about and for others. Now the transgender community and other marginalized groups are our focus, but then, the new focus of the time within HIV was the straight community, people of color, and bisexual guys, the so-called MSMs (men who have sex with men). New stories were around how they were transferring the virus to their straight partners through having unsafe sex. They kept their behavior secret and with it, their feelings of shame and guilt. Such secrets led to dishonesty, made them hard to reach with information, made them more vulnerable than gay men to ill health and death.

Another strand of positivity was that there were many community heroes in our group. They were survivors, some of whom had been positive for twenty-five years. This group, battle-scarred and uncompromising, owned a wisdom that demanded celebration. I saw a celebration of life in those people, and a strong motivation to teach us about staying disciplined in our sex lives. We set out to do an optimistic, even slightly triumphant show that was about *living* with HIV, rather than dying of it. It had strong story-telling potential, and it was also fertile ground for musical repertoire.

As before, what follows is an account of the main programming and artistic decisions we took. A recurring theme is how we took songs that had meaning in one context, and used them to reveal new meaning in another. Also note the balance of musical concerns, such as key and style, with story-telling ones.

An opening that plays with expectations: In a good program, at least one set of expectations is a set-up that will later be subverted to surprise the audience. Here at the incubation stage we brainstormed around the life experience of someone we knew, who had decided to take control of his own remaining days as a musician, by choosing the music for his own funeral. We decided to open with a funeral, a dramatic opening that would allow us to get the death of previous shows, which was usually at the end, out of the way early. We would then become unexpectedly joyful right away. The person's choice was Morten Lauridsen's "Sure on this Shining Night." It seemed luminous, spiritual, chorally conventional, and interesting in that it was unexpectedly slow for an opening number.

A few bars before the end, we did an abrupt segue into an upbeat, double chorus, spectacular version of the 1970s pop-rock hit "Life Is a Celebration" (from "Kids from Fame"), some of which was in 7/4 time. In this "bait and switch," we moved the audience from death to life, ballad to upbeat, from night into day, from classical to pop, and from a meditation about the universality of mortality into a hedonistic, joyous, and specific present. With careful planning, we also stayed in the same key to provide some aural continuity.

Two patterns of recurring material: Like a good meal, most good performances have through-lines. A musical ingredient or a narrative element will recur, creating a pattern—perhaps an instrument, a period, a composer, or a style of singing. Here, we had two patterns.

First, we used some medium-tempo jazz, Gerry Mulligan's classic "Blues in B-flat," sung wordlessly exactly as written, and learned mostly by ear. This was chorally surprising, in that it is rare to hear a 300-strong TTBB chorus sing in this style. Once we got into the instrumental improvisation, the jazz became the backdrop for an actor, who spoke in the style of a David Attenborough wildlife show, and introduced as the "wildlife" the "Homosexual of the Lower Manhattan Region." Musical purists would say we ruined the jazz by having people speak over it, but the early 1960s jazz, sophisticated in itself, also provided the perfect quizzical, cerebral mood for the story of how dating occurs to unfold. To create the pattern, we sang different segments of the same material twice more later in the show, and used the segments to signal a moment of storytelling by speech. To do musical justice to the style, there was some instrumental and vocal improvising later too.

Second, we also needed a song that was about statistics, and counting. We needed material around which to project numbers of HIV infections and deaths on a screen, in a light, humorous but factual way. Again, the music and statistics recurred several times. Almost immediately, the director came up with a short kids' song called "Twelve," familiar to many who were 1970s US kids from the show *Sesame Street*. "Twelve" also fit, because it created a new pattern around 1970s polyrhythmic pop. It enabled us to contrast deep feeling with emotionally cool statistics in the form of numbers of infections and deaths. The song also had cultural resonance for a particular 1970s generation, and subliminally signaled the free love mores of the time, in counterpoint to the chastening infection numbers being shown.

The re-imagined song: Sometimes recreating a piece of recent pop music as performed is perfect, and gets people excited in itself. At others, it is not enough. Here, we knew we needed a song that would tell the story of the spread of the virus, and how that occurred through switching sexual partners. "Crazy in Love" was a megahit in 2003–2004, eight years before. It had become a pop classic, in part because of Beyoncé's steadily increasing status in the LGBTQIA+ community, the international black community, and across pop culture. The music had a slightly manic intensity about it, and the lyric was about how when in love, we take "crazy" decisions that we know may be wrong and we may later regret:

Got me looking so crazy right now, your love's
Got me looking so crazy right now (your love)
Got me looking so crazy right now, your touch
Got me looking so crazy right now (your touch)
Got me hoping you'll page me right now, your kiss
Got me hoping you'll save me right now
Looking so crazy, your love's
Got me looking, got me looking so crazy in love

Originally about black women's experience, the context of HIV risk took the lyric to a whole new place. At an incubation meeting, our choreographer said he had recently been doing some work on tango, which he was really enjoying, and soon after that our director independently came up with the idea of Beyoncé's "Crazy in Love." I quickly came up with a sketched arrangement of the song as a medium tempo tango, and we had our core idea.

Next, we developed the staging to include a series of same-sex couples dancing an elegant, flamboyantly sexy, almost aggressive tango while the chorus sang. The passionate dance pointed toward the taking of risks. Dancing couples swapped partners, and white scarves were passed during the choreography, to indicate how the virus was transferred. The tango also inspired the unique timbral color and intimate, unplugged feel of the band, which included piano, bass, drums, accordion, and improvising violin. We used them throughout.

The choral moment: Next, we kept our audience on their toes by going into an a cappella song by Ysaye Barnwell, made famous by Sweet Honey and the Rock, called "Would You Harbor Me?" A campaigning song with strong African American associations, this song introduced the concept of the HIV positive person as alone, an outsider. In our context, its message was that it was no longer necessarily white gay men but more likely bisexual people of color who found themselves outsiders, facing the triple threat of racism, homophobia, and HIV status. Chorally, the song was an a cappella, texturally interesting opportunity for us to showcase our vocal technique.

The moment of risk: Many shows need a moment of risk, where the point we are making is revealed in full, and the audience are faced with an extreme emotion. If your shows don't have one, they may be a little tame currently. Here, we chose the song "Totally Fucked" from the then-current Broadway musical *Spring Awakening*. It felt risky to many in the group, and some initially refused to sing it at all, until we explained why we were using it.

Again, we reimagined the context of the song. Getting regularly tested for HIV is the right thing to do for the sexually active of all kinds, and remains a recurring feature of the lives of many gay men. Our emotional focus was the moment after

Programming, Repertoire, and Show Design   **115**

taking your test, when you wait for the result in the cold hospital waiting room. Your past life passes before your eyes, you remember intimate moments when a sexual risk might have been taken. The first line of the song goes: "There's a moment you know . . . you're fucked!"

Singers had to sing the word "fuck" over fifty times in the course of the song. We had to workshop the word itself so it felt comfortable in the mouth, and after early misgivings, singers went with it. This was the second-to-last song of Act 1, ending with a moment of hard rock climax and a sudden silence. I remember an audible gasp from the audience. In the silence, the five solo singers were sitting semi-staged on simple chairs in a row, in front of the chorus. Four were given the all-clear and are led away, but a fifth stayed on stage, in shock, newly aware they were positive. This singer then led the group into "Take Me Home," the final song of Act 1, a brand-new commission by composer and now Hollywood producer Our Lady J. The tragic, childlike lyric included the following:

> *Thought I was a young man, thought I was a strong man, thought I was fine*
> *Take me from here, I don't wanna be here,*
> *I don't wanna see here, Take me home.*

Act 1 ended in a fortissimo choral scream of pain.

The opening of Act 2: The first twenty minutes of a second act can be the hardest zone to program. The audience has already been there a while, and you've laid out an initial set of ideas, including many of your strongest. Yet there is still thirty minutes to the finale, which is often the part that comes easiest. You have to make a new start, but stay on theme.

In this case, we devised a tableau of two songs: the Jackson 5's "Stop: The Love You Save (May Be Your Own)," and "You Can Be as Loud as the Hell You Want (When You're Makin' Love)," a then current musical theater hit from the musical *Avenue Q.* The two upbeat songs were interwoven, but in tension. One was sex positive and encouraged lack of inhibition in the bedroom, while the other urged caution. One was 1960s Motown, and the other contemporary Broadway.

The 11 o'clock song: In his play 'Endgame' (1957), a Samuel Beckett character says of life: '*The end is in the beginning and yet you go on'. Put another way,* the key to the end of a good story is returning to where we started, but now with a signal difference, because something has changed. The so-called 11 o'clock song, then, the song right before the finale, needs careful thought. I like to return to earlier music, perhaps reprising a song in a new form, or revisiting an idea. In this show, we returned to the theme of regrets for past choices, set up with "Crazy in Love," and sang Edith Piaf's famous "Non, Je ne Regrette Rien" by Charles Dumont. We returned too to the idea of "Nothing has changed; everything has changed," from our earlier Act 1 commission.

Previously ashamed, now the singer is freed, but has learned to live with the mistakes they made. Life will never be quite the same, but the choir sings

116   Transforming Choral Singing

triumphantly of moving forward, having processed earlier anger, sadness, and struggle. This song was originally programmed as a full chorus arrangement, but at our soloist auditions, the perfect singer appeared. Three weeks before the show, in an example of iteration and later creativity, we rewrote the arrangement around their solo voice, only bringing in the chorus later.

The hopeful close: Another tough decision is where to leave an audience at the end of a choral performance. The cliché is to end with hope, but not all stories end happily, and when a performance is about change, we don't always want to leave an audience in a happy place. At the end of Act 1, we had taken this show's audience to an emotionally dark place, and it would have been possible to leave them redeemed, healed but not exactly joyful after "Non, Je ne Regrette Rien."

Our initial thought was then to reprise Lauridsen's "Sure on this Shining Night," as a peaceful and sublime conclusion. The show would truly have come full circle, and earlier tension would have been resolved. After hot debate, we instead moved the audience from redemption to optimism and finished with an upbeat, still uplifting but lesser-known Sting song called "After the Rain," whose key lyric went:

> *After the rain has fallen*
> *After the tears have washed your eyes*
> *You find that I've taken nothing, that*
> *Love can't replace in the blink of an eye*
> *After the tears have fallen, there'll still be love in the world*

Encores (in this case, none): Often we plan with an encore in mind, but this show had such a clear arc, so no encore was programmed. Elsewhere, I found myself doing encores that contrasted with our finales, and therefore were often ballads. Another approach can be to reprise a song from the show literally in the moment—one that the audience applauded especially loudly that night. Above all, acknowledge the applause and respond to it—an audience won't like you to leave too soon.

Again we finish with some questions, to help you apply these ideas to your own context. What are the social or political issues around your choir that have similar story-telling potential? Post-COVID, homelessness is an important example in US cities. So too, at the time of writing, is the rise of the far-right, and the potential for war. Thinking more locally, what issues are in your local news? What communities could you represent? Here in San Diego in 2022, we are near the border with Mexico, so there are many immigrant stories to be told. What are the local organizations with whom you could partner around, say, a choral show about home, or about immigration? We found our local ones welcomed us with open arms, as a new way that they could get their messages across.

Programming Tips

Curb appeal: As with buying a house, a listener makes an initial decision about whether they are going to enjoy a performance within the first minute or two so curb appeal matters. The programmer has to grab the audience's attention with their opening gambit.

Embed tension and release in your programming form: In most good art, from symphonies to novels, tension is created that is later resolved. The end, as Beckett says, is embedded in the beginning, but with a signal difference. In this case, we expect it to be a sad show about HIV, but it turns out more hopeful than we thought. Again, don't be afraid of tension in your programming choices, as it adds contrast and helps the release songs to breathe.

Explore a range of show length: Most contexts have norms about how long a show lasts. In pre-COVID New York, our concert programs were expected to be in two halves of forty-five minutes or possibly fifty and thirty-five minutes, with an intermission. Programs are sometimes too short, but much less often. We also tried a single act of seventy-five minutes, with a Q and A afterward, and this worked well for us. Online, lockdown programs I have seen tended to be one act and even shorter, lasting between twenty and forty-five minutes.

Both narrative and musical content should be fertile: The strongest themes lead you to a fertility of programming and show design ideas for both narrative stories and musical ones. Four or five years ago, queer activists were convinced that employment rights was the next new fight. However, it was hard to find ninety minutes of varied songs and stories that would make a compelling evening around that theme. We did a ten-minute segment instead. Likewise, I personally love 1950s jazz, for example, have specialist training in it, and would love to do a whole show, but I could rarely find a choral performance where it would fit.

Don't get too personally invested: Art is also about good judgment and knowing your audience. So beware of programming a song that is too personal to you. If we become too invested, we can lose perspective and become self-indulgent. The ultimate skill (and sometimes luck) is in finding music that aligns with our group's purpose *and* our personal preferences.

Take risks: Our work needs to be stimulating at minimum, and ideally cutting-edge. As with the clutch in a stick shift car, there is a "biting point" of taste to be found, where the clutch engages and the car suddenly moves forward. If your taste is too conservative, your show can lack energy, cohesion, and interest. If it is too controversial, audiences and singers may be offended, and walk out of the auditorium. Above all, be prepared to shock people enough, as that is where change (and indeed the most interesting art) happens.

Follow your gut: Sometimes a song may not land with your singers initially. On its own, it can seem too dark, too light, or too "out there." The exact fit of a song in the

118   Transforming Choral Singing

program may not make sense until the bigger picture of its flow emerges. Whatever the context, you will sometimes face reasoned and passionate argument against a song choice, but there are times you should program it anyway. Know the impact you are trying to create, check with listeners, but then follow your gut.

Watch your music licensing budget: Licensing can be an unexpected cost, as some of the most familiar songs are also the most expensive. Start planning early, and be flexible in your choices with extra songs in your back pocket, as some will be refused or too expensive.

C. Workshops

> Before you leave the house, look in the mirror and take one thing off.
>
> —Coco Chanel

We turn now to three programming workshops that will help you explore the programming of your own choir. In line with this Coco Chanel quote, editing your ideas is key to them all. The first is about creating a fertile store of new show concepts, that can develop gradually over a three- to five-year time span. It also focuses on the relationship between art and mission. The second is more granular, a group task about ordering and editing a pre-defined set of songs within a single show. This one helps to reveal our programming habits, and provokes discussion about show flow and the impact of individual songs in particular positions within a program. It would work both with your singers and advisory groups. I have also used it in consultancy work and at choral conferences, to give choral directors and others a rare space to compare approaches collaboratively, and learn from each other. The third involves discussion of a set of programming templates.

Workshop 1: Developing a Store of New Show Concepts (4–6 hours)

This day-long retreat is great for engaging everyone with the artistic process. Assemble a group that reflects your choir or chorus's community ecosystem. It should include: yourself as conductor and deviser of the program; your executive director (or main managers and budget holders); one to two board members or organizational leaders, one to two audience members, and two to three singers from inside the group, across a cross-section of age, gender, race, etc. If possible, add two to three outside people who do not know your work, but will have refreshing perspectives: perhaps conductors of other local choirs, composers, marketing experts, or influencers from your community. Workshops like this can be a great way to involve those whose voices have not been foregrounded in the past. There are four tasks, taking a total of around four hours.

Programming, Repertoire, and Show Design **119**

Task 1: Opening Briefing (45 minutes)

Set the context and objectives. Before the session, ask people in the room to prepare to cover the following topics, or present them yourself. Keep this part moving along.

1) **Introductions:** Lay out and agree objectives for the day, as above. Point out toilets, break times, finish time. Introduce your board members, staff, and volunteers, their roles, and who does what. Welcome guests, and ask them to introduce themselves, what they do, preferred gender pronouns, etc.

2) **Your mission, vision, values (See Chapter 2):** Lay them out clearly, and ideally give them out in writing. They are a given, and create the context in which you are working, so there is no need to discuss them here.

3) **Your current artistic year, structure, and artistic goals:** This will often start from the number of main shows a year, what kind of art you make and in which venues, number of singers, level of skill, audience size, likely show content. If time, allow brief comment on what has worked and not worked in the past. Stick to two to three examples, stay positive, and don't get sidetracked into debate or unnecessary detail. This part just sets the context.

4) **Financial and administrative overview:** How have the past couple of years been? Your business leaders should identify past artistic and financial successes and failures across shows, fundraisers, etc. Also identify your overall budget size, and how you may be intending that to change in the coming couple of years.

Task 2 (45 minutes): "Your Changing Context," and "Dreaming about the Artistic Future of [Your Choir]'

(This starts similar to Workshop 4 in Chapter 2, but focuses on programming)

Divide into small groups. Explain that you are going to move fast here to get a flow going. Then discuss these two questions:

1) **New artistic developments:** What new developments are there in your artistic area? New repertoire, songs, ways of programming, kinds of ensemble, vocal sounds, ways of performing. Is a cappella all the rage, are virtual choirs passé? What music is trending now in choral singing? What would the next level look like for you?

2) **New social issues:** What is changing in your community, or your social and political context? What issues are coming up for your singers and audience right now, and how have those changed over time? Examples for my choir at different times over the past fifteen years might include: increasing division and polarization, bullying, teen suicide, marriage equality, addiction, PREP, discrimination in the workplace.

120 Transforming Choral Singing

A plenary is not necessary here, as this session is really just stimulating thoughts for later. Have a brief one, if valuable. Break if needed.

Task 3 (90 minutes) Create Eight to Ten Show Concepts

Define the idea of a "show concept," which for the purposes of the workshop consists of three ideas:

1) A show title: for example, *Accentuate the Positive*
2) Three to five song ideas that fit with the show title: for example: "Life is a Celebration" (*Fame*), "Sure on this Shining Night" (Morten Lauridsen), "Totally Fucked" (*Spring Awakening*).
3) A sentence or short paragraph which summarizes what the show is about, and its journey. For example:
   This show celebrates with joy the lives of those who have been living with HIV/ AIDS, and highlights their wisdom and their insights as LGBTQIA+ people.

Divide into small groups of four or five. The job of each small group is to work fast, and create eight to ten possible show concepts, for the group to consider performing over the next three to five years. Write each show concept on one sheet. Stick all eight to ten sheets on the wall or noticeboard of the workshop room at the end of the session. Hold no whole group evaluation yet—this is incubation, so all ideas are useful.

Next is LUNCH, and an opportunity for all those involved to examine all the show ideas on the wall informally.

Task 4: (90 minutes) Evaluation and Conclusions

1) **Memorable concepts:** Ask each group member to identify their most memorable show idea of the day, and say why. Are there ideas that were liked by a number of people for different reasons?
2) **Top ten ideas:** As a group, assemble and prioritize your top ten best ideas.
3) **What have we learned?:** This is about where we are artistically, and what we now know about how we will implement our mission in the next few years. Your discussion may also have revealed useful insights about the processes of your group, what the possibilities are, what your limitations are, and what you do well and badly. Identify which potentially exciting shows were proposed, but which your group cannot do because they lack certain skills or resources.

As well as being great brainstorming opportunities, these four exercises are especially useful for us as artistic leaders, because they allow us to take the cultural temperature and so establish new, more current priorities. They also spread debate and therefore engagement about your group's artistic agenda across your management team and school, college, or church context.

For my group, the priorities we established changed over time. Our new priorities in 2011–2012 included bullying of LGBTQIA+ students, changing the agenda on HIV, "where next" for the US post–marriage equality, and a new goal to do collaborations with guest choirs at regular intervals. When we did a similar exercise in 2017, our priorities could not have been more different. After the election of Trump, the optimism in our community had been replaced by sadness and anger. Priorities then included expressing a new anger in the trans and BIPOC communities; a fear to be on the streets at night, after homophobic attacks in previously safe areas; and a sense that we were under attack and needed to fight back.

Our show concepts changed markedly to reflect this. One was called "I See Fire," and featured the famous Ed Sheeran song from *The Hobbit*. It was about seeing a menacing fire coming toward us as we sit around the campfire, and the need to gird our loins and prepare for battle. We also invited transgender composers to write for our group, and featured transgender performer and songwriter Justin Vivian Bond in our holiday show, to highlight how Christmas time is not always so rosy for those thrown out by their families, and how chosen families can play a role.

Workshop 2: Creating a Concert Order (2 hours 30 minutes)

This workshop is best suited for your whole artistic team, but could involve others too. As with Workshop 1, it can enable others whose voices have traditionally been less heard in your group to have a say. I have also used it with groups of choral conductors from different choirs. It enables us to learn new programming concepts from each other, and to become more aware of our own thought processes and our conventions and clichés as programmers. There are three tasks below.

Task 1: Program These Items into a Concert Order (20 minutes)
Divide into small groups of four or five. You will be given a pile of cards. On each card is written a description of a single program item. Read them through. Here are the rules:

1) Your concert is in two acts of approximately forty minutes.
2) You will need to omit or edit some items.
3) You may wish to add some new items of your own.
4) You have twenty minutes to program your concert.

The task time limit is intentional, as it will make your group make fast decisions and discuss less.

Below is the list of program items, each printed on a separate card in the workshop:

- A big fun choral show tune arrangement, involving the whole group (fast) (6 minutes)
- An Elton-John-style heartfelt ballad about remembrance of "you," featuring your key soloist (slow) (5 minutes)

122   Transforming Choral Singing

- A "feel-good" gospel song (fast) (4 minutes)
- The fundraising speech to donors by the chair of the board or similar organizational leader (5 minutes)
- A newly commissioned piece: a little uncertain, it came in late, it's too hard, the membership is not quite sure about this, but it cost a lot of money. (3 movements, medium tempo, ends slow) (15 minutes)
- A guest appearance by another choir (10 minutes)
- Twelve minutes of highbrow a cappella choral material. Four short madrigals (medium tempo) (7 minutes in all)
- An extended piece of harmonically complex late Romantic music (slow) (5 minutes)
- Comedy skit 1: likely to be very funny (5 minutes)
- Comedy skit 2: less likely to be funny, because less well written (could be split up from comedy skit 1, or placed together) (7 minutes)
- A spectacular but accessible multicultural set of three songs from South Africa, involving drumming and dance (fast–slow–fast) (6 minutes)
- A singalong number (4 minutes)
- A speech by a nonprofit executive about marriage equality or a similar issue, to be followed by a song about that issue (8 minutes)
- A song from a contemporary TV hit show we all know (3 minutes)
- A stunning and complex piece in eight parts that you've been working on for two concert periods—your showstopper (slow) (5 minutes)
- An appearance by your small group, two cabaret songs (3 + 3 minutes)
- An overture by the band (2 minutes) As a group, your task is to order the cards on a table or on the floor into two columns, as the two acts of your concert.

Task 2: Debrief: Discuss Your Decisions and Identify Habits and Assumptions (45 minutes)

Next each group presents their two-act program to the whole group. All have used the same cards. Then discuss these questions as a whole group:

1) What was the first song you programmed, and why? Which did you find easiest to decide about?
2) How did you end each half?
3) Where did the ballad go? Why?
4) What did you leave out, and why?
5) What did you add, and why?
6) What other issues did you consider?

Then zoom out to discuss these questions:

What programming conventions/habits you noticed yourselves using?

Programming, Repertoire, and Show Design   **123**

Do other groups you know in your region use different ways of working that you might want to steal?

Is there any repertoire in the task that previously would have been acceptable, but you omitted because it would now be seen as cultural appropriation?

Workshop 3: Templates (1 hour)

This time, a chance for some individual reflection, again followed by a plenary discussion. Below is a list of six programming templates. They may be presented on cards individually, or in a digital presentation on separate slides. Read all six through silently as individuals. Then discuss the questions that follow.

TEMPLATE 1: An example full show

ACT 1

Opening piece:	Establishes mood/tone, welcome; Often upbeat (7 minutes)
Core repertoire	(Likely to be more high-brow, prove we can sing) (8 minutes)
Contrasting section 1	Variety, light and shade (8 minutes)
Contrasting section 2	Variety, light and shade (7 minutes)
Guest star/small group	Another contrast, more intimate (10 minutes)
Finale	With choralography. Often upbeat (6 minutes)

ACT II

Opening	Takes us to a new place (5–8 minutes)
Danger zone!	Audience more tired. More of the Act 1 material?
	Could be less focused. (10–15 minutes)
Speeches/ "necessary" items	(8 minutes maximum)
Something funny:	Soloist, small group, or guest star returns (5 minutes)
11 o'clock song	Emotional keynote, ballad. Moment of tension, dark, healing,
	intimate, dramatic change (5 minutes)
Act 2 finale:	Tension released. Move back toward feeling good. Public,
	celebratory (10 minutes)
Possible post-finale encore:	EITHER a little a cappella farewell, touching
	OR go up another level of energy, chorus often ends up in
	the audience (5 minutes)

Figure 6.7

124 Transforming Choral Singing

TEMPLATE 2: The Four Tenets

Make them laugh

Make them cry

Some moments of really fantastic singing

A moment of challenge

Figure 6.8

TEMPLATE 3: A holiday/Christmas show

Give the audience their holiday/Christmas

Some Santa and elves

Some winter

Some Christian birth stories

A moment of inclusion, compassion, charity

Always sing SOME traditional material

Figure 6.9

TEMPLATE 4: A pop/singalong show

Connect with the audience

Singalong medleys in audience keys

A loose theme: '70s, boy bands, Britpop

Please your singers, and make sure they have fun

Engage your community

Figure 6.10

Programming, Repertoire, and Show Design   125

> **TEMPLATE 5: A themed/explicitly political show**
>
> An artistically fertile theme: addiction, racism, marriage equality, holocaust, oppression
>
> Songs about struggle
>
> Political anthems
>
> Songs of remembrance
>
> New commissions

Figure 6.11

> **TEMPLATE 6: A choral, eclectic show**
>
> Songs from non-Western cultures
>
> Mixtures of high-brow and low-brow
>
> Juxtapositions
>
> Songs in other languages; tends to be shorter
>
> Engage other musicians

Figure 6.12

Discussion Questions

- Which of these templates do you recognize as part of the way you work?
- Which do you find your group using most, and which are not part of your approach?
- Are there other similar templates you like to use? Do you overuse them?
- How do you currently feel about your own programming? If you are pleased with it, what is great about it? If not, what strategies can you use to keep your programming fresh and innovative?
- What programming templates do you find especially valuable? Which are the ones you use a lot, that you now want to change?
- What new ideas have these templates generated, that you could apply in your own programs?

Notes

1. In what follows, I draw especially on the ideas of John Cleese, Malcolm Ross, James Webb Young, and Mihaly Csikszentmihalyi.

126 Transforming Choral Singing

2. Ross, Malcolm (1978), *The Creative Arts* (London: Heinemann Educational Books), 87–121.

3. Livermore (1988): 154.

4. John Cleese (2020), *Creativity: A Short and Cheerful Guide* (New York: Penguin Random House).

5. There are a number of different versions of this model of the design process out there, often deriving from Graham Wallas's seminal *The Art of Thought* (1926/2014). For more on one similar to mine, see the Interaction Design Foundation website here: https://www.interaction-design.org/literature/article/design-iteration-brings-powerful-results-so-do-it-again-designer

6. Adapted from Cleese's classic video, "John Cleese on Creativity in Management," by Video Arts, especially from 17 minutes in. https://www.youtube.com/watch?v=Pb5oIIPO62g

7. Csikszentmihalyi (2008).

8. Nevala-Lee (2016).

9. For further ideas and resources, the work of the community music movement, spearheaded by Lee Higgins and others, is another fertile source of similar ideas around artistic leadership. Higgins (2012) focuses on how musicians facilitate the voice of various communities, through work in prisons, day care centers, women's groups, and minority ethnic communities of various kinds.

7

Teaching and Learning in Rehearsal

Being a choral director is about performing but it is also about education. Sometimes we are the maestro, making the grand gesture or bringing out the nuance of a pianissimo "oo," but at others we are often the best kind of elementary school teacher, setting standards of behavior and using our complex teaching skills and musical experience to support our singers' learning. In schools and colleges, the best choral educators use singing to nurture human beings and help them grow, change, and flourish, as well as facilitating rehearsals and performances. As James Jordan wrote in *The Musician's Soul*, "A love of community and care for each singer is paramount in any music-making activity."[1] The best also encourage active Freirean reflection, action, and transformation in their singer-students.[2] Just as the best music-making is always change-making and grounded in community, so too is the best music education.

This chapter is about rehearsal—what it is, and how we can use teaching and learning strategies to make it a place of connection and bonding, a place of effective and socially just learning, and a place of impactful music-making that takes account of social context and facilitates growth and change in whole people as well as in their singing. In earlier chapters, I focused on the musical practices of choral singing, including vocal sound and pedagogy rhythm skills, improvisation, and programming. From this chapter onward, the focus begins to move gradually toward our social practices too. Here, then, there is renewed focus on the way musical and social practices entwine into a single way of working that helps our singers learn musical material and prepare them for performances.

Workshops in this chapter are organized in four batches, around the journey we take toward a show. They start at the warm-up, move through from the initial teaching of a piece to the reviewing, running, and refining phase, and finish with final performance preparations. Learning and rehearsing by ear *and* from notation is a recurring theme.

I want to begin, though, with some thoughts about learning style, the relationship between formal and informal learning, and the way in which our principles of connection, impact, social justice, and stylistic openness can be integrated into our pedagogy as the rehearsal process unfolds.

Learning Style

Education researchers outside music will tell you the conventional, though by no means universal, view that there are three main learning styles: visual (by looking),

Transforming Choral Singing. Charles W. Beale, Oxford University Press. © Oxford University Press 2024.
DOI: 10.1093/oso/9780197657775.003.0007

aural (by hearing) and kinesthetic (by doing, or perhaps feeling).[3] Unless we have an impairment of some kind, they contend, all of us will use all three, as the best musical activity requires visual learning, learning by ear, and learning by doing and feeling. Thanks to a combination of nature and nurture, one learning style may tend to be more dominant, and in my experience of choral singers and jazz musicians, this also interacts with the pedagogy of certain musical styles, so some musical styles tend to align with particular kinds of learning.

For some choral directors, learning style is something to consider but not a primary concern. At many mainstream choral rehearsals, there is one dominant way of learning the piece—the score. Using a score foregrounds visual learning, in that singers are often looking at "the music" on either iPad or paper, and singing along with others doing the same. They of course hear the music too, and feel the voice, rhythm, and groove through the body, but common practice classical music is almost impossible to learn to a high level without reference to the visual. Notice a relationship between a style of music and a style of learning. The ear is involved, but the eye is the key means by which sound is initially encoded and transmitted. We even call the staff notation "the music." This gives the visual learner a huge advantage in classical and other related kinds of choral singing, and more to the point, disadvantages musicians who may be highly skilled but learn in other ways.

I am more of a visual learner myself, as, I suspect, are many musicians who are successful in the classical tradition. I loved to read as a child, and as a singer in classical choirs, I even used to memorize music by mentally "taking a picture" of the staff, imagining that picture and reading the part back from it. My jazz and pop experience took me in very different directions in my twenties. Then, I was forced to learn without notation much more of the time, and the notation used in those contexts looked the same but was interpreted differently. I sang in choirs that learned and then modified parts by ear, and I played in bands where there was no music on the bandstand, and your main encoding tools were your ears, your musicianship, and your musical memory. The style of the music again has its analogue in a different learning style, which foregrounds spontaneous interaction by ear in the moment and inventing your part from a given mental map. The classical music skills of memorizing a specific part from a score and reproducing it precisely "as written" (in fact inventing it according to a different set of rules) were not required in that context.

For a while, this approach sapped my confidence. Although I had a "good ear" in classical terms, I found working by ear deeply deskilling. I felt I was failing and at one point worried that jazz was not for me. As a teacher later in my career, I found the same deskilling phenomenon in my students. Teaching jazz to classical piano teachers, I found that even the most successful and experienced educators with perfect pitch and twenty years of getting students into top colleges found learning by ear hard. Many commented that they felt were not suited for jazz as a whole. In fact, it was not the musical practices themselves, but the way we learned by ear and the configuration of rhythm, melody, and harmony within the musical material that was

Teaching and Learning in Rehearsal **129**

hard for them. Likewise, singers coming to classical music from "by ear" traditions like jazz and pop music can find the focus on staff notation hard. In their case, there is the added pressure that if you do not "read music" (and even if you read chord symbols really well but don't know figured bass), you can be treated as if you are somehow not a "complete" musician. Of course I generalize, and some jazz and pop music is transcribed, written down, and reproduced from staff notation too, with varying degrees of authenticity and precision. My point about learning styles stands, however.

In terms of choral singing, although notation is often helpful, it is possible to learn all kinds of choral music by ear and sing with expression, individuality, and authority at every level, from beginner to professional. Singers who primarily learn this way may find sight-reading harder, but they are just as effective as learners, and can also be equally expressive and impactful as performers.[4] How a singer in your choir learns their music is really a side issue, irrelevant to their core musical skills of vocal performance. They can read from the score, or learn from an mp3 on their phone. A recent survey of ninety-five singers in my San Diego group revealed that 15 percent of them learned their parts "mostly from the sheet music," 29 percent learned "mostly by ear, in rehearsal and using the rehearsal tracks," while the remaining 56 percent "used an equal mixture of sheet music and learning by ear."

To drill down, neither is a perfect means of learning on its own. Staff notation symbols do not express the tonal nuance of any style well, and contain little expressive nuance beyond basic "dynamics, articulation, and phrasing." Meanwhile, learning from a recording can also lead to unsatisfactory rigid copying. Both are simply tools to learn the part, after which the singer always needs to define the character of their unique performance through aural interaction with other singers and the conductor. Music is, in the end, an aural medium.

When we teach in choral contexts, then, how should we use our knowledge of different learning styles to help engage all our singers, so everyone has an equal chance to grow? A key theme in this book is the need for flexibility. In the context of teaching and learning, flexibility means that in every rehearsal choral directors should offer the widest possible range of ways into singing, so that regardless of the singer's cultural experience, learning style, or prior experience of music education, they can learn effectively. This leads directly to greater participation, engagement, and success by singers who would otherwise see staff notation as a barrier into choral singing, and it also facilitates engagement by singers with learning challenges of various sorts, and those whose primary learning style is not visual.

Let's take each learning style in turn, and identify strategies. Visual learners can benefit from strategies that include: bringing a pencil and writing information down; the use of smart boards and video screens; phonetic spellings of words and lip shapes; and visually present music symbols, as appropriate to the style. Meanwhile, aural learners can benefit from exercises involving inner hearing and critiquing singing. Silent singing while "thinking" the piece in your head can be especially useful, so their inner map develops. So too can regularly learning new warm-ups and melodic phrases, to develop skills of aural memory. Exercises involving listening to other singers, the whole group, or each other also work well, followed by verbal discussion. Listening to recordings of quality choral ensembles can also help aural learners to identify aspects of sound and style.

Finally our movers, feelers, and kinesthetic learners learn best in contexts where they can communicate, emote, and engage their bodies, for example by using their hands and arms to draw dynamics and phrase shapes, or pointing to accents with their fingers. Again this is automatically built into some styles, but not into others. Encourage them to get the pulse or the rhythm into their bodies, and allow them feel what a regular pulse is via proprioception (see Chapter 4). Exaggerate those movements to make this clearer. It can also help their learning to ask these singers to conduct themselves as they sing, to hear their physical gestures come alive in the singing of others, and to engage their breath, faces, and bodies in the emotion, meaning, and storytelling of a song. Solfège, Dalcroze Eurhythmics, and the Alexander Technique all contain great insights in this area, because they combine visual, aural, and bodily skills, and enable singers to feel the importance of posture, alignment, and ease in their bodies.[5]

In their so-called "Ear Playing Project," Maria Varvarigou and Lucy Green have recently revolutionized thinking about learning styles specifically in learning popular music by ear. Focusing on classroom-based musicians who learn and copy parts, Green identifies four learning styles, which I have found useful in my choral teaching. Below I paraphrase, summarize, and simplify in places. How many of these learning styles you recognize in your singers from observation of them working by ear?

Impulsive: "Impulsive" by-ear learners dive in right away. They essentially "make it work" or "fake it until they make it." They make a rough mental map of the whole gestalt first, and then color it in. They sing as they learn, and improvise the parts they can't hear initially, starting from rhythm and then moving to melody. Over several repetitions, these learners' attempts gradually become more accurate, and less improvised.

Practical: "Practical" by-ear learners will not sing at all right away. Instead they will listen through to a part several times before they attempt to copy it. Then they try to break it down into its component parts, getting one particular phrase accurate and then building out from there. It will seem like they are taking longer, but this does not mean they are less able. They are simply working in a more detailed way from the start.

Shot in the dark: "Shot in the dark" by-ear learners are more haphazard, and Green found they tended to learn more slowly. Often fearful, they were less confident while they were learning, and tended to guess or stay silent, but got there in the end. They needed more encouragement before they would attempt to sing or play a phrase back, even though at the moment of performance they knew their parts well.

Theoretical: Theoretical by-ear learners tended to use verbal strategies. They would talk more, asking each other whether a phrase was "high or low," identifying how many notes there were, and how often notes were repeated. Like "shot in the dark" learners, they tended to be less successful initially, and took longer to learn parts in pop songs.

For me, Green's work immediately revealed insights in relation to singers I meet in rehearsal. There are those singers who shoot themselves in the foot by talking analytically about the piece while it is being played to them, rather than simply trying to sing it back. You may also recognize those singers who dive in, make an overall schema, gradually color in melodic detail, and then need your support to remind them how a part they had mislearned earlier actually goes. Then there are those who go slowly and methodically note by note or phrase by phrase from the beginning in order. They take longer to learn their parts, need more repetitions, and find it harder to allow wrong notes at any point. In the workshops below, I offer a number of practical strategies that build on these ideas.

What then are we really saying here? Overall, musical learning is by its nature a holistic encounter, a rich experience that encompasses all the senses, and where potentially all kinds of learning styles can be implicated. All of us learn through our eyes, ears, and bodies to some extent. That said, in the end choral singing is an aural medium. With or without staff notation, it is now music education orthodoxy that your singers will learn fastest through direct musical experience, that is to say, through listening to and making sound rather than talking or reading about it.[6] This requires from the choral director a primary focus on teaching through sound alongside symbol. It also requires endless creative variety in the pedagogy they choose, and ideally the ability to teach through sight, sound, and physical movement all at the same time. Such pedagogical variety can be hugely helpful in engaging singers from the widest possible range of cultural traditions. It will immediately contribute to equity and inclusion and stylistic openness, by providing opportunities for all kinds of singers to succeed in your choir. If in doubt, your key teaching strategy is not to talk, but to ask your choir to sing some more, and empower them to make mistakes and fix them themselves. Then they will do most of the learning for you.

Formal and Informal Learning

Interviewer: How do people find their song?
August Wilson: I think . . . they have it. They just have to realize that. And then they have to learn how to sing it.

—quoted in Giving Voice, Netflix 2020

Another key bifurcation in music pedagogy occurs between two sets of learning practices, known as formal and informal learning. In choral singing both occur, and both are useful, but it is worth identifying the difference, and again using strategies

132 Transforming Choral Singing

to enable your singers to learn both ways. Again, musical styles and their cultural contexts can predispose learners to work in certain ways.

Formal learning occurs in the context where there is a teacher and a taught, and a curriculum that is systematized, such that there are certain narrowly defined "things to be learned," whether they be concepts or skills. These hierarchies have been critiqued from Basil Bernstein to Freire.[7] The student's own ideas are conventionally less valued in this way of working, and power relations can be strongly skewed in favor of the educator. In classroom and rehearsal contexts, questions from the director are more likely to be closed, with defined answers, that are, for example, easy to identify as right or wrong. The good "student," then, will tend to produce a result that is very similar to those around them. Uniformity is often the result, and individuality and difference are less acknowledged as part of the educational experience.

Informal learning, by contrast, tends to be more holistic and student-centered. It often occurs at the pace of the learner, through encounter with musical experiences, rather than through being proactively taught. In its purest form, informal learners find their own level, set themselves tasks and find their own solutions. The educator is still crucial, but pedagogical strategies are focused on guiding a student toward their own result, and enabling them to take their own decisions as learners. The curriculum is more open, individuality and difference are more possible in the educational outcome, and power relations are much more equal.

The student is in charge of their own learning and their own assessment of it. The learner is in control, and the educator is like a sheepdog. They shepherd the student, re-inforce their own learning approach, and challenge them to make demands on themselves by offering new tasks and support that align with the student's own direction of travel. Learning is more individualized, messier and noisier, in that they are encouraged to ask more questions of themselves and of others around them. The good student will tend to produce a result that is different from those around them, and a range of responses, based on culture, background, age disability etc. are acceptable and indeed encouraged. There is much more room built into this set of education practices for individuality, and difference is valued within the pedagogical space. Informal learning is likely, then, to be more socially just, and can enable educational success and effective learning in singers from a broader range of cultural backgrounds and learning styles.

How useful is that range of outcomes in choral singing? Perhaps, you may be thinking, we always want uniformity of choral blend, and after all the choral director has to be "in charge," right?

The two models I set out above are archetypes of complex and multilayered sets of learning practices. As with learning styles, both formal and informal learning will occur to some extent in and around every choral rehearsal. In rehearsal itself, the power relations are ostensibly skewed in the director's favor. We are after all in control of the pace of learning in the choral rehearsal itself, and we control the order in which elements are learned and the pace of the interaction. However, a choir is not a unified entity, but a set of individuals. Some learners will always be able to go faster than we do, while others would rather go much slower, or learn in a different way. Some will be more encultured in one repertoire, and some in another. So in order be equitable (but also to be the most effective and get *everyone* ready to perform), all singers should learn informally too. We need to be aware of how they learn best, provide them with formal and informal learning opportunities, and be demanding in asking them to take responsibility for their own learning.

Homework, or at least learning outside the rehearsal, is therefore incredibly useful. Digital technology empowers the individual learner. My singers, for example, would record themselves singing in rehearsal on their phones, and then critique their own performances at home. As adult learners, they would often learn their parts in the car or on the subway while commuting to and from work. They would also get together in informal learning groups over a drink, sometimes alongside or instead of coming to my more formal sectionals. As educators, we should encourage and even insist that singers create for themselves a range of learning environments, from whole group learning to small group learning and individual learning. This helps every singer to thrive, and empowers them to decide for themselves how they learn best, and then learn that way.

I want now to bring back in my earlier points about how learning style and music style can align. As with learning style, musical style is also a factor in the balance of informal and formal learning singers use. One star singer of mine with a pro musical theater background, for example, would show up like on day 1 of the rehearsal period as if for a professional show, knowing every note of the entire show by ear from memory. Others with pop, rock and gospel backgrounds would sometimes have no notation skill at all, while others had a range of ability at staff notation reading. Their tendency was to learn the song through a combination of ear and elementary reading skill, listening and joining in alongside those reading from the part. They would "know when it goes up and down," and read the lyrics. In my experience, informal learning of this kind is key for those musical theater and pop singers, as it is for the large minority of classical singers, who read staff notation less well. All would learn the music one way or another in the end.

With regard to formal and informal learning, the educational journeys of jazz and pop musicians are definitely configured differently to those of classical musicians. My own academic research on the experiences of jazz players and educators found that all jazz musicians learn using some combination of formal and informal music education, from the turn of the 20th Century right up to the present day[8]. Jazz is a primarily but not exclusively African American style, and an oral tradition where improvisation and creativity are valued above all else. In the 1910s to the 1930s, for example, New Orleans musicians, mostly people of color, would initially learn informally, sitting alongside their peers in bands, and the assumption was that this was the only way jazz musicians learned. As they became professionals, however, we have documentary evidence to prove that early jazz greats Barney Bigard and Sidney Bechet[9] took formal lessons in solfège and clarinet technique from a classical clarinetist in the New Orleans Opera House orchestra. These days, jazz is taught in colleges conservatory style, just like classical music, but any jazz educator will tell you that crucial informal learning still occurs on the stand in order to create a truly rounded professional improviser who knows the culture and musical practices of jazz performance. Almost all musical learning, then, emerges from complex combination of formal and informal approaches.

Green's work and my own experience as a player and performer both suggest that top-down formal pedagogy is both less common and found by learners to be less useful in non-classical styles.[10] Learning in the small vocal groups common in jazz and popular music bands tends to be more informal and collaborative. Singers sing along with each other and work with other instrumentalists by ear, often teaching each other parts and devising harmonies peer-to-peer. Crucially, their learning is also guided and motivated by a strong sense of ownership. These are songs that they like and belong to them culturally. They often write them themselves. Again, this correlation between musical practice and learning practice in popular music requires us to be pedagogically flexible as choral directors.

Where does all this analysis leave us? First, the silence of the disciplined choral rehearsal often masks that there will be many different learning styles and practices taking place simultaneously. Choral learning is messy and complex. When singers arrive in your choir, they can be used to learning in a range of different ways. We cannot expect our singers to be trained in a single way of working, or respond only to one teaching approach as "correct for choral singing." Second, patterns of learning style and of informal versus formal learning are in part based on the individual's abilities, and in part on their home musical style, the way that musical style is most easily learned, and the learning style that comes easiest to them. Some will thrive if you use formal pedagogy and visual cues and tools to teach them exactly how it goes. They feel safer if there is a person in authority providing structure, and they do as they are told. Others, perhaps encultured in other styles, will do better if they invent their own structure, go at their own pace, work out for themselves how their part goes, and then ask questions. Most will be somewhere in between, and all equally have something to offer to your choir. Almost all of your singers will use all three kinds of learning style and can adapt to formal *and* informal learning practices to some extent. In this context, what is your role as a choral director? For me, to only use the pedagogical approaches common in classical music education in a choral rehearsal is to exclude too many singers who deserve to be in your choir and can vastly improve it. Through flexible pedagogical choice, in essence being a better teacher, you can greatly enhance the connection and impact of your choir's work, widen the styles it sings in, and make it more socially just, by including singers from a much wider range of social and cultural backgrounds.

Love Your Choir

No part of great teaching involves insults.

—Stephen Sieck

"Love Your Choir" was the title of a session I attended at a conference around twenty years ago, facilitated by James Jordan. At the time, I nearly decided not to attend. It sounded too vague, too "woo-woo" to be serious, but in the end, I went along. I was so wrong. In that three-hour session, I learned deep lessons about being a better choral director and human being that have stayed with me ever since.

For me "loving your choir" can happen both on the level of the individual and on the level of the group. As with musical learning, choirs contain many kinds of individual personalities. Some compliant, helpful, and proactive contributors are easy to love, while others can be more challenging on all kinds of levels. On the individual level, you should at least learn everyone's names over time, and get to know all your singers. Who owns a cat, who has a degree in music, who broke their arm a couple of years back, who is a teacher, who can find and book an emergency rehearsal venue, and who is the one volunteer you can trust in a crisis are key. Stephen Sieck (2017) is very emphatic about the importance of seeing singers in your group as individuals, with their own intersectional needs, cultural backgrounds, struggles, and marginalizations. He is right, and this is a key part of the social practice of being a choral director. I find even learning everyone's names can be a challenge, and like everyone, names that are unfamiliar are harder for me. Our principle of equity requires, however, that I challenge myself to love everyone in the room equally.

Similarly, the group as a whole will have its own unique personality. My London group's behavior was less orderly and therefore more chaotic, a little restrained emotionally but overall more compliant and adventurous. The New York group by comparison were more outrageous, attention-seeking, and childlike in performance. They were often much less compliant, but they were also fiercely loyal, and emotionally open in performance, and at times unexpectedly conservative.

Rather like a marriage, a choral director's encounter with their choir is in some ways analogous to a one-to-one relationship. You can behave to your choir like the adult, the parent, or the child, and it can too. Your behavior as their director can get the best out of them as a group, or the very worst, depending on how loving it is. The same applies to the experience of every individual singer. As individuals, many in the group may be welcoming, progressive, and even activist, but as a whole, the group can still, for example, be experienced as racist to those inside it. I found that loving them simultaneously as individuals and as a group not only resulted in rehearsals that were more effective but kinder, more inclusive, and less conflicted.

Our goal, then, is to love everyone in the room equally, but truly equal love requires both director and directed to be continually checking themselves for bias. We are all the product of our environments. Are you more emotionally open with men or women, for example? Do you make assumptions about the energy and aptitudes of younger people, or the wisdom of older ones? Which races and ethnicities do you find it easier to communicate well with? Which seem to present you with fewer ways into a loving and musically effective conversation? Who are you more likely to have brief conversations with in the break, and why? Who comes up to you to ask questions, and who does not?

Certain people will probably need a little extra love, to feel as loved as everyone else. They can be the ones who sit alone, the "elders" I refer to later in Chapter 8, or those who a group can decide are "problematic" for one reason or another. They are often the ones who need to feel most heard, but also the ones from whom you can learn the most. If they feel uncomfortable, your presence one-to-one as a listening leader, even if only for 30 seconds, can give them the foundation of positivity they need. If done without tokenism and with persistence and lightness of touch, your ability to show up for a singer consistently can be the reason why they remain in the group.

Within your musical practices, the same can apply. Jordan focused a lot on being grateful to the choir as a whole, for their sound, their hard vocal work, or their sense of team. Positivity was key, as was finding ways of couching learning opportunities to the group so comments were never about blame, shame, or anger. Rather than, "Tenors, you are flat at bar x. Fix it or else," he suggested, "Tenors, that was an amazing effort. Let me see if I can help you be more in tune at bar x." When things go wrong, then, the first place the director should look is to themselves, to discover what they could do better to help their choir improve. If a section sings flat or repeatedly makes the same timing or pitch error, it is never because they willfully want to, and rarely because they are not doing their best. Instead, most often it is because the director has taught the phrase to them in a particular way, or because of circumstances outside their control. Perhaps they are tired collectively, they can't hear each other well or the energy in the room is low. Either way, any moment of failure is a time for learning and positive reinforcement, and never a time for making singers feel worse about themselves, as humans or as singers. That loving approach, then, should underlie all pedagogical interaction, and can pay huge dividends both in the personal relationships of the group and its musical ones.[11] It is also a core value that underpins our principle of social justice.

Workshops

What follows is structured around four key areas of a rehearsal period that every choir is likely to need. First, we briefly cover the warm-up, because most rehearsals should start with one, long or short. There are no warm-up workshops, as they have already been covered in Chapter 3, but I offer suggestions and tips. Second comes three workshops on the early part of your rehearsal period. They cover the introduction of new material, and this section includes suggestions and tips on using rehearsal tracks. These workshops also introduce the importance of story-telling as key to explaining the purpose of our work, and they cover detail on working by ear as well as from sheet music. Third are two workshops on the tricky middle part of your rehearsal period. Here, although there is still more material to learn, the main rehearsal activities are reviewing and running material, and refining character

The Warm-Up

From Robert Shaw on,[12] the warm-up has been an essential part of choral rehearsal. Focused, fun, and short warm-ups can have huge value. They create a sense of group, and gather your singers psychologically. They focus singers mentally and physically, make them aware of their voices and their listening, and prepare them for the very specific demands of the choral singing task. If you can use activities that cover all three learning styles in your warm-ups, you can wake up all your singers.

I used to be obsessed with warm-ups, and would spend much longer than I do now on a very detailed opening session lasting up to twenty minutes. I would use it to introduce my concept of the voice. Sometimes that can still be useful, just as it can in the one-to-one vocal lesson. That said, I found singer feedback was divided, and both beginners and more advanced singers felt the need to "get to the songs" sooner than I pedagogically wanted. As Deke Sharon points out in "Maximizing Rehearsal Time,"[13] it can be more efficient to get into the main rehearsal quicker. While singers of all levels need to develop their vocal technique, and warm-ups are like the calisthenics of singing, these days I see warm-ups mainly as a shorter, introductory device. Instead, I drop technical exercises into my flow later in the evening, closer to songs they relate to.

Every community has its own rituals, the mental and physical activities that everyone knows, and that bind the group together. I found that above all, my vocal warm-ups acted as rituals. Their effect was as much psychological and even spiritual as it was musical. They were familiar introductory activities, part of the social practices of the group, that took people out of themselves, and reminded them that this was the start of a special part of their week. The activities were vocally and musically useful, but they functioned mainly to allow the subconscious mind to emerge, for the thoughts of the day to order themselves, and for that calm that leads to better artistic thinking, emotional flow, and unified mental focus to take place. In other words, good warm-ups can in themselves facilitate musical and social connection.

A thirty-second moment of silence holding hands, for example, can be immensely useful in a warm-up, and can be followed a vocal exercise that everyone knows how to do without thinking. So too can a moment of extreme sound, which can allow people to vent and feel free of restriction, hidden amongst the sound of others. Finally, the best warm-up sessions should include a moment in which you explicitly focus on connection through listening, blending, and singing together in a way that unifies the group. For a range of other specific warm-up exercises, check out Chapter 3 on vocal sound.

Suggestions and Tips

1) **Define a clear structure and goals, and check outcomes:** You and your singers should both understand why you are doing an activity. Welcome their critiques, though not necessarily in the moment! Also monitor how useful a warm-up really is. Don't assume that because your singers went through the task, your goals (musical *and* social) were achieved. Sometimes we think we are achieving an outcome with a warm-up, when in fact singers are going through the motions of your carefully honed activity, but little change is achieved. Listening without making assumptions is key.

2) **Ask a member to run a set of warm-ups for you:** Perhaps this is a section leader, or a singer who has approached you with some ideas. Create a culture where anyone can make a suggestion, so you enable future leaders to emerge. It also adds variety to get a range of different voices leading.

3) **Be demanding, specific, and fun:** Check whether your singers are doing an exercise right, and that everyone is enjoying themselves while they do it. Don't be afraid to insist, be demanding, and explore the full range of the voice.

4) **Start on time and normally take no more than ten minutes:** Avoid unnecessary repetition, which can wear the voice out, and don't use up crucial music learning time. Move fast, as attention spans are short.

5) **Singing the right song can also warm up the voice:** It can be just as useful to warm up by singing a less demanding song early. It gets some early fun in the room, and can focus the group on a particular vocal challenge in the song.

6) **Ask questions:** During rehearsal itself, don't ask questions, but request that singers direct queries to section leaders, so rehearsal can keep moving. But in warm-ups, as in sectionals, why not welcome questions, and encourage singers to be active learners?

7) **Vary your rehearsal start routine:** Vary your routine, so sometimes warm-ups are long, but sometimes get into the material quickly.

8) **Time of day is key:** Choral rehearsals are often in the evening, and people have been using their voices all day by that point. They may not need much warming up.

Learning New Material

Often in a conventional choir rehearsal, it makes sense to move straight from a warm-up into some musical detail, or at least some singing. If there is one moment in the rehearsal when people will be likely to learn new or more complex musical material effectively and efficiently, it is early on. Again, singing is the main activity and main learning tool of any rehearsal.

Workshop 1: Telling Stories (15 minutes)

Impactful choral performances are always about telling stories. So while we want to get the choral detail quickly, it is always useful to talk for a few minutes about the story a song tells, and why we are singing it. I use the term "story" literally and metaphorically here. This workshop asks you to identify several kinds of story that you might tell in a rehearsal, to engage your singers with a new piece.

Choose a piece of repertoire that you need to prepare for a rehearsal. Then think about:

1) **The lyric story:** what the song is about, what story the words tell. This is not the whole story, of course, but it is often where a singer and indeed many listeners will start.

2) **The melody and routine story:** where the main tune is, and its musical shape—what I call the schema. To make it memorable, it helps to identify about a musical feature that you like best. There is that story to the form of a piece, its map, which goes: "There is that cool bass line part at the beginning." "Then it goes verse, bridge and then double chorus." "Don't forget the round and round section, which today will go around twice, so we hear that gorgeous part I love where . . ." and so on.

3) **The story of the character of the music:** The musical character also has its "story," relating to the narrative of the musical gestures, and can build excitement about what you are about to sing: "It starts quiet but calm, and then builds to a massive climax. From there it suddenly bursts out into polyphony . . ."

4) **The story of the emotional intent, and values being expressed:** Emotion in rehearsal can be just as powerful as emotion in performance. It motivates singers to know "why" we are singing a piece. You may also be doing a show about a concept, say, old age. If so, the emotional intent might fit into a longer narrative structure at a particular point. For example, in a series of songs about growing older, a song like Joni Mitchell's "Both Sides Now" might be a summary song that celebrates the wisdom and insight of older people, or highlights feelings of anger in the face of young people's lack of respect. Every song contains an emotional story as well as a purely musical one, and your singers' commitment to that story also needs to be rehearsed.

Discussion

As choral directors, we need to have rehearsal strategies that help choirs tell these stories. By highlighting them, you are expressing the social purpose of your singing from the podium—what you are advocating for. A discussion of older people might then lead into a fruitful five-minute "hands-up" activity, and sometimes a brief break-out into pairs, around singers' experience of getting older. My experience is

140   Transforming Choral Singing

that a "why" discussion will almost always lead to the growth of meaning around a song, and a deeper understanding of why the musical gestures were chosen. At a run-through that follows, look for feelings of added emotion in the room, and even tears. This work around social impact early in a rehearsal period is motivating, and supports quicker learning of technical musical features later. It clarifies "what we are saying," and enables singers to envision the social impact of their singing.

Should you sing first and then chat, or chat first and then sing? My priority as a choral educator is always to get people singing first. This is more educationally efficient, and discussion always takes up more time than you imagine it will. Often, after we have done half an hour on the key melody or the overall geography of a song, singers will have more specific questions. They will also begin to see what a song is about for themselves, which can save time later.

On the other hand, some songs need an initial explanation, because they are potentially controversial, and immediately challenge the singer. Recall that my example from the programming chapter, "Totally Fucked," involved the singers in singing the word "fuck" around fifty times. Some explanation was needed before we sang it, as to why this lyric was artistically justified. Others just needed psychological preparation to say "fuck" in public at all. You can imagine some of the hilarity that night, as we sang vocal exercises that got us used to the word in our mouths.

A second example of a song needing explanation before singing was in a singalong show we did about New York City, where we sang a K-pop song called *New York* by a band called Mamamoo. Much of it was in Korean.[14] It was a doable but fun challenge for our mainly white, English-speaking singers, and an opportunity for Korean speakers in our group to lead. Again, it was a song that demanded a chat and a brief listen to the original *before* starting to sing, and we did start to learn by singing the four lines that were in English!

Now, two more short workshops containing strategies for learning new material.

Workshop 2: Just Words, Rhythm, and Character (15 minutes)

Early success and a level of early accuracy is crucial for singers to get a first impression that they can learn from, and will motivate them to continue. So if the musical material is challenging, or there are many starting pitches to find, try working on words and rhythm alone first. Words and rhythm work also focus the singers on a song's story right away.

Begin by finding a piece of repertoire that you want to teach initially by ear. Then try the following strategies:

1) **Say the words to the rhythm:** As a first run, ask singers to "Say the words to the rhythm."

2) **Identify the story told:** Ask singers to analyze from the lyrics they just performed what the story is about, and which are the important words.

3) **Discuss the musical character:** Now add performance of the phrasing, noting any accents, longs and shorts, and stressed and unstressed syllables. Relate the phrasing to the way it helps tell the story. Also note any builds and dynamic changes over, say, thirty seconds to a minute. Repeat words and rhythm, emphasizing telling the story by adding phrasing detail, but still without any pitch.

4) **Work on vowels, as if singing:** Check for evenness, resonance, and blend, using relaxed speech voice. Also work on clarity and length of consonants. Repeat with better vowels.

5) **Add a sense of performance:** Ensure you go at the real tempo. Explain the meaning and impact, and relate it directly to the words. This final time, still without pitch, ask singers to exaggerate the expressive features of the performance, so the full meaning comes across. Conduct with performance-level intensity, and expect the same focus from your singers.

6) **Finally, color in the pitch gradually over the coming weeks:** You'll be amazed by how the musical character remains in place, and how much easier and quicker learning the pitch is for some singers, if they achieve rhythmic and emotional confidence first. Now they can go back to the rehearsal tracks or score, and understand better the meaning of the musical gestures.

Workshop 3: Listen and Repeat (15 minutes)

When learning by ear on a song they don't know, singers need the pitches to be played to them repeatedly in short segments. Singers who *do* read benefit from this too. The following painstaking approach, in line with Green's "practical" learning style, can be helpful. In spite of the strict "top-down" hierarchical pedagogy, note the elements of autonomous learning:

1) **Start with the most obvious and catchy melodic segment:** Perhaps this is the chorus of a pop song, or a unison moment in a classical piece. Break it down into small chunks.

2) **Establish especially careful listening:** Announce, "I sing first, then you repeat." Make clear that this is a separate mode of work, that involves especially intense concentration. Ensure absolute silence. With younger children, I find it useful to say something like, "Turn 'record' on in your brain." Be specific about, "Repeat back EXACTLY what I sing." Adults appreciate the clarity of this approach too, but use different language. To allow failure, announce, "Mistakes are good, and you are not expected to get it right first time. If you haven't got it yet, that's absolutely fine, you will! Just keep singing." This

142   Transforming Choral Singing

enables learners to work autonomously, monitor their own mistakes, and adapt as they go.

3) **Sing the first two bars accurately, and repeat:** Wait for silence, count yourself in, and sing your first two bar chunk. Singers should repeat exactly what was sung, in time, like a question and answer. Support the aural experience with hand signals, to indicate pitch rising and falling, and solfège if you and the group know it. Sing it CORRECTLY to your singers the first time. Repeat two to three times, until 70 to 80 percent secure, aiming to keep the pulse going if you can.

4) **Add the next two bars, and put them together:** Then move on to phrase 2. Once that is secure, stop. Restart, with the cue, "Now phrases 1 and 2 together." As before, you sing phrases 1 and 2 first, then they repeat. At each stage, singers are deciding for themselves what they have got right, and what still needs to be learned.

5) **Add phrases 3 and 4 in the same way:** Do the same for phrase 3, then phrase 4, then 3 and 4 together. NOW try phrases 1, 2, 3, and 4. Many will have forgotten phrases 1 and 2, and will need to review. Continue until, say, a key eight-bar chunk of the whole piece is memorized in its entirety. Stick with the approach painstakingly even as concentration wanes, as early success on even a short passage will pay dividends later.

6) **Add countermelody or bass line:** Now start on the second part down, a countermelody, or perhaps the bass line that goes with it. Suggest that those singing the actual melody continue to sing, hum, siren, or even imagine their part silently on each repetition, while you teach other parts.

7) **Sing through the eight bars in its entirety:** Sing through from memory right away, in glorious four-part harmony. Give praise, as the level of concentration and often patience in singers will have been intense.

Suggestions and Tips

1) **Listen and judge whether to go on:** Listen carefully for the level of security in each part, as you go. Is it around 30 percent there, around 60 percent, or the 80 percent you need to carry on? If unsure, ask your singers, "One more time?."

2) **Get singers to help each other:** People learn at different speeds, but this does not necessarily make them better or worse performers in the end. To encourage informal learning and build community, say "If you think you know it and are bored, sing it louder to teach it to the people on either side of you, who need your help."

3) **Encourage phone recording:** Encourage singers to record their own singing and even the whole learning process on their phone. Make clear the recording is for personal use only, and is not to be copied or shared.

Teaching and Learning in Rehearsal **143**

This brings me to recordings in general. As we have seen, recordings are key to facilitating informal learning in the vast majority of singers, whether they use notation or not. They allow them to go at their own speed, and can reveal detail about how their voice actually sounds, which may not be evident in rehearsal, when they hear their own voice partly distorted through the skull, and in relation to the rest of the group, which can be loud. Two more sets of suggestions follow. The first is around recordings and videos of rehearsals:

1) **Buy a quality all-in-one recorder and a separate video camera:** Clarity and good recording quality are key. Ensure your recorder has good condenser microphones, plugs into an outlet, or has batteries that last a long time. Place it on the podium, so it picks up the whole rehearsal, including what you say when you are teaching. Wear your own microphone too, if your recorder has more than one input channel. Also video the director as they teach, and ideally have a second camera and microphone on the singers.

2) **Enable your singers to use the recordings and video:** Make recordings available privately on the web, and perhaps stream them live as well for those who can't make it or are perhaps sick at home. The truth of how your group sounded in rehearsal, good and bad, will be more transparent, and will lead to productive conversations. If a singer misses a rehearsal, they can watch how you taught it, listen, and sing along. They can also privately practice choreography once they know the form and sound of the song.

3) **Use the recordings yourself:** After rehearsal, listen back and remind yourself how the song sounded, and get inside the singer experience. When you listen back later, new details will stick out to you. The objective truth of how your singers sounded can be surprisingly comforting at times, and equally horrifying at others(!). Either way, it will help you prepare a more considered and singer-focused rehearsal for next week.

4) **Play parts of a rehearsal recording in rehearsal:** Singers often find it easier to understand choral issues when they hear them directly played back in a separate occasion. It can be hard to hear the full picture from the fourth row of the sopranos. Ask them to describe the musical character, identify what worked well about a run-through, and what issues they hear. Point them to your own concerns too. If possible, send them a link, and set homework, so they can continue to listen repeatedly and in a more intentional way outside rehearsal.

5) **Listen to the song or piece as recorded by the original artist or choir:** Turn up the volume, and suggest they listen without singing. This works equally well with Katy Perry and William Byrd. The recorded arrangement may be in the wrong key, but for this exercise, this doesn't matter. Singers will pick up the musical character, and can hear for themselves what vocal approach and phrasing is needed.

6) **Listen again later in the rehearsal period:** Sometimes it can also be helpful to listen to original artist recordings later in the rehearsal period. Once the

144   Transforming Choral Singing

musical material is essentially learned, singers may still fail to "get" something about the musical character, and indeed be readier to hear the original sound. Listening to a recording can focus your choir on a sound better than you trying to describe the issue, and in rehearsal can unlock a new energy.

Prerecorded rehearsal tracks can also be invaluable help, especially for informal learners. Here is a second set of suggestions specifically around rehearsal tracks:

1) **Allow enough time:** Putting together really excellent rehearsal tracks is time-consuming. Even for a professional singer, a single song can take three to four hours, and editing can increase this even further. Consider asking your more experienced singers and section leaders to help you put them together.

2) **The trade-off between quality and usefulness:** Be realistic about how much time your choir has to produce quality tracks. For many years I directed a less-well-off chorus, and our compromise was to produce quick rehearsal tracks, generated straight from Sibelius. The result was without any lyrics, simply inexpressive computer-generated pitch and rhythm, but singers found them adequate, and they were inexpensive, quick to produce, and used by a majority. In other groups, we spent money on getting tracks produced that were accurate, stylish, and vocally considered. They were of course used by more people, but it may or may not be worth it to you to work that way.

3) **Use tuning software:** Autotune software is your friend, used judiciously. I also know some directors who sing every part, soprano to bass, in its eventual register, using tuning software. You will sound like a robot, but at least you can set the tempo and enough of the musical character will come across. As a male-identifying baritone, I can also sing them a soprano part at pitch. Thankfully, choirs are surprisingly forgiving about their director's own voice.

4) **Licensing:** To stay on the right side of licensing law and ensure confidentiality, keep rehearsal recordings of all kinds private, and use them only for educational purposes. Ideally make your rehearsal recordings streaming, rather than downloadable.

5) **Public-facing voice:** Make sure that you as the director are disciplined around what you say when the recorder is turned on in rehearsal and elsewhere. Use public-facing voice only!

Reviewing, Running, and Refining

When I used to sing in choirs, I remember often being told, "We've already covered this" by directors, when all they had done was teach it once. There was an assumption that there was no need to reinforce, or that somehow learners had to do the rest themselves, without support. In fact, in the second half of a preparation period reviewing and running material is crucial, to get it into the muscle memory and mental schemas of your singers. Again, aural learners will benefit from hearing the group sing the song, and will grow gradually in confidence. A higher standard is also expected as the rehearsal period goes on, so singers sound more emotionally committed and add a second level of detail and understanding to their performance. At the same time, you still need to teach new material, so you have to get more efficient, and use time wisely.

Marketing professionals will tell you that you have to communicate something six times for it to register. Never assume that, simply because you have taught something once, it has actually been learned. Instead, teach it six different ways. It can be invaluable to verbally explain previous points taught visually, reinforce key heard ideas by moving, and in different ways insistently hammer home how the song goes, and what it is about. I used to overthink, and add more and more demands to a task, often to the confusion of my singers. Now, I give one clear focus in concise language, such as "Better diction, please," and sing it again. When performing from memory, a performance can lose detail once memorized, so double-check and reinforce key details of dynamics, routine, and musical character.

In longer rehearsals, spend time running, reminding, and checking, even when singers are tired. Also, try positively reinforcing a song not sung for weeks. "Well done, that's coming along nicely" can be useful in itself. The run-through has done its work, and singers will be individually assessing what they need to remember and have forgotten. By the last two to three weeks before a performance, increasing time is spent running and running the material, to reinforce, add layers of security, and internalize the emotional journey. This all adds the eventual relaxed ease of a well-prepared performance.

When working from memory, there is the "books down" moment, not essential but often desirable, where your singers finally put the music away. Learning style is again key, and I have done this different ways with different groups. With my New York group, I found it useful to leave our "books down" date very late, until perhaps three weeks before the performance. Different learners go at different speeds. There was always a lot of material to learn for their shows. Their performances also had theatrical elements, so there were many bells and whistles to add, from the detailed choreography on four or five songs to the eight-part arrangements, speeches, and costumes. With other groups I have been more structured, got them off-book sooner, or done a phased memorization.

In Chapter 6, I covered the need to leave some space for late creative decisions, so we can respond to events or modify an arrangement if it is not going well. As a result, I prefer singers not to memorize too soon. There is nothing worse than the collective anger of a choir who has memorized a song faithfully only to find that the song changes or is even cut entirely later in the process. Those decisions are deeply demotivating and can undermine the credibility of a director very quickly.

Next are two workshops around reviewing and running material.

146   Transforming Choral Singing

Workshop 4: "Three Things to Remember"

As performance time approaches, we never have time to cover everything we want to again and again. You often have two options: run a song, or rehearse specific places. There is rarely time to do both. If "rehearse" is your choice, try one of these "three things" strategies:

1) **Three points in a one-minute talk:** If you are really short of time, verbally remind your singers of three things to remember, with no actual singing. For example, in a few seconds, you can say:

   "3 quick things. Remember that bit at Letter C, where it gets really quiet. Got it? Watch out for the diction on the word "SSSSSing" whenever it occurs. Say "sssssssssssing." Great! And tenors, don't over-sing at this point here, as you sometimes stick out. Instead, enjoy the sound of the altos. If you can't hear them, you are too loud." Remind others to "go back to the rehearsal tracks and check . . ." so informal learners feel included. If that's all you have time for, so be it. Reinforce the same points next time.

2) **Three points in five minutes:** If there is a little more time than that, sing those three short segments, for literally thirty seconds to a minute each. Don't sing the bars before or after, as it wastes time. Move fast, with focus and urgency, and insist that those aspects you mentioned absolutely have to be in place. Don't add extra demands, or get distracted if something else goes wrong. Those three segments will suffice to put the whole song back in their heads for that rehearsal, and take five minutes in total. You can efficiently cover four songs in twenty minutes that way.

3) **Make a note to run later:** Note publicly that in a future rehearsal, you will need to run the entire song. The diligent will prepare, using whichever learning styles they feel are most useful.

Workshop 5: Fast-Forward

Running through is incredibly useful, but can also be time-consuming and unfocused. The following strategies can speed things up and focus attention better than a standard off-book run:

1) **Double-speed run:** Announce that to save time, we will be running the song double speed, off-book immediately. (Sometimes the accompanist will be able to play along, sometimes a cappella is the only way). Go right into it! Remind the singers that although words, pitch, and rhythm are the main things to

remember, we are treating this run, hilariously, as a performance run too, that is to say all dynamics, phrasing, and choreography should be in place and clear. For added hilarity, allow body movements for kinesthetic learners.

2) **Rehearse your conducting:** Conduct these runs, as this is also your chance to memorize, and to discover what the singers need support to remember. Note the places where the singers thought they knew the material, but some aspects are less secure than they imagined.

3) **Reminders:** Once you have done a double-speed run and are even off book, try going back to the score. Remind singers briefly of key aspects to improve, which will be fresh in their minds, and get them to write them into the score. You can sometimes finish there, and you will have done good and memorable work. From the learning style perspective, you are going in spirals, returning to the visual even as you focus more on the aural.

4) **A final run at tempo:** If time, do one further run at the real speed, aiming for an extremely expressive and confident version. Simply running twice, you'll often find a piece markedly improved.

Closer to the Performance

As a performance approaches, singers tend to feel they know the pieces we are singing, and can plateau. As a result, their work can feel more fixed and even deteriorate slightly, the nearer to the performance we come. The consistency of that fixedness will create a sense of security and a relaxed authority to the finished show. But if that fixed set of pitches, rhythms, and lyrics is all that a performance is, your audience will leave unfulfilled. As ever, impact and connection are the goals, so with the material largely under the belt, the three new elements to add as you approach the performance are expressive freedom, communication, and ease. Here now are two more workshops which focus on these three final elements.

Workshop 6: Developing Ease and Freedom

1) **Conductor free rein:** Ask the group to sing a whole song, but tell them that the conductor has totally free rein to play with the tempo, dynamics, etc. in the moment, to "mess with" the performance. As in tai-chi, the goal here is that your singers should listen and respond in the moment with ease and flexibility. Some find these exercises easy, while others will find changes in the moment unsettling.

2) **Sing through with no conductor:** Ask the group to sing through a whole song, but this time without conductor. It should start on its own, by breathing together, and continue, leading itself through tempo changes, dynamics, and blend issues. The run won't go exactly as you or they wanted, but they will

148   Transforming Choral Singing

have learned a lot through having to respond spontaneously to what happens without you. Note where they need your help, and where they are doing fine on their own. Praise the group for its ability to self-regulate.

3) **Making ensemble changes:** Repeat a run with no conductor. This time give a verbal instruction to change the performance in a certain way, but to do it as a group, without you. For example, suggest they sustain a new faster tempo, or perhaps take longer over a ritardando.

Again, this is a revealing moment for you and your singers. Are there ingrained habits that prevent such tempo changes, for example? Did they manage the ritardando themselves with skill? Sometimes you can find your work as a teacher is done. At others, you will need to provide that extra layer of detail, emotional commitment, or surprise, to stop singers from switching off their ears.

Discussion

There is a view of performing that values consistency and reliability, and implies that there is one perfect performance, the same every time, which is our ultimate goal. This gives singers security and ease, but fails to allow for a level of freedom. As an improviser, I believe all performances, even of the most hackneyed oratorio, are in some ways constructed afresh in the moment. In all music-making, there is the fixed and the free, and the free is where the essence of connection in performance happens. For example, an audience can tell when a choir is under-rehearsed, because of hesitancy in the attack, and a general lack of freedom and commitment in the vocal gestures. They can also tell when a choir is singing on "automatic pilot," and when it is confidently creating a brand new performance for them in the moment. Under-rehearsed or on automatic pilot, your choir is not entirely free.

The truth is that there are freedoms even in the strictest of recreative classical performances, just as there are fixed elements in the freest of free improvisations. A good choral ensemble will not only know its part really well, but will also use these freedoms. They will know the material well enough to be free to respond in the moment to the energy of a change in personnel, a larger crowd, a different night, or an error that means we start a song in an unexpected way. All these situations can cause an ensemble challenges, if it is not free to respond to them. Having to respond in the moment can also create unexpected moments of choral magic.

At its best, a choral performance from this point becomes a complex, spontaneous interaction of between conductor and singers. All are well prepared but alert and relaxed, and both conductor and singers collaborate, giving up some control to the other to achieve the best result. There is maximum freedom and flexibility in the performance itself, and control flows back and forth in the moment, stretching like a rubber band to suit the given musical situation.

Workshop 7: Communicating Meaning for Social Impact

There comes a moment when a performance needs an audience. Connection skills come to the fore, as we begin to look outward. Singers begin to imagine the audience, and say, "This song is going to make them cry," or, "I hope they find this moment compelling/hilarious/touching" etc.

These activities are about how we tell our story:

1) **Eye contact, face and body language:** Perhaps three weeks before a show, sing through a song that feels "ready" musically, asking singers focus entirely on how they use their eyes, face, and body. The goal is to *over*-communicate with the body. Suggest the singers use hands, faces, and whole body to "explain" and even "dance" the song to the audience. Discuss what went well and badly. Invite strong communicators up on stage, to demonstrate what they are doing to others. Then dial it back, defining an appropriate level of physical movement for that song.

2) **Invite listeners in, and rehearse telling your story to them:** The following week, invite some people to a preview. Invitees can simply be a few friends you trust to come along, say nice things, and be honest. Or you could organize a formal preview performance in a venue, with an invited audience of school kids, elders or deserving community members who want to come. Go to them, if they can't come to you. Tell singers to consciously rehearse speaking to them in the performance.

3) **Listen for audience response, then discuss:** During all performances, the audience will guide you through, if singers know the cues to listen for. Discuss these questions with singers, all of them around noticing the impact they have rather than the technical quality of their work:

   i) How was the quality of a silence during a performance? Did it hold people's attention, as you expected it to? Is a song falling flat unexpectedly, and if so, why? How was the quality of a silence before the applause, but after the piece ends?

   ii) Are listeners responding well in appropriate places, for example laughing at jokes? Are there even places that you did not realize would be funny, that they are now laughing at, and you could make more of? Could some jokes be cut?

   iii) Where in the performance are listeners moved? Where are the actual tears? Were you unexpectedly moved yourself as a conductor? Did your singers become emotional themselves? Were there "goosebump" moments, of musical beauty rather than emotion? Again, were those moments at the moments you expected, or possibly at other places?

150 Transforming Choral Singing

    iv) Did you as singers feel any connection with each other? Or with listeners? How was it for them? What songs are having the most impact in your view?

Discussion

This final focus on communication is in some ways the most important of all. It is not the icing on the cake. It is what we are all about, because it is what causes the change in audiences that makes for all successful art. There is a vital distinction between rehearsal, where we look in, and performance, where we focus should be exclusively on looking out, to communicate and feel the connection and impact of our work. Performing is so much more than simply laying out a musical text in its purest form. Every performance is an entirely new construction of a piece of music from scratch, however well known it may be. As in jazz, spontaneity, flexibility, responsiveness to an audience, and mindful engagement in the present moment are the key to achieving maximum impact in choral singing.

Notes

1. James Jordan (1999), *The Musician's Soul: A Journey Examining Spirituality for Performers, Teachers, Composers, Conductors, and Music Educators* (Chicago, IL: GIA Publications), 94. See also the video, "James Jordan: The Human Connection," https://www.youtube.com/watch?v=sBKo pHh8koM&list=PLZQqNNHsg4fBHmj5ktQVxuiWUqsFEYWlc
2. Hess (2019), after Freire (2000).
3. In his article about using learning styles in choral rehearsal, Don Ester (1994) describes them as visualization, audiation, and locomotion. Beheshti (2009) uses visual, auditory, and kinesthetic/ tactile; other models include Gumm (2004), who was working specifically with choral singers, and identifies accommodator, divergent, convergent, and assimilator learning style types; Some also add reading and writing as a fourth learning style.
4. Beheshti (2009) writes: "These students are usually more open to different styles and genres of music, such as folk, jazz, Celtic, [and] traditional," and later, "The weaknesses of auditory learners tend to be in the area of note-reading skills . . . unless they have an exact recording to match what they are seeing on the page. . . . Sight-reading is also a weak skill for auditory learners. Until they hear the music, the written score is not very useful."
5. Ester (1994): 20–21.
6. For more on experiential learning theory, see Kolb (2005), after Dewey, Lewin and Piaget, and Swanwick (2011) on "Teaching Music Musically," which specifically starts from an ontological approach to what music is.
7. Bernstein (1996: 97) famously talks about students as "the controlled," while Hess (2019: 16) discusses the exacerbation of "power hierarchies between teachers and students," and how that relates to colonialism, cultural appropriation, and stereotyping.
8. C. Beale (2001), *From Jazz to Jazz Education: An Investigation of Tensions between Player and Educator Definitions of Jazz*, PhD thesis, University College–London.
9. Kinzer (1996).

10. Green has some fascinating suggestions for formal music educators "for adopting and adapting informal music learning practices within various formal music educational settings, not as a substitute, but as a complement running side by side with existing approaches" (2008 (1), 130).
11. In "The Musician's Soul," Jordan (1999: 172) writes (of a non-denominational spirituality): "Only in fully, penitentially, and self-emptyingly loving the other—loving the singers and the composers, and above all loving the God who is himself the fullness of every other love—can he begin to draw near the miracle [of stillness that all great music possesses]."
12. http://robertshaw.website/speeches
13. https://www.youtube.com/watch?v=NB3TTGSOpwM
14. Mamamoo "New York": https://www.youtube.com/watch?v=OucgyzOKLWM

8
Directing and Leading a Choral Community

Music-making starts and ends with people. Your singers are your main resource for achieving artistic success, and that artistic success is itself driven by your leadership, and the positive and collaborative personal relationships that your leadership creates. The way you run a rehearsal and direct from the podium models the kinds of personal relationships you and your choir aspire to.

In this chapter, I want to explore what it would look like, if your main job as a choral leader was to influence those musical and social practices to facilitate connection and impact, and to prioritize stylistic openness and social justice. I believe these principles can profoundly change how a choral director approaches directing a group, and how they lead the community that surrounds it. This chapter is organized in two contrasting halves. In the second, we focus specifically on leading music-making, but we begin with the personal and organizational aspects of directing and leading a choral community.

A. Personal and Organizational Aspects of Choral Leadership

Connected Artistic Leadership

Conventionally (and slightly hilariously), let's begin with the old nineteenth-century myth that a single charismatic, highly temperamental, but somehow visionary choral director drives singers and audiences mercilessly on a unique journey, which they have conjured up through their musical expertise and creativity alone. Authority here rests on their personal persuasiveness and their specialist training and knowledge of the great canons. The direction of travel of artistic impact is indicated by the dotted arrows:

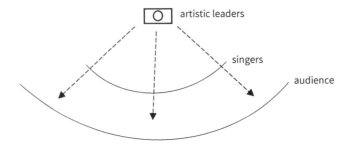

Figure 8.1

Connection in this model, if it exists at all, will tend to be one-way. Authority resides solely in the visionary artistic leader, while singers and audience bow down in respect. The choral director is on their podium, revered but alone.

Developing my community ecosystem idea from Chapter 2, I want to start this chapter from the very different premise that the choral director is at the center of the community ecosystem, a complex network of musical and social relationships that facilitate continual in-the-moment communication. Starting from this premise, again as indicated by the arrows, the communication is two-way.

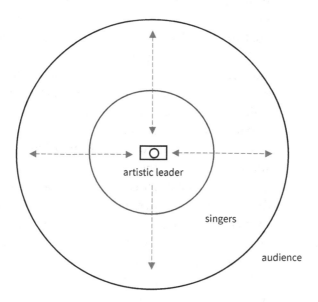

Figure 8.2

Let's take the musical realm first. When I conduct, I am a lighthouse that sends beams of light out in all directions toward my singers, in the form of physical, emotional, and mental energy and musical information. My singers, boats floating on the calm or choppy musical seas around the lighthouse, need to know the geography and how they should act on their musical journey. But to leave the analogy behind, they also send their energy and information back to me, in their sound, their eye, contact and their faces. That physical communication to me is key. I hear where they are in the music, and judge how to behave at every level in response to the data they present me with. That data takes the form of how they look, sound, and behave in the song.

In this ongoing two-way process, I listen and empower them to make their light brighter, more focused, and precise. I have to be musically alert, but also emotionally open, both to give and receive feeling in the music-making. I must feel their energy. Although there is only one lighthouse and everyone relies on it, my job is to unite them, keep them out of danger, and reflect their light back to them. The brightness of that light is then reinforced and multiplied by the number of people in the group.

The result is a complex collaboration, which only works because I share power and let light and information flow back and forth. When this collaboration is working at its best, my group leads me as much as I lead them. Without them, there is no singing. Without me, the rocks loom, and our performance lacks character, precision, and unity. We depend on each other. We fuse into a single ensemble. We connect.

That same back-and-forth is necessary in the personal and organizational realm. We need support from our production team, our marketing team, our singers, our donors, our audience, and our board, pastor, or faculty head. Indeed they all need to be able to lead and contribute fully in order to make our operation work to its fullest potential. We also support them. As in the musical process, the choral director sits at the center of a network of two-way relationships, not at the top of a hierarchy. They lead a choral beehive that is fluid, ever-changing, and interdependent. The bees give the queen bee control, but the hive as a whole is only at its most effective and powerful when every singer, volunteer, and senior manager is equally powerful, and can lead and make their own decisions. As Stacey Abrams famously put it, "Good leaders are always at the ready. But not always at the front."[1]

Regardless of context, such networks of two-way relationships embody the musical and social community of the choir. The director's role as leader is to nurture and grow them in all their aspects in both directions. These networks carry knowledge, skills, understanding, feelings, attitudes, and relationships, but above all they are the means through which the music is enacted, and the music embodies all of what that network stands for in sound. When training a conductor or choral educator, I am interested of course in what they know in the score, but much more interested in their musical and social antennae, in what they discover through listening, feeling, and hearing from their group. A good director will give energy, but will also show exquisite sensitivity to the feelings, aspirations, and values of their network, and will know how to empower their singers so the energy *from* them grows brighter and stronger[2]. This is perhaps most obvious in schools, where the educator role is foregrounded, but equally present in community and college contexts too. A skillful artistic leader receives a huge amount of musical and social data from their networks, distills down the key insights, and devises art. That art then reflects not only the leader's own voice but also the voice of their whole network, whether that be a community of school children, Bach lovers, churchgoers, or LGBTQIA+ singers.[3]

When we lead well in this way, the exponential increase in connection that happens is truly magical. Energy radiates outward. Word goes around. Singers join in larger numbers. A larger audience attends, because they recognizes themselves in your art. The choir's financial bottom line will benefit and the impact of their work will start to spiral outward in ever-increasing circles. Learning in school and college choirs deepens, and worship in communities of faith takes on new energy. That impact could not occur without the choral director, but it is created by everyone.

Returning to our social justice principle, the hard part is that we are all different. No choral director will connect equally to every person in the room. Where they lack the lived experience to empathize fully with the identity or personality of their singers, a director is less likely to attract them, communicate well with them, or present art that fully empowers them. Identity and culture play a crucial part in such connection. A fifty-year-old director may find it harder to program music attractive to twenty-five-year-olds. A white, straight, cisgender choral director may find it harder to connect with black trans singers in an empathetic way. An able-bodied choral director will struggle to truly get inside the mindset of a singer who uses a wheelchair or see the barriers that may be preventing them from fully engaging. They may even ignore them entirely, because their experience is not present enough to them. If connection is key to all good choral singing, there is learning work for us to do as choral leaders, to ensure that our networks include everyone equitably, and that honest and authentic two-way communication occurs with all our singers. This involves acute self-criticism and self-awareness, to understand and acknowledge publicly exactly what it is that we do not know. Connected and equitable choral leadership, then, is always about learning, and about facilitating a learning culture in your group.

Who Do You Want in Your Choral Community?

Good singers: Obviously, you will need good singers, but how good, and good at what? Good classical singers, for example, are not the same as good pop singers, but both are good, and both can be a good fit in any choir, if they are open and curious to learn. We also need choral singers more than soloists. They have the connection skills. In choirs, we see those loyal, hard-working, connected but above all selfless singers, both kids and adults, and we love them especially. As one stalwart told me, "I just enjoy to sing. Put any music in front of me, and I will sing it well."

Good volunteers: Whatever your context and budget, logistical volunteers who get there early, set out the room without prompting, hold clipboards, and tick off names are vital. So too are social volunteers who will quietly connect with new or younger members, organize social activities, and solve problems resourcefully.

Good community members: Your choir's relationships define who the group is, who is attracted to it, who stays with it, and who in a community context becomes a lifelong member. So you need singers with open body language, emotional intelligence, and a smile, who will proactively oil the wheels of social discourse. You also need team members who "play nicely with others," and naturally establish and model the social rules we will all play by. We know those singers who may object to standing next to certain people, or have problematic personality traits. We welcome them too as they need us, but should unobtrusively identify these issues before they arrive in the group, and bear them in mind.

Good activists: You also need passionate and proactive activist leaders in your group. They are the change-makers, and the guardians of your social values. They believe in the school, love the music for its own sake, or just want to help people through singing. Whatever their age, you need a few disruptors, people who will

156   Transforming Choral Singing

demand the group gets better, and that it sees the world their way. You don't need many of them, and they will not always agree with each other. Your activists are in it because they see the change your group makes in the world, and they believe in it. Managing their energy can be a challenge, but when we find those people, good leaders hold on to them and channel their energy for the good.

Leading from the Art

Leading a choir or an arts organization is a unique responsibility. On one level, you alone can coalesce the artistic vision and devise the choral product that fulfils the mission and is the reason your group exists. At the same time, for the art to be the very best it can be, you must be fully engaged in supporting other leaders within the school, college, community of faith, or nonprofit your choir embodies. This too involves communication and collaboration.

Your art is less likely to thrive, for example, if someone above or beside you lays out a budget first, and insists you work within its arbitrary limitations. The best choirs are led from the art, and a better process begins from a clear, well communicated, appropriate but flexible artistic vision from you, which provides your colleagues with the direction they need. The more they can be responsive to your art, the more impactful that art will be, and the more successful the group will then become in fulfilling its purpose.

The values expressed in your art are what will get funders interested, so you can support your fundraiser by being clear about that. Your group's brand, marketing, and PR necessarily align with its product, so the assets they create should support the show and showcase its point of view. Even if you say little, your presence at key finance, HR, marketing, fundraising, logistics, and senior management meetings will infuse their process with your vision. We lead, then, by being present and connecting people to the artistic vision. We do a kind of dance constrained by the time we have, the resources available, and above all the quality of our communication with others.

It is also the choral director's job to compromise the most. As artistic leaders, we should be very used to having people say no to us. If we are any good, we learn to adapt, and understand the creative opportunities and challenges we face. The paradox is that we must lead from the front and simultaneously serve our singers and our school, faculty, church, or community. We only operate with the consent of others, and are utterly powerless without them. Once our ideal show is conceived, we need the skills of compromise, to hone it down into a more specific version. That version has to create impact in a specific school, college, or city, with a specific audience, at a given educational level, with a given amount of money, and with the resources the group can realistically muster.

On one level, this is the death of our personal vision by a thousand cuts. Nevertheless, we cannot have ego. This necessary interaction will improve our art by making it especially apt, impactful, educationally appropriate, and unique. Good programmers, educators, and artistic leaders already have their ears wide open and anticipate compromise. Their personal artistic choices are always molded by what is possible, and by a clear sense of what art is needed by their community.

Just as our group makes demands on us, we should be making demands on them. It is part of our role as leaders to insist on certain standards, and to earn respect by being disciplined, reliable, professional, and flexible. Choral directors are not the only arbiters, but we are often the only people qualified to judge whether our art is impactful or achieving its educational objectives. Just as we are held accountable, we should be empowered to hold both our singers and our colleagues to account. There is no need to be "difficult" or "temperamental" as a leader, but at times we do have to be persistent.

Here is where our flexibility needs to show itself across the whole organization. Art is not always predictable, so it is important that a director can add resources where they are needed. They should be able to add a song, a video screen, or a confetti cannon to a show, just as they can reduce a budget, if it turns out they have less cash than first thought. Too often, I have found myself forced to do the latter, and unable to do the former. If all I am is flexible, the whole group is not making the most of its opportunities. If all I am is self-indulgent, the group will go over budget and not be able to continue. Above all, when issues arise, the director should not become isolated by losing communication with the key people we depend on for help. The dance is complex.

Vulnerability is also key to leadership. An artistic director has to make themselves vulnerable to their group, in order to serve them. We share personal parts of ourselves and our community members in our art. Likewise, the group has to make itself vulnerable to its artistic leaders. A good artistic leader will be able to "hold" a group while a problem is solved, a group emotion is processed, or artistic risks are taken. The better a group is, the more it will make itself vulnerable structurally and financially for the good of any extra artistic or educational impact that could be generated. Choral directors should feel heard, supported, nurtured, and defended, because they make themselves vulnerable on everyone's behalf.

Next a few thoughts about *being* managed. How should you expect to be treated by your group? First, you should expect your ensemble to be demanding. Your manager should challenge you to have ideas, and then give you the resources to carry them out. Second, all art requires a fertile personal vision. So your choir or chorus should also enable self-care for you, and be proactively enabling you to grow as an artist. You should be encouraged to interact with other directors, go to conferences, discover new skills, indulge your personal stylistic preferences, and learn about styles you know less well. Your manager's main role is to nurture, support, and protect their artistic leader, rather than place barriers in their way.[4]

If a choral director shows signs of lacking personal zest, or they begin to repeat themselves, this can often be a sign that they need more freedom and self-care, not less. Your manager should be checking in regularly that you have the freedom and resources you need, and if necessary provide extra professional development in the form of new ideas, contexts, and artistic stimulus. If you need more structure, they should provide that too. Then again, if your creative curiosity is truly exhausted, you are no longer connecting well with others, or you feel there are just too many barriers, you may be ready to move on. It is their job to note that, and take steps to help you relight your personal flame.

Often groups give up on their choral leaders too easily. Sometimes, they can simply fail to nurture or challenge them sufficiently. Others define them as somehow "difficult" or not suitable, without really exploring the underlying issue. Black colleagues of mine have suffered this one especially, but it has also happened to many colleagues of mine of all races. If their director is doing a good job, managers can also assume all is well, not search for data, and take them for granted. Because we are musicians, we are often assumed to be magicians. If we are successful, it can look as if we can magically continue to solve all problems and keep ourselves energized and motivated, even if we are overworked, endlessly repeating ourselves, or given too few resources to creatively explore.

In reality, like any employee, we can only work well, grow, and thrive with the stimulation, reflection time, tools, resources, and above all the deep, collaborative, and honest relationships we need. Do you deserve a sabbatical after ten to fifteen years' service? Support them by asking for it. What nascent skills do you have that they can develop, so that you continue to grow, to the benefit of all? Ask for training in working with a different age-group or community. It can be hugely supportive and motivating when you and your managers devise and agree a plan for your growth as a musician, leader, and educator.

Some questions about your own practice: How much time do you spend working on the art, as opposed to developing community, or managing logistics? What would be the best balance of both in your context?

How much do you feel your group values you as a choral director? What more could it do to support you and challenge you in your work? Are there even barriers in your way? Talk honestly and with humility to your leadership about that. How are you feeling personally in your work? Are you feeling energized about your artistic process? What are your next steps, to ensure you stay stimulated and fertile as a leader?

Fellowship

A few years back, my sister visited me in New York and came to rehearsal. I would always arrive early to set up and chat to people before it all began, so she was able to mingle and observe the singers' arrival into the space. They would greet each other in twos and threes. There were hugs, light kisses on the cheek—her comment was that there was "a lot of quiet affection."

That story is about a community choir, but whatever your context, rehearsal is not just the time where we sing, but also the time where singers have fellowship.[5] A colleague of mine once described being a choral director as like being the pastor of a church. Our singers come to sing, of course, but they also come because the choir holds a space for them that expresses and represents who they are and what they

Directing and Leading a Choral Community **159**

believe. Marginalized high school and college students know this especially well. It is a key part of the director's role to curate that space, because it is the space in which singing can facilitate growth and personal change.

Storytelling is a recurring theme in this book, and a great way of leading fellowship is to plan a storytelling moment during rehearsal. In the second half, as a break from the focus of rehearsing, I might find a reason to tell a joke, relax people, and make them laugh. In my choir, I might speak about a singer who had been doing especially amazing advocacy work, thank someone for volunteering, or talk about where we would be singing in future, and why. In yours, why not celebrate a student's recent success, explain why a hard decision has been taken, or make yourself vulnerable by telling a personal story about what is going on with you spiritually? Such stories engage singers personally in our values, ethics, and social mission, and bond them to each other.

No space is entirely safe (see the next chapter for more on that), but we should aim for a space, where our whole community can meet what LGBTQIA+ people call their "chosen family." Many in our group had been excluded from their biological one, and some were thrown out onto the street. Many more had been made to feel tolerated rather than entirely celebrated, because of their sexuality. For them, rehearsal was as important as performance, and in some ways more so. The rest of the world can seem hostile, unwelcoming, and lonely, and there is huge pressure on us all to be a certain size, look a certain way, and belong to a certain social tribe. The same is true for bullied students in schools, synagogue and church community members, and college students struggling with mental health issues.

Rehearsal should be that special place, the one time in the week when singers feel safe to truly be themselves. In mine, there were greetings at the beginning, chats in the break, plans to meet for coffee at other times in the week, and (theoretically!) secret dates set by text message during rehearsal. When there were birthday celebrations, singers would sing "Happy Birthday" wholeheartedly, and there were special songs to be sung when someone passed away in the group.

There would sometimes be a lot of identity performance. At one point I had forty-five drag queens in my group, who at different times would arrive and sing in their finery. A couple of leather guys would consistently arrive at rehearsal in little else than black leather vests and revealing leather trousers. The majority might be coming from work in what we called their "corporate drag." Trans people in the group might be confidently displaying their identities, or tentatively exploring new ones by simply wearing their home clothes. All were proactively welcomed as their full queer selves.

The teens in your school choirs need that same freedom as they discover themselves, and so too do our college students. Our welcome and engagement with marginalized ethnic groups will always need care and intentionality. In the end though, we all come together to sing. It is not your job to reflect the lived experience of everyone in the group, and that is not possible. It is your job to reflect the group's purpose and values, in ways that all can hear and act on.

Art has to reflect community life, and we did a number of shows that were directly or indirectly about suicide, addiction, and other self-destructive behaviors. Musical

160   Transforming Choral Singing

material should trigger emotion and be challenging at times, but where emotion is triggered in rehearsal, it is our job to note this sensitively and ensure that someone nearby can offer a tissue or a hug. In doing so, we set a tone of compassion and respect in the room, and directly model the kind of society we wanted to create.

In my groups, there have also been a number of occasions where a song made some singers feel uncomfortable because of their cultural background or previous experience. In those situations, we should lean into the situation, support those concerned, and make sure everyone feels heard. After rehearsal, it was also important to follow up with a call, to check how those singers were feeling. Your crucial network of two-way relationships is unlikely to flourish if, in that situation, your response is: "We don't have time, so everyone stop expressing yourselves, keep quiet and sing."

All of this is not peripheral. It is core to our purpose that choirs provide personal and social support for our singers. My experience is that this fellowship work has huge benefits for the quality of our sound, its resonance, its blend, its dynamic range, and the passion and unity with which we sing. People frequently described my choir as both looking and sounding like a community. Our singers looked free to be themselves, and sang wholeheartedly as a result. When a community ecosystem is regimented and closed down, so too will be their sound. If conflicted, the vocal sound will become equally conflicted and uneven. Get the social cohesion of your group right, and every aspect of the musical process will also be more focused and precise, from listening and blend to diction and attack. In a truly unified choir, singers will place a single note exactly together, and the resulting musical gesture will be magnified exponentially, as will be the impact of the piece.

This kind of choral leadership is a balancing act. You are not a social worker, a coach, or a therapist, nor is it your job to be the savior of all. Nevertheless, you hold the space within which the fellowship aspect of the work is made real to everyone in the room. If you see your leadership in narrowly musical terms, you can quickly close down those personal connections and alienate your singers. Choral directors lead choral communities, both for the good of their art and because it is ethically the right thing to do.

Empowerment

One rehearsal, I spent a persistent ten minutes searching for a particular vocal result. Suddenly it clicked. I remember, without thinking, jumping up and down and dancing a little dance on the platform in an uncharacteristically expressive way (I am British after all!). I am told I also yelled, "Yeeeeeees!" at the top of my voice. I achieved laughter and ease in the room, and when we sang the song through five minutes later, the group's entire sound had grown. Such positive reinforcement, spontaneous or not, empowers your singers, and is vital to your artistic and mission success. An empowered group can sing as loud, as quiet, as happy or sad, as simple or complex as it likes. It has greater vocal capacity, flexibility, and expressiveness.

Some choirs can sing with great refinement, but their directors tend to function as inhibitors. They hold the sound in with their gestures rather than enabling it. As a result, dynamic range and characterization can become muted, and storytelling can lack punch. Starting from a place of empowerment, I learned over time to reinforce singers' good vocal behavior more of the time, and say no to them less, both in my verbal interactions and my conducting gestures. Increasingly, I listen for alignment between what I need singers to do and what they are giving me back, and start there in my comments. This increases the percentage of moments where I can positively reinforce their actions, and beckon for more. As soon as I started doing this, I found my singers more responsive and engaged. I had given them agency.

As I mentioned before, another empowering teaching mantra I discovered was: "I don't sing in the concert." It was a way of thanking them for their work, but it also said, "I trust you; you have to take responsibility now." A choir is only ever as good as its conductor, but it is also only as confident as its singers. Our choral art is utterly dependent on their morale, and the quantity and quality of the work they do. If a director is being incompetent or communicating poorly, the impact of this is first felt by the singers. Their lack of empowerment is, if you like, the canary in the coal mine. On the other hand, if singers are enjoying themselves, showing up on time, attending regularly and giving good feedback about the art, this will quickly spread to your audience figures and finances. A board, pastor, or school management team messes with this illusive chemistry at their peril.

Where else does empowerment start? Your singers need a voice. Ours elected their own leaders, who helped manage auditions and administrate the group, and dealt with member concerns. They also had a say in the hiring and firing of our artistic and educational leadership, myself included.

With regard to programming, there are two undesirable extremes. In the first, singers or other managers assemble a repertoire list, decide on a concert theme, and perhaps consult the director for their views, and say, "Conduct this!" This often results in dull outcomes—shows written by committee to please everyone, and often the lowest common denominator. The opposite undesirable extreme is that the choral director chooses every song. We have all seen choral shows that say more about the tastes, personal predilections, and previous experiences of the conductor than they do about the needs of either singers or audience. Entire evenings by a single obscure composer, half-heartedly sung by loyal singers who feel ignored, will not inspire members of your community ecosystem to attend, applaud, and give back. Somewhere in the middle is the right path.

On the one hand, singers and others should have a chance to suggest themes, concert titles, and individual songs. High school singers can be particularly creative, and will often help you create the programs that will attract other high schoolers. Singers also need a say as rehearsals progress. Sometimes they like to please and they trust you, so even if there are issues, they keep quiet and gamely carry on. At others, there may be gathering resentment or festering anger, and silences in rehearsal may take on a very different quality!

162 Transforming Choral Singing

College students can have short fuses where there are issues. Check in frequently on how the learning is going, and whether the material itself is hitting the spot and fun to sing. Again, once the concert is over, give your singers the chance to give feedback on programming, rehearsals, arrangements, conducting, and accompaniment. If you have it, also ask about band sound, space on stage, lighting, sound, dress, choreography, and stage management. Where you are being successful and making singers comfortable, you will feel affirmed, and there is always something new to learn.

Finally, there are some members of your singing community who you disempower at your peril: singers of any age, they are what I call your "elders." Crucial opinion-formers and influencers, they are not necessarily in formal leadership positions, but they nevertheless have great insight and informal power. They "get it" somehow, and they have earned a particular kind of ownership in the eyes of your group. Present in all kinds of choirs, they may not be part of the core social group, or its current main leaders. Perhaps they have just joined the group and are immediately marked informally as its future leaders, or they choose to "just sing." These key singers hold the conventional wisdom of the group. Their opinion is likely to have validity, and is shared by many. To ignore them or to inadvertently tread on their metaphorical toes is to lose cultural capital. By learning their stories and harnessing their energy, regardless of channels of formal authority, you are ensuring that the message and values of your group has continuity.

That said, there are also times of era change where a year group leaves, a director moves on, and those opinion formers are replaced by a new generation. A choir's beehive is usually a multi-generational community of singers, and sometimes a large number of them can become disillusioned or move on. Your elders will stay. They care about the group for its own sake, and will never feel entirely loyal to you. They will, however, tell you the "real" story and keep you on track.

Coalitions

As choral leaders, we build not only communities, but also coalitions. Compared to my concept of community ecosystem, a coalition is broader. It is likely to include allies of various sorts, including other singers, listeners, influencers, donors, ensembles, and organizations outside your own. In a coalition, a school collaborates with another school, college with college, church with church. Any choir can work with a local social organization or nonprofit cause. Your coalition partners will be different from you, but will share, at least in one aspect, your values and common interests, and do similar work. For us as an LGBTQIA+ choir, such allies included other nearby choirs, and other arts organizations and associations. Outside the arts, they also included other LGBTQIA+ organizations, schools, colleges, welcoming and affirming churches, and so on. The broader your coalition is, the more powerful you become. At the same time, broad coalitions take work to keep together, because the range of opinion and values within them is wide.

Coalitions are more likely where you can identify a win-win for both sides. For example, we did a show called *Four Choirs and a Cathedral*, where we hosted all four queer choirs and choruses in our city in the spectacular and gigantic cathedral space of St. John the Divine. The win-win here was a chance for all four choirs to sing in this gigantic space, to do joint songs that we could not have done separately. We also made a joint statement about our solidarity as a movement, but in a religious space where our community cannot always assume a welcome.

Another of our most complex and effective collaborations was the one New York did with our younger sister gay men's chorus, Coro Gai Ciudad de México. I first met their leaders at a conference in 2016, and had an immediate sense of a synergy and some possibilities. Culturally we were very different, and we were at different stages on our LGBTQIA+ journeys, but both groups came, after all, from huge, vibrant, and diverse cities, with big arts scenes and subway systems. Both cities were hubs for large communities of gay men, who were drawn to their city in part by the promise of fellowship, self-expression , and by the homophobia they faced. Our collaboration itself lasted approximately eighteen months, began with a joint performance in March 2017 in New York, and ended with a joint performance in Mexico City in June 2018.

Again there were many win-wins. We New Yorkers were able to make a unique statement about social justice, standing alongside a large queer Mexican choral group in our city two months after Trump's election. We sang together for queer equality, and for the cause of breaking down walls. The Mexico group's main need, they said, was that they felt they were growing too fast and lacked infrastructure and resources. Our joint show in Mexico sold out, and they were left with a pot of money, and much enhanced brand recognition and profile, that they could use to build capacity. Lasting friendships were made at singer level, a new international community of singers was built, and our show attracted considerable media attention in both cities. By creating a coalition, both choruses achieved their own objectives. We devised a project that was bigger, more artistically successful, and more impactful than either of us could do on our own. We worked in ways that gave all parties an equal say in the process, and provided equal but different benefits to both. We sang their repertoire, and they sang ours. Both groups learned, both grew, and both achieved their respective purposes.

Within your own community, which are the musical and non-musical organizations with whom you could collaborate to create a win-win situation? What would such a collaboration look like?

B. Musical Aspects of Choral Leadership

We turn now to musical matters. Choral music education has not always been effective in teaching directors how to lead effectively in non-classical styles. This has left everyone from high school teachers to professional choral directors lacking the stylistic knowledge or the music teaching tools to do their jobs well. It has also left them less in touch with large sections of their potential singers. We can no longer put up with the tacit assumption that once you have the skills and understanding to direct classical music, this will miraculously suffice for every other style. Classical musicians would certainly never accept directors leading them who did not have the cultural background or knowledge to do it well. There is more to stylistic openness than simply doing more popular styles.

From the social justice perspective too, the majority of choral directors in schools and colleges across the country are white, and are expert in the styles white people know. As such, their training rarely covers the core musical competencies that will enable them to truly engage and educate singers from a range of ethnic, religious, and other backgrounds.

So we switch gears now, and turn to the nitty gritty of choral directing itself, focusing specifically on choral leadership, and how our practice as musical leaders might need to change to align with the principles of stylistic openness and social justice.

Watch for several recurring themes from earlier in this chapter. First, the director is at the center of a complex network of relationships and leads by connecting. Second, your choir's musical practices are often a direct analogue of their social ones. Third, it can be more efficient and effective to solve an issue in the moment in your musical behavior, rather than using words to "tell someone what to do." Finally, the same leadership qualities of collaboration, flexibility, and empowerment of everyone in the ensemble are central here too.

This section also follows on directly from the rhythm skills work of Chapter 4. There we focused on strategies for singers' rhythmic development, while here the focus is leading and directing in popular and especially groove-based styles. This is another area covered less in conventional choral trainings. Just as the musical gestures are modified, so too must the leadership style of the director change, and the ways in which they communicate. As with earlier chapters, there is not the space to be comprehensive, so this section focuses mainly on areas of our conducting where important differences occur, and where overlaps can be seen. As with previous chapters, what follows is practical, but because of the nature of the work, content is presented here as several sets of suggestions and tips for conductors, and not as workshops. They cover pulse, beat, and tempo; leading a rhythm section; form and routine signals; directing phrasing and musical character; conductor positioning and levels of control; conducting gestures; and aspects of singer choreography.

Suggestions and Tips

1) Directing Pulse, Beat, and Tempo

With regard to the pulse, the conductor remains that musical lighthouse, the enabler of the group pulse, transmitting and receiving musical and emotional information. In all music, responsibility for the pulse is shared to some extent, and earlier we covered how every singer is responsible for locking in and for leading the groove. This first section explores how, as the director, you may need to modify your conventional conducting gestures when working outside common practice classical styles. Getting singers and conductor to externalize pulse and gesture in their bodies is also key.

Count-ins: In jazz and popular styles, though less in musical theater, there is often a verbal count-in from the conductor, or a one- or two-measure count-in from the drums. An out loud count-in establishes not only the tempo but also the musical character. Sometimes two bars can be too much in performance, but at others a longer count-in sets the tone, and can actively save time in setting a new tempo in rehearsal. Practice giving two-bar count-ins in 4/4 at different intensity levels and speeds by saying, "One . . . two . . . one, two, three, four," clicking your fingers on 2 and 4 as you go.

In-breaths: In classical choral conducting, attention is rightly given to the anticipatory gesture. Conventionally, we signal the in-breath before the choir begins to sing, with the body or hands. In many non-classical styles, the music literally breathes differently, and melodic gestures have a different rhythmic function. The music requires new breathing habits from your singers, and this can affect when and how the conductor signals in-breaths and indicates legato.

Rhythmic gestures outside the "box": Key to some choral methods is the "conducting box" idea,[6] that all gestures should be made in a space roughly three feet by three feet, directly in front of your face and chest. This is effective with certain sorts of repertoire in all styles, as it draws in the eyes of the singers, focuses conductor energy, and keeps both sound, phrasing, and tuning buoyant and "up." Gestures are kept simple, clear, and relatively small. That said, even in conducting classical repertoire, there are times when the area outside the box is expressively useful, as Trecek-King notes. Where groove-based music is concerned, the whole body is more often engaged. Hip sways, leg movements, and finger clicks are key to demonstrating a groove's character. I find clicking on beats 2 and 4 at waist level is more natural, and indicates a relaxed ease. It can look strange and become more physically tense to click your fingers higher up, at chest or ear level. We return to this under "Phrasing and Musical Character" later in this chapter.

2) Leading a Rhythm Section

A substantial portion of the choral conducting tuition I received was around beat patterns and ictus. The goal was for the director to clarify for their musicians how many beats were in each bar, exactly where each beat is on the pulse, and how much

166 Transforming Choral Singing

stress there should be on that beat. The model was that we controlled the pulse and rhythmic character. This is solid training, but when working with a rhythm section, leadership is by convention more collaborative. Even where I am beating, say, 4, I am often reflecting the drummer's tempo to the singers more than leading them. Choir, rhythm section (bass, drums, percussion, guitar, and piano) and conductor all share control of the pulse as individual rhythmic units. Rhythmic delegation and open two-way communication are again crucial.

Rely on your band for the groove and time: Rhythm section members conventionally define and keep the groove steady without a conductor. Having a conductor at all can seem unnecessary and even strange to some players, so negotiate your role carefully. They essentially *are* the rhythmic conductor. Once you set a tempo and a groove is established, empower them to play that role, even if you are still sharing the ictus with your singers.

There is sometimes no need to conduct the beat: Once the piece has begun, conducting the beat at all can be unnecessary. This can also be true conducting a classical orchestra, of course,[7] but much less often. Instead, lead by giving more entries and phrasing cues, and signal the character of the groove in your face and body.

The language of directing the groove: The director still needs to communicate a clear and detailed vision of the groove. Musical language can be crucial, to avoid losing credibility as a leader and communicating poorly. Refer to grooves by name, just as you would an "minuet" or a "presto." "Two-feel" and "four-feel" swing, jazz waltz, salsa, samba, bossa nova, eight- and sixteen-beat rock, show 2, rock ballad, Motown, soul, and hard rock are common examples of terms.[8] Each groove term is really a flexible template, so also specify the character of, say, a bossa nova. Is it perhaps a more conventional '60s Jobim bossa, or something more contemporary and freer, like Bebel Gilberto? Also crucial to directing grooves are terms around feel, including "laying back," playing "on the front" and "locking in."

Italian and other terms: In popular styles, all of the terms above sit alongside a sprinkling of the standard classical Italian ones, which most of your band members (and singers) will have some knowledge of. Their experience of classical music may vary hugely, so I code-switch, reinforcing my use of *p*, *ff*, and *crescendo* with their modern equivalents ("quiet," "very loud," "get louder"). Italian terms representing character, like *grazioso* or *furioso*, are less useful(!).

Agreeing on the texture of the groove: In an initial play-through, rhythm players will offer you a multilayered texture involving a complex combination of sixteenth, eighth, and quarter-note patterns. These textures are really your players' opening gambit, a serviceable groove template, but not necessarily the most interesting, specific, or appropriate. As they rehearse, what they play will become more unique to your performance. Focus on levels of intensity and density. As a way of achieving a "quieter" result, try asking for the musical space to be a little emptier, rather than asking for less energy or loudness.

Levels of freedom: Another expressive quality to consider is the level of freedom players have to embellish around a groove. In pop music and some musical theater, players will usually stick exactly to the part, however repetitive. In more improvised contexts, however, including jazz and other kinds of pop music like funk and some hard rock, the part is only a guide. Players can and often will add individuality, and embellish what is written. A player who is empowered to embellish will engage more, make more interesting rhythmic decisions, and be interactive with the embellishments of others.

Check the rhythm section can be heard by the singers: The drummer and bass player can only lead the singers' pulse and groove for you if they can be heard. Position the band so the singers can hear them clearly, but avoid rhythm section spill into the choir microphones. One crack from a snare can obliterate your entire choir's sound, if the snare is too close to a choir mike. If they can't hear the band, a choir may gallop ahead, and become significantly out of sync. Foldback speakers well positioned and well balanced are your friend, as are well positioned and angled directional microphones.

Other rhythmic power struggles: Even where they can hear well, a band groove can also start to run away, or band and singers can feel the rhythmic gestures in entirely different ways. If a choir is in danger of rushing ahead of its rhythm section, for example, anticipate this. If not, you will have to choose in the moment whether to rein in your choir, or ask your band to speed up. If they tell you that a groove is not "sitting" but you don't hear it yourself, ask band members to explain, and act to rectify it. A choir will feel a groove in a particular way itself, and, to add complexity, individual drummers and bass players sometimes tend play on the back of the beat, while others will play on the front. Find players that are flexible and feel the beat in the way you like. Then empower them and trust them to solve these issues. Intervene only where necessary, helping band and choir to negotiate pulse, rhythmic detail, and groove amongst themselves.

3) Form and Routine Signals

Repeats: Where there are repeats, your role can vary. Sometimes, you will want to obey what a score says. At others, you will want to prescribe the number of repeats, and announce, "We are going around four times here." You may want to stay flexible, so you can decide in the moment to build tension or allow a vocal or improvised solo to continue longer. These compositional decisions, affecting the tension and release of a performance, are rare for classical conductors.

Round and round signals: I signal "We're going back" by pointing behind, and "We're going on" by pointing forward. Even without a repeat in the part, I will sometimes signal a "round and round" by taking one finger and circling it above my head (or in front of my chest so the audience can't see it). The groove needs time to deepen further. On the last round of the repeat, I signal "We are going on this time" by pointing with my index finger directly forward.

Backings: Backings are another compositional feature of riff-base styles. During a "round and round," an extra backing gets added to the texture, again to build tension. Touch your back with one hand to indicate, "Backings are about to come in, but

168   Transforming Choral Singing

we are still going round and round." Then count down from a few beats before the backing begins, and bring in the section singing the backing. I have been known to use the fingers of one hand at my chest, to give a "4, 3, 2, 1" into the entry, that cannot be seen by the audience. Err on the side of clarity, rather than confidentiality.

4) Directing Phrasing and Musical Character

Warm up your singers by getting them moving: Movement can encourage flexibility and ease. Try warming up your singers by singing a song while actively marching. Suggest singers lift the knees high in time to their own singing, while touching each knee with the opposite hand. You will find it loosens the body and the breath, engages the torso, and markedly increases volume, vocal energy, and musical character.

Move to the groove: Earlier in my discussion of rhythmic education, I discussed how as choral directors, we are sometimes taught to stand still, and we teach our singers to do the same. Conventionally, we think "forward and up" as per Alexander technique, and model physical stillness below the waist, for better posture and grounding of the breath. This is good initial practice in many contexts. However, I established earlier that groove-based music tends to be dance-based, and this can help rhythmic learning. At times then, we have to literally dance the musical character to the singers. Once you do move your hips, your singers will mirror and begin to move too, and this will improve their feel, rhythmic learning, and vocal phrasing. On the level of vocal technique, such movement is seen by some as disrupting the vocal support, but in my experience, the concept of "anchoring" to create an engaged column of air is entirely consistent with moving the hips and legs.

Choose your focus: It is impossible to communicate everything about a song in your conducting. Rhythm, pulse, and groove are crucial, and achieving the exact feel of a pop song (or a Strauss waltz!) can be much more important than giving entries or indicating phrasing. So don't be afraid to prioritize the groove in what you communicate in your body, and once the groove is in place, switch your conducting focus back to other areas.

Hand and facial gestures: Liberated from the ictus for at least some of the time, your hands and face are free to indicate other features, including:

Attacks and releases: I use little explosions with my hands for attacks, and sometimes cutting and pointing gestures to indicate hard attacks.

Dynamics: Indicate hairpins by holding the sound between both hands as if holding a balloon, and expanding and contracting the space between them.

Stressed and unstressed phrasing, syllable by syllable: Indicate stresses with weight in your hands, and sometimes by mouthing syllables. To indicate stressed and unstressed syllables, I often mime a "waa-waa" trumpet mute using open and closed hand.

Short and long notes, including staccatos, legatos, and accents: I indicate a long note or legato phrase by pointing my hand toward the group and then doing a

Directing and Leading a Choral Community **169**

gesture toward the singers, as if a plane is taking off. Against the advice of some classical textbooks, I find short notes and accents can be communicated best with stabbing, pointy hand gestures, which intentionally break up the legato line and can also disrupt perfect vocal fold closure. The rhythmic precision and variety of resonance is the expressive goal. Where I need a beautiful legato, fold closure is the highest priority, and I direct differently.

Variations in vibrato and straight tone: I use a horizontal flat hand held steady for straight tone, and wobble it at different speeds in the moment for vibrato. With practice, your choir will really listen and look, and you can control vibrato intensity and speed in real time.

5) Conductor Positioning and Levels of Control

Earlier I pointed out that there is often no conductor in pop music—for example in a Coldplay song, or one by Pentatonix or Ladysmith Black Mambazo. In these musical situations, the choral sound should be disciplined and tight, but the director often needs to get out of the way. You remain in charge but free your singers to own their power as communicators and be the (rock) stars of the show. Try these strategies to vary your level of control and free up your positioning:

Stand to the side: Try standing either fully stage left or stage right, perhaps with your band. This makes the communication between choir and audience more immediate. Singers can still see you in their peripheral vision, and can be instructed to turn their heads or full bodies toward you to see key cues. Your triangle of power remains directly in front of you, so you angle yourself toward the center of the choir when you want their full attention. You can also instruct your choir to angle toward you where needed, although their primary focus should always be the audience.

Stop conducting: We discussed earlier not conducting in rehearsal, as a learning exercise. As trust develops, try giving your singers full control of the tempo in performance, once a song starts. Next, stay on stage, but delegate the start of a song to your choir too. With practice, even with a group of one hundred or more, you will find they can bring themselves in and start singing without you, even a cappella. If your group is larger, slight head movements (from you or from carefully positioned singers) can help. Aim to make your expressive gestures and tempo indications superfluous, by baking them into the performance. Also point out those places where the ensemble will absolutely have to watch you.

Leave the stage altogether: In some styles, the choral director may not need to be present at all. An even more provocative move is to leave the stage altogether, where appropriate or logistically possible. Audiences love it, because it presents physical evidence of your trust in your singers. It also shows your ensemble's confidence, and again gives the singers full eye contact with listeners, which aids connection. The element of musical risk will also draw listeners in, and keep your group alert.

6) Conducting Gestures

Set the tone with only face and eyes: Try directing the group, using only your face and eyes. As well as cuing that way, set the tone with a facial expression—peaceful, playful, groovy, intense, etc. Try smiling, nodding your head, bringing sections in with your eyes, increasing the dynamics with facial gestures, and so on. You'll be amazed at how little effort is effective, and your rhythm section will feel freer.

Facilitate listening across the ensemble: Less experienced singers can be blissfully unaware of other parts around them. Scan across the group, and use your eyes and facial expression to show you are listening intently to all sections. This will help (and sometimes force) them do the same, and can lock in the groove without you saying a word or proactively "conducting."

Add vocal light and shade: Also important in directing choirs in these contexts is control of resonance and tone in the moment. Develop shorthand signals for particular kinds of sounds. For example: I make a relaxed fist near my belly to indicate engaged anchoring for "belt"; I flap my hand in a particular way to add vibrato; and I hold my nose for "twang."

Evaluative pose: Explore being only in the more distant role of a thought partner to your group, an outsider listener. Try using an evaluative pose, perhaps one hand at your hip, head on one side, stroking your chin with the other hand. Again, singers will listen harder and be more autonomous, modeling your behavior and thought patterns.

In-the-moment telepathy: I remember the first time I thought to myself, "It would be nice to have a crescendo there," did nothing at all with my body or face, *but the crescendo happened anyway!* When I later asked why they got louder, singers said something like, "It felt right." I had trained them, by often asking for crescendos in similar contexts. Once your group knows you well, such in-the-moment telepathy and proactive leadership on their part without being asked is invaluable, again saving rehearsal time and words.

7) Choreography and Movement

Choreography is an authentic feature of non-classical styles of many kinds and adds visual interest. Although it is not strictly the choral conductor's responsibility, I am including these suggestions here, because movement affects how your choir sings, and there are definitely better and worse ways of devising and teaching it.

Start to teach choreography from week 2: The first time they learn a song, notionally in week 1, your singers should focus solely on the music. They need to know the geography of a song first, how the different sections are laid out, so movement is learned in relation to an existing lyric and melody map in their minds. However, if the choreography is added too late, there is too little time to memorize and develop song and movement together. Add choreography in notional week 2, once the outline of the music is in place, but before too much detail has been set in mental concrete. Then gradually refine both, hand in hand.

The **"bedding in" phase:** Once you begin to review and run material, focusing on choreography can reduce vocal confidence and precision. Both are physical, so this is to be expected. In this "bedding in" phase, work on both separately. Sometimes singers should "think" the song, perhaps mouth words, and focus on movement, and at others sing the song full out, but "mark" or omit the choreography. Ask for both to be precise together later. Avoid changing the choreography once it is learned, as this can disrupt learning and morale very quickly. Work out snags privately before teaching your singers.

Remedial choreography for good singers with two left feet: We do not audition our singers for their ability to move. Some will have rhythmic challenges, and others will not be natural movers. Position singers carefully in performance, and provide short extra sessions for singers who need more practice, perhaps run by members themselves. Five minutes of one-to-one help from an experienced dancer can often unlock an issue.

Ensure that the gestures of choreography and singing align: Music and movement can sometimes fight each other. Perhaps the top of a vocal phrase requires an accent, while choreography asks the singer to implode into their body. Conversely, when a bodily movement aligns well with a vocal gesture, they can powerfully reinforce each other and improve the sound. Where a vocal gesture is passed from part to part in counterpoint, it is easiest if the move does the same. As above, try out choreography on the body while singing the song *before* you teach it to your singers.

Some final questions for self-reflection, around you as a choral leader: Do you see your own choir primarily as a community? Or primarily as a musical ensemble? What does your group need next as a community, and as a rehearsing and performing group? What simple steps can you as leader take to move the group forward in both of those aspects? What can you as a conductor do *less* of, to improve your group's performances? To what extent do your programs and performances belong to your singers, and to what extent do they belong to you? How could you make them belong to both? What is your own natural leadership style? Are you more of a listening counselor-leader, for example, more of visionary, or more of a driver-manager? How could you vary your leadership style more moment-to-moment, so you could lead better in all of the above ways, and more?

Notes

1. Abrams, quoted in Cole (2021).
2. Dag Jansson (2019) describes this aspect of choral leadership as "singer perceptions"
3. Jeremy Heimans and Henry Timms (2019) see this bottom-up connection between community and culture as a fundamental characteristic of twenty-first-century cultural life. For them, this is an expression of "new power values" (18), = characterized by self-organization, opt-in decision-making, collaboration, crowd-wisdom, sharing, open-sourcing, radical transparency, maker culture, more overall participation, and short-term conditional affiliation.
4. Harriet Simons (1983) refers to this aspect of our work as the "self-actualizing conductor.

172 Transforming Choral Singing

5. I hesitate slightly to use this word because it feels gendered to me!
6. Trecek-King refers to it here, but it often appears elsewhere in the choral conducting literature. https://www.trecekking.com/conducting-for-educators-part-2/
7. I am reminded of a famous clip of Carlos Kleiber conducting the Vienna Philharmonic in a Strauss polka here: https://www.youtube.com/watch?v=ExBzl7mvPDI
8. If you lack confidence or experience in this area, try buying a professional drum kit textbook which lists and notates all the grooves for you. I still have my student copy of Norman Grossman's (1972) *The Complete Book of Modern Drumming* (Lancaster, PA: Amsco), and a more complex but comprehensive one would be Mick Berry and Jason Gianni's (2012) *The Drummer's Bible: How to Play Every Drum Style from Afro-Cuban to Zydeco* (Tucson, AZ: Sharp Press).

9

The Daily Practice of Equity and Inclusion

Social spaces such as choirs are often unkind and treacherous for BIPOC, LGBTQIA+ and other marginalized people. The same social space can feel perfectly safe to some, but fraught with danger to others. We do not always know when we are discriminating against our fellow singers, or being offensive, unfair, or simply unkind to them. We can choose to ignore this, "just sing," and hope respect will somehow improve over time, or we can become proactively anti-racist, and make the fundamental changes necessary to our social practices.[1] Enacting those changes can be messy and painful, but brings huge rewards.

I am a choral director not only because I love choral music, but because I believe in fairness, compassion, and humanity. It is self-evident to me that because we are *all* human beings, we deserve equal respect, equal rights, and equal opportunities, as we make our way in the world. In the words of Maya Angelou, after Martin Luther King, "The truth is, no one of us can be free until everybody is free."[2] Choirs are a fantastic way to help make that principle of social justice a reality, and I have seen it happen. Such a focus can have a transforming effect on the empowerment and belonging your BIPOC and other marginalized singers experience in your group, and can radically change the perceptions, behavior, and language of the white majority too. This overall transformation can in turn deeply affect your choral sound, your teamwork, and the identity your group shares as members of the ensemble. I begin by laying out some key concepts that underlie Diversity, Equity, and Inclusion (DEI) work. Later, I offer workshops, suggestions, and tips that can help make your group kinder, fairer, and more equitable for all, whether it is in a school, college, community of faith, or other community setting.

Let's begin with diversity. In my jazz days in the UK, I once had a post-gig drinking conversation with a fellow musician with a disability, that has stayed with me ever since. We were chatting about the London neighborhoods where we felt comfortable to live, and he said with characteristic British understatement, "Personally, I never live in areas where there is too much of one sort of person." Diversity, then, is about not having too much of one sort of person in your choral group. In fact it is about ensuring that you have the widest possible range, and realizing that the ethnic and other demographic make-up of your group communicates powerful messages about your values to your singers and your audience. Whether you realize it or not, your choir is representing, "saying something." So you cannot avoid the question of what you want to represent.

Importantly, no one person can somehow "be diverse" or add diversity to your choir. Diversity is good, because it demonstrates that you have done the work to

---

Transforming Choral Singing. Charles W. Beale, Oxford University Press. © Oxford University Press 2024.
DOI: 10.1093/oso/9780197657775.003.0009

ensure that no one has been excluded. Everyone has to work together, and everyone has the great advantage of experiencing and learning from people different from themselves. Diversity also ensures that the group is taking full advantage of the range of vocal talents available to it.

Equity, by contrast, is about proactively achieving fairness. It is needed because we are all different, and need different resources and opportunities to ensure equal outcomes. Where there is equity, everyone is treated justly, regardless of who they are and what they believe. In a choir that is equitable, for example, a choral director should give everyone an equal chance to sing well, whether they read music or not, and regardless of their style. Individuals and groups can be selfish and competitive. Inequality is baked into our experience as human beings, and racial inequality especially so. So there have to be systems in place to proactively ensure equity occurs. Without equity, diversity is unlikely. What might that mean in your choir?

Inclusion takes many different forms, depending on your group. It starts from welcome, and moves toward engagement, and then to belonging (see Workshop 3 in this chapter). Where people feel included, they tend to feel welcome, comfortable, and enabled. They are more likely to engage, and will tend to feel they belong. A choir where people don't know your name, can't speak your language, call you fat, or take no account of your mobility challenges is unlikely to make you feel included. Nor is one where everyone is superficially friendly and possibly deluding themselves that all is well, but you realize white people are self-evidently being foregrounded.

The DEI field covers many areas of identity, and is developing constantly, so what I write here may already be out of date when it is published. Here I will focus on seven areas that feel most apt in the current climate, and in the context of choral singing. They are: race and ethnicity, gender identity, sexual orientation, age, body type, socioeconomic status, and disability. As elsewhere in this book, I acknowledge I have left out some areas entirely, but hope the principles outlined below indicate a direction of travel, and will have general application.

This chapter is in three parts. The first considers why you might want to do this work at all. It unpacks the most common and central DEI concepts, including privilege, intersectionality, and the challenge of holding space for marginalized people. The second moves from theory to practice, and lays out some workshops to help you to implement those concepts in your choir. The final section offers suggestions and tips, simple things you can do persistently, to help you and your singers make your choir a truly equitable, welcoming, and respectful social space.

To finish this introduction, here is an important disclaimer: As a cisgender white gay man, I am in almost every regard the *last* person who should be writing this chapter. I can claim hardly any authority or authenticity in the area of minority rights. I have only experienced marginalization, discrimination, stigma, and bias as a gay man. Racism, sexism, and other kinds of exclusion and inequality has not been my lived experience. The most I can hope for is to set a good example to other white directors, and hope that I have neither patronized nor offended the very people, my fellow humans, who this chapter is intended to support.

Why DEI?

Let's begin with a "lightbulb" joke, which I offer here with huge respect for therapists:

Question: How many therapists does it take to change a lightbulb?
Answer: Just one, but the light bulb has to want to change.

Many groups and organizations can feel a heavy-hearted need to engage with DEI out of duty. Rather like health and safety or governance structure, they know that they *should* have at least a statement and some regulations in place, but there is a lack of urgency and specificity about their approach. They have not thought through why they need to change, and exactly what changes would benefit them. There is a lack of both urgency and clarity.

One BIPOC inclusion consultant who I spoke to about this said that in her experience many organizations doing this work did not begin from a place of firm belief. They had not examined in detail what their DEI needs actually were, in relation to their activities and the demographics of their group. She went so far as to say that it was often better *not* to work on DEI at all if your organization was not ready for it. For example, if your choir is going through a major financial crisis or a change in leadership or membership, DEI is unlikely to be your priority. Wherever your group is, then, embark on your DEI journey wholeheartedly, with clear objectives and with honesty and authenticity.

All of that said, if you are still ignoring the world of DEI, you have not been paying close attention. Incontrovertible evidence of lack of equality and violence against marginalized people is rife across the Western world, and so is the impact of that inequality on our fellow human beings. Hate crimes from anti-Semitic attacks[3] to murders of transgender people[4] are rising fast. The savage and random killings of African Americans in the US continue unabated, including in 2020 alone Ahmaud Arbery, Breonna Taylor, George Floyd, Tony McDaid, and others who for space cannot be named, but should not be forgotten. Even if it is not yet present in your choir, there is a deep sense of urgency across the non-extremist political spectrum that enough is enough. We have reached a tipping point, and to take no position is to be complicit in the many inequalities of the before times.

Art reflects life, and many in the arts are embracing diversity, equity, and inclusion as the core concepts of the age, and telling stories in their art that reflect that. The anger is real, as are the barriers to equity and inclusion that many face. The real question facing your group, then, is not *whether* to implement DEI practices, but *how* to respond to current inequality in a way that is appropriate to who you are and what you uniquely do.

Privilege

I began with the idea that certain kinds of people tend to do well in our society. They have what we call "privilege." For some having privilege is just fine. While I am not complacent about those people, their values are very different to mine, and I suspect many of those in the arts and arts education. Others with privilege may see themselves as liberal and compassionate, and may speak and act at times in compassionate ways. Nevertheless, without the persistent application of DEI practices, they will find it hard to change life for those less privileged than themselves. Indeed, they will tend to perpetuate it, first because it is not in their interests, and second because it is hard wired into our way of life, our language, our behavior, and our institutions. It is systemic.

So, for example, there is a huge store of numbers and a vast historical literature to suggest that white people tend to be better educated and be paid more than black and brown people. Black and brown people are more likely to be in prison, get stopped by the police, or get shot by them, and they have less access to everything from mental health services to voting opportunities. Likewise, straight people get to live their lives more openly and freely than those in the queer community, and they can generally love whoever they want without fear or shame. Women are paid less than men, and tend to take on unequal work in the nuclear family. Cisgender people (whose gender identity and expression match the biological sex they were assigned at birth) can be themselves in their bodies much more easily than transgender, non-binary and other gender-fluid folks. The middle class, who have more money, education, and other opportunities to begin with, tend to be given more opportunities, unless society actively intervenes to give working class people a leg up into the system. You are less likely to be a model or be successful in show business if you are older and your body is not a certain shape. People with disabilities and the neurodivergent tend to have more trouble getting access to the facilities and resources they need to lead full lives.[5]

History is written by the winners and creates how we see the world. It foregrounds the voices and stories of the privileged, and erases those who have less. As a result, people with privilege, whose stories are foregrounded in this way and who have been taught these stories, often wrongly assume they understand everyone else's lives too. In fact, to be blunt, they are often simply ignorant of them. They haven't experienced them because their privilege has meant they didn't need to. While they do have more power, this does not entitle them to speak for others.

There is no substitute, then, for education and a proactive approach. Everyone should hear and learn from the authentic voices of those whose lived experience is different from their own, and especially those who are less privileged. Art, of course, is an incredible way for those voices to be heard, which is one reason why choral singing is so important. The best art also requires the skills and cultural experience born of privilege or at least long periods of hard work, so our choirs will tend to be full of people who have it. DEI practices are a great way to counterbalance that tendency, and are especially necessary in the arts for that reason. How does privilege appear in your choir?

Intersectionality

I was working for what was then called LGBT Equality in London with my choir, when we won a vital legal battle for civil partnerships in 2005. Our programs became hopeful anthemic celebrations in that period, and we started a custom small group to sing at gay weddings. I then switched continents at just the point that enabled me to fight the same political battle all over again in the US! So in 2015 I found myself conducting another choir in New York, this time celebrating the legalization of gay marriage.

Both times, we felt we had achieved those new legal rights as a victory for *all* LGBTQIA+ people. Legally we were correct, but in fact, of course, things were more complex and unequal than that. The LGBTQIA+ population is by no means a single unified community. In our euphoria and arrogance, we forgot that many of our black and brown brothers and sisters were still suffering from acute homophobia, unable even to come out of the closet, let alone get married. In New York, for example, in Harlem north of 96th street in Manhattan, across the Bronx, and in many other more ethnically diverse and less gentrified neighborhoods, hardly anyone had the option to get married, and homophobia was almost as rife as ever. We also completely omitted trans people from the story we told ourselves. In parts of South London, the story was much the same.

This occurs because identity is intersectional. So a black *and* queer person has two strikes against them. They will find it harder as a black individual in a world where white people make the rules, *and* harder as a queer person in a homophobic world. A lack of intersectional thinking skewed our view of success. African American queer people, Latinx queer people and others were left behind in our movement, because most of its leaders were white. So too were transgender people of color, who were ignored despite being so key to our movement early on (Marsha P. Johnson and Silvia Rivera, for example). They got left behind because white cisgender gay men, themselves committed activists who did great work, were too dominant in our movement from the 1970 to the early 2000s.

In Chapter 1, I argued that through connection choral singing has the potential to create "community," and I quoted Ken Burns, about how choral singing is a radical, change-making act, because, from a "me" and a "you" it creates the potential for a new "us." The concept of intersectionality problematizes that idea, and challenges Ken Burns's concept of "we." It helps us to critique our idea of "community." In fact, communities are multi-layered, and, just as with learning style, they are made up of individuals from a range of backgrounds, with a huge variety of levels of privilege. Those individuals often choose to come together to sing or find fellowship in our

178 Transforming Choral Singing

choirs in spite of those inequalities, and the conflicts they can create. The complex identities of those in our choirs and choruses are made up of series of overlapping *wes*, and the amount of privilege and power each singer possesses will depend on a variety of identity factors. You can explore this further with your group by doing Workshop 4 later in this chapter.

Recognition of intersectionality does not mean that the idea of community and coming together as a unified group is now somehow untenable, but it does make it much harder and more complex. For me, singing remains a hugely powerful tool to break down barriers, heal division, and connect with people who were previously marginalized. The key to facilitating that healing and connection is the daily practice of DEI. What identities do you find in your group's members? Which may be hidden? How do they intersect in the individuals you see before you?

Brave Spaces and Microaggressions

The foundation of DEI practice in our choirs is to agree a set of standards for respectful behavior, and make them explicit. As directors, we are used to holding the space in which our singers interact, and rely on common sense and decency of the old fashioned sort to ensure everyone's comfort. Explicit standards simply take that process one step further. Your DEI standards create what used to be called a safe space, and is now called a *brave* space, in recognition that complete safety for marginalized people is almost impossible. This is not politically correct cancellation of certain behavior, but a simple assertion of higher standards. Your group, you assert, should be *especially* welcoming and you will do what it takes to make the artistic and social space comfortable for *all,* and indeed more comfortable than an increasingly uncomfortable and divided outside world.

A brave space gives singers some clear rules of the road, if you like. It ensures we all interact as respectfully as we can, helps us acknowledge that this can be hard, and enables us to challenge each other in honest but intentional ways that do not cause lasting damage to our community as a whole. The goal of a brave space is not just to create a set of woke rules and regulations, but to create an inclusive and equitable culture that is self-sustaining and self-correcting, built on compassion, belonging, teamwork, and love.

From time to time, because society is unequal and we do not share lived experience, we are bound to offend each other, or act in ways that are unfair or unkind to our fellow singers. Some offenses will be large, egregious, and need to be dealt with firmly and ruthlessly. Others will be smaller, and come into the category of what we call microaggressions. Microaggressions are still significant, and the media is full of examples of people have lost their jobs over the smallest incidents. When microaggressions occur, our choirs need mutually agreed steps to put them right. Explicit standards in themselves create a sense of a unified "us," around "This is the way we do things," and so can minimalize the dehumanizing effects of feeling marginalized. No new outsiders are created by an issue, and we create trust via a civilized and transparent system that all have signed up to. Small examples of disrespectful behavior can have big negative consequences on a whole community, and likewise small examples of compassion and respect can be transforming. Can you think of examples of microaggressions occurring in your group?

How do we make a start? First, we need to collect good demographic data on our singers (and ideally our audience too), to find out who "we" currently are. We also need to know who we are currently attracting, who is not attracted to our group who could be, and why. If anyone leaves, we need to find out why, in a way that allows those people to be honest with us. See Workshop 3 in this chapter for more on this.

Next, every change that you make toward making your group truly diverse, inclusive, and equitable needs to be followed through across every activity of your group, social and musical. Welcoming singers who use wheelchairs, for example, requires you to consider and, where needed, rethink every aspect of performance, rehearsal, and selection of venues. This might include access, mats, ramps, signage, door locks, concert dress, seating arrangements on- and off-stage, restroom access, usher training, seats without arms, mobility buddies, and so on. Where is the best place on the risers? How might you modify your choreography? What about learning methods for blind and partially sighted singers?

Likewise, truly welcoming transgender and non-binary singers requires new thinking around voice tests and auditions, the effect of hormones on pitch range, resonance, and vocal pedagogy, restroom access, and so on. If you set out on a well-intentioned DEI journey but do not follow through, you will have made things worse, and been dishonest to exactly the people you want to be fairer to.

If all this feels like a lot of extra work, remind yourself that this work is already taken for granted by the privileged people in your group. It is only fair that everyone has an equal chance to succeed. Remember too that success is like a flywheel. Once your choir has become more inclusive and as long as that work continues, it will attract and retain more new singers of all kinds in perpetuity.

Diversity, equity, and inclusion, then, is not something that can ever be said to be "completed." You can't just do a course in it, establish a set of standards, and then move on. As the title of this chapter implies, instead, it is set of ongoing daily practices. If those practices are truly embedded, they should be fluid, and your choir should be continually revisiting them, and update them regularly. Over time, new situations will arise, new language will develop, and your ways of keeping your artistic space fair and equitable will become even more refined.

The Learning Leader, or "Being White in Charge of a Choir"

Rightly or wrongly, most choral directors of mainstream choirs are white. I am white myself, as is roughly 60 percent of the US population. I can say little of value, then,

180 Transforming Choral Singing

that will somehow apply to *all* choral directors in this area. What I can explore, though, is the idea of leading an inclusive and equitable choir while "being white." We have a specific, not-always-blame-free cultural experience, and we bear a special responsibility to lead in ways that are proactively anti-racist. This is not without its unique challenges. So in this next section, I want to address directly the thorny topic of what proactively anti-racist leadership looks like for white choral directors.

First, the obvious part, which is by no means the easiest: It falls to us to learn how prejudice and bias expresses itself in our groups, and watch with eagle-eyed attention. Then, wherever we find it, we should proactively and consistently challenge racism, sexism, homophobia, and other discrimination. We may think we know what it is, but because we have not lived it, we are more likely to miss it or be wrong about how it makes those affected feel. In the current environment, all racism and other bigotry needs to survive and grow is inaction. Where we see and sometimes simply feel implicit racism in our groups, our job is to name it publicly. We should do everything we can to put it right, even if that means changing our group's structures and long held traditions.

Because we are also more likely to make mistakes, white people must be doubly prepared, so that we can respond with openness, empathy, and authenticity when questions arise, as they will. This work involves taking personal and professional risks, and many of us start from the position of being fearful of saying the wrong thing.[6] Such fear leads directly to the all too familiar and often disabling defensive response of "white fragility."[7] Such risk-taking is much easier once common standards are in place, and such fear is reduced.

Remaining alert in this way is an *especially* important part of the job for white people, because they have upheld the racist status quo for so long, (mostly) unknowingly perpetuating systems of oppression that they have not experienced themselves. These issues have relentlessly affected black and brown people in countless ways throughout their lives. They must now equally affect ours.

Again, this is an area where social practices and musical practices should align. A song itself can be experienced as a microaggression, or worse. What should you do if, in rehearsal, a song is prompting an unexpected reaction in, say, your BIPOC singers, and they read it as racist? How exactly should we show leadership in these situations, as the person in charge but also in a position of privilege? Previously, I would have trusted my musical instincts, asserted formal authority as director and taken a solo decision. We are now in a world where that simple, hierarchical leadership style is hard to justify. It seems arrogant. It implies that I as a choral director can arrogantly speak for people in my group whose lived experience I don't share, and cannot therefore deeply understand. It assumes I own the artistic perspective of everyone in the room. It feels white to me now. In summary, the key to effective leadership in these situations is the exact opposite—white humility, lack of assumptions, and collaboration. So, to answer the question, we act by leaning into the issue, listening intently, having the debate transparently with all our singers, apologizing publicly if necessary, changing the song and only then moving on. To return to a key theme in this book, as choral directors we do have to act.

As white choral leaders, we have something to prove, which is that we understand what true diversity, equality, and inclusion looks like, and can enable them in our group's relationships and ecosystem. Because of the way we were brought up, many of us don't start with that understanding, and because of past history, BIPOC people are likely not to trust us when we say we do. That doesn't mean we can't learn. Instead, it means we no longer have the option to be the assumed authority. Instead, we have to present ourselves as learning leaders, and be servants to our singers, unafraid to empower the full range of voices in our groups. We should lead by empowering others and then getting out of the way, so other voices can be centered.

BIPOC people have had to do a different but equally demanding kind of work for years, just to get into our choirs, and in order to get their names out there as composers, singers, and human beings. When inside our groups, they have often been "othered," celebrated as exotic, or asked too many questions, as owners of cultural knowledge that the majority do not have. They have effectively had to act as white people to get along in our groups, and simultaneously had to be better than white people to get the same opportunities. They have been the ones to work twice as hard.

Now, they need to be able to be their full selves, as white people have taken for granted for so long. They are entitled to relax and feel empowered. It is white people's turn to do the work, to learn about what they have been through, and to actively advocate for our fellow directors, singers, and listeners to do the same. It falls to us to lead a choral group which may include people with lived experience radically different from our own, and where to some we begin as the oppressors. This is an especially hard job, and one that above all needs love, authenticity, and humility.

In previous chapters, I have covered in outline the application of social justice principles in our musical practices, including programming design, facilitating vocal sound, rhythm, improvisation, teaching and learning, and leadership. We turn now to four workshops that demonstrate how such social justice principles can be applied in the social practices in your choir's work. This is followed by a set of suggestions and tips.

Four Workshops

These workshops are designed to work with a range of choirs in school, college, community of faith, and other community choir contexts. As a result, they are a little generic, so adapt them as needed.

182 Transforming Choral Singing

Workshop 1: Six Respect Practices (Two 30-minute sessions)

I first came across this workshop at New York City's LGBTQIA+ Community Center Youth Enrichment Services. It is a great first step and lays the groundwork for your DEI work, and, as I hinted at the top, it can tease out the level of motivation your members really have for this work. Many of your members will embrace the six key practices right away. The challenge of course is how to implement them. These concepts and activities are often part of educator and corporate training, and indeed the training of kids in school homerooms across the country. The workshop works best in groups of no more than ten people.

Session 1 (30 minutes)

In this first session, go through each practice. In the second, after your participants have had time to process, ask for stories that exemplify the concepts in action.

1) **All sit in a circle:** on chairs or cross-legged on the floor. The leader is also in the circle. A simple presentation on a screen displays these words:
   Confidentiality   Respect   Attentiveness
   Openness   Sensitivity *Not* Making Assumptions
2) **Stress the importance of these six key practices:** Explain how they are at the core of the values of your choir or chorus because they have such a transforming effect. Beyond common-sense good behavior, stress that they will make your choir into an *especially* brave space, and they are vitally important and thus expected of singers, staff, volunteers, and senior managers at all times.
3) **Announce and discuss each practice below one by one:** Ask participants to share what they think each principle might mean in the context of your choir. Collect responses on a white board or shared Zoom presentation. Then summarize and agree on the main idea and move on. Spend around five minutes on each.
   i) **Confidentiality:** We sing about our lives, and we also encourage people to get to know each other at a deep level. So there will be some in your group who will be sharing private feelings, thoughts, and actions that may make them feel vulnerable. Because of this, we all agree that what goes on inside our group will remain confidential. That way, we all feel safer, can share more without fear, and respect each other's privacy.

   Examples might include:
   Life experience: Some may have been arrested in the past, have addictions, experienced violence or abuse, attempted suicide, had relationship break-ups, or have had other life experiences that they feel uncomfortable sharing.

The Daily Practice of Equity and Inclusion **183**

Taking pictures, tagging, or posting on social media: singers can inadvertently reveal someone's location or who they are with by taking pictures and posting on social media. Use social media with consent and permission only.

Coming out in an LGBTQIA+ choir: Some in the group may not be out to their family, workplace, or indeed to anyone when they join.

Health status: Some in the group may have HIV, sickle cell, a hidden disability, or other health conditions that they do not want shared elsewhere.

Immigration status: Some in the group may not yet have formal permission to remain in the country.

If visitors are invited that day: Make people aware ahead of time, and give visitors badges to identify them.

ii) **Respect:** This is in a way the most nebulous concept, but also the most central. Being respectful involves making good judgments around language and behavior that acknowledge and honor others. Easy to say but hard to do, respect is about continually learning about others who may have a different sense of what is respectful than you have. Respect is also about communicating clearly.

Examples include:

Choosing appropriate greetings, to suit the culture of the group

Avoiding making others feel uncomfortable through, for example, language used or inappropriate physical touch

Calling everyone by their preferred name and gender pronoun

Listening carefully at all times

iii) **Attentiveness:** Being attentive is in part about being present for others in the room. We should quite literally attend to whatever is going on, whether it is the rehearsal or a discussion with another singer. Being attentive can also be about persistently making small but loving acts of kindness and compassion to everyone in the room. Over time, attentiveness can transform a group's culture, and it is initially likely to make everyone keenly aware of their language and behavior, until it settles in. Attentiveness also implies a group responsibility to monitor language and behavior, so that everyone benefits.

Examples include:

Noticing that someone's arm is in a sling, and asking them if they need help with anything

Not talking during rehearsal, and quietly encouraging that in others

Helping others near you with vocal parts they are unsure of

184   Transforming Choral Singing

If you enter a rehearsal late, waiting until an appropriate moment before entering the space quietly, without disrupting the musical activity

Unsolicited giving of small gifts, perhaps at Chinese New Year or another religious celebration or festival

iv) **Openness:** Being open is in part about being present mentally, and in part about making oneself emotionally available for whatever may go on. Sometimes, an unexpected feeling may arise in the room, or we will sing a song that triggers someone. Rather than closing them down in that moment, openness is about allowing difficult feelings in the musical and social space with flexibility and emotional intelligence.

Examples include:

Stopping the rehearsal to talk about singers' emotion around a song

Clarifying why a certain decision was taken

Being honest about a song we find difficult

Acknowledging that there are people in the room who may have very different views from ours, and creating the kind of open space where two views can interact with honesty.

v) **Sensitivity:** Like attentiveness, sensitivity is about empathy, and about noticing difference where it occurs. Sensitivity also demands that we change our behavior in response to what is in the room. One can be sensitive to gender difference, sexual orientation, or age, for example, or sensitive to others' personal feelings around a range of musical and vocal issues. Sensitivity creates a culture where singers trust that if they ask for change, they will be heard.

Examples include:

Sensitivity to a person's vocal quality in rehearsal, by consciously adapting to their sound

Sensitivity to a person's presentation of gender and sexual orientation, if they are, for example, exploring a new aspect of their identity or expression for the first time. This can take the form of *not* raising it, if it would cause embarrassment or dysphoria.

Responding to a request for help from another group member.

vi) **Not making assumptions:** We all come to rehearsal with assumptions about who our fellow singers are, and what their lives are like. This is particularly true of strangers. Our brains have to make predictions of some kind on the basis of assumptions, when we initially meet people. If someone is a certain age, we may assume certain things about them. People are complex, so some of those assumptions will undoubtedly be wrong. Later we learn more. An older person may have the latest tech skills, for example, and a larger person may still be a trained dancer with fantastic flexibility. The kind of space we want to create is one where everyone is treated as an individual, rather than as a member of an identity group. Stereotypes emerge because society reinforces assumptions about people. Our job, then, is continually to challenge our own assumptions and those of others.

Examples include:

Assumptions about where a person is "from"

Assumptions about a person's lifestyle based on their gender, race, age, sexual orientation, etc.

Assumptions about people's musical likes and dislikes based on what we see or hear about them from third parties

4) **Close:** Close by asking group members to bring a story to Session 2 from their own life experience about when they experienced respect or disrespect.

Session 2 (30 minutes)

Begin in a circle as before, with the same group of ten people.

1) **Write stories on cards:** Remind the group that they were to bring their own stories. Give out cards and pens, and begin by asking them silently to write their stories on the cards and turn them in to the facilitator. They will not be telling those stories themselves.

2) **Tell stories and discuss:** The facilitator then chooses the best three or four stories, and reads them out, or if appropriate asks the person if they feel comfortable to share themselves. After each, make time for discussion, feedback, and if appropriate Q and A.

3) **Reiterate all six practices:** Finish the session by reminding the group of all six concepts, as some may not have come up.

Close by reiterating the importance of the choir as a uniquely brave space, where we try harder than in everyday life to uphold high standards of respect.

Discussion

Originally designed for youth contexts, these introductory practices can be hugely beneficial to the respect culture in your choir. They form the foundation of the special nature of your choral space, and because they are made explicit, they allow everyone to be themselves. Repeat in groups of ten until your whole group has done both sessions, and from then on, take newly invited singers through them before they come to their first rehearsal.

186 Transforming Choral Singing

Workshop 2: "Oops" and "Ouch" (45 minutes)

Microaggressions are those small but significant everyday slights that members of marginalized groups experience when around other group members. Like the rules of the road, "Oops" and "Ouch" are two simple but highly effective things to say. After this workshop, they will take on special meaning in your group's day to day interactions.

1) Introduce the Two Main Practices (15 minutes)

"Oops": You should say "Oops" if you realize that you have been offensive to another person in what you just said or did. Saying "Oops" out loud enables the person concerned to acknowledge their error. Once noted to the potentially offended victim, they should apologize immediately, and briefly talk it through.

"Ouch": You should say "Ouch" if you are offended by a term or behavior another says or does. Saying "Ouch" signals that some something was said or done that hurt, and felt disrespectful. Note that it can feel disrespectful, regardless of the intention of the person who said the phrase or did the action. Again, once an "Ouch" occurs, an apology is almost certainly appropriate. Again, a short conversation can lead to healing and learning.

2) Discussion in Pairs (30 minutes)

Divide the group into pairs. Project each of the following textbook microaggressions on a screen.[8] Ask each pair to discuss why the language used is a microaggression, and then identify how they might use "Oops" and "Ouch" to note the offense, apologize, and learn from it.

Microaggression 1 (to a person of color): "You're so articulate": This might appear to be a compliment, but when a white colleague tells a colleague of color "You're so articulate" or "You speak so well," it suggests a racist expectation that they would be less articulate. Arusha Gordon writes, "Speaking as a white person, when we register surprise at a black individual's articulateness, we also send the not-so-subtle message that that person is part of a group that we don't expect to see sitting at the table, taking on a leadership role."[9]

Microaggression 2 (to a trans or non-binary person): "You're transgender? Wow, you don't look it at all": Telling a transgender person that they don't "look trans" might likewise seem to be a compliment. After all, we might think, they wanted to "pass," didn't they? However, while the speaker may have good intentions, it is offensive because it implies being trans isn't in itself desirable. It is normative, indicating that the speaker expects all trans people to look a certain way, when really, they should be free to present any way they want to. They may not be interested in "passing," and will almost certainly be anxious about their gender presentation. By commenting, the speaker will have increased that anxiety and drawn attention to a sensitive issue. Veronica Esposito writes that this kind of comment "implies that erasing my transness from view is a cause for celebration, and that I can't be beautiful and feminine unless I conform to cisgender standards of what a woman should be. In short, it assumes I can only be valid if I erase who I really am."[10]

Microaggression 3 (to a person of an ethnic background other than your own): "Where are you actually from?": The openness of this question makes it seem innocuous. On one level, it implies openness and curiosity to get to know someone. However, it "others" the person, and implies a strong assumption that they do not truly belong in your home country. Rakshitha Arni Ravishankar writes: "Being asked where we're from carries implicit assumptions about our race, caste, ethnicity, nationality, etc. Often, it translates into: 'You don't *seem* to (already) belong here.' It validates existing beliefs about social identities and can be quite patronizing."[11]

Microaggression 4 (to a person with a disability): "The way you've overcome your disability is so inspiring": This is an example of what Stella Young calls "inspiration porn."[12] The implication, she notes, is that we have "such low expectations of disabled people that we are congratulated for getting out of bed and remembering our own names in the morning." Instead, she asserts, we should have the same expectations of everyone.

Microaggression 5 (to a person of African descent): "Is that your real hair?": African American hair is key to African American identity. The texture of black hair is often seen as "less professional" than smooth hair. For black women and some men, the bias against natural hair results in higher levels of anxiety about their appearance. In Darian Dozier's *Insider* article, Briana Williams comments: "I tend to have issues with microaggressions when my hair is big and curly . . . People tend to run their hands through without asking, and I've been asked if I could put my hair in a bun instead."[13]

Microaggression 6 (to an older person who forgets something): "Are you having a 'senior moment'?": There is an assumption of empathy here, but forgetfulness is not simply a characteristic of age, but something that can affect us all. Anti-ageism campaigner Ashton Applewhite jokes in recent TED talk, "'Senior moment' quips, for example. I stopped making them when it dawned on me that when I lost the car keys in high school, I didn't call it a junior moment!"[14]

Discussion

Regardless of race or other aspect of identity, many of us commit microaggressions all the time, and so many have written about the pain they cause.[15] Because they are small in themselves and victims stay silent, we are often unaware that they have caused offense. Like the six respect protocols, "Oops" and "Ouch" enable a culture where offensive moments can be publicly acknowledged and become learning opportunities, hopefully with less lasting rancor. There is an assumption of good intentions on both sides. Where repeated microaggressions occur and no learning is taking place, there are clearly deeper issues of thoughtlessness, ignorance, and bias to be addressed. "Oops" and "Ouch" are not appropriate practices in the event of a

188   Transforming Choral Singing

truly egregious racist, sexist, or homophobic event. Are there everyday slights used in your choir's language and behavior, where "Oops" and "Ouch" might be useful?

Workshop 3: Welcome, Engagement, and Belonging (90 minutes)

As written, this workshop is more appropriate to adult and community choir settings. It aims to develop an awareness within your group of three key concepts: welcome, engagement, and belonging. It can bring up issues which need carefully handling by a facilitator, but can be highly productive.

1) What Do We Mean by "Feeling Welcome," "Feeling Engaged," and "Feeling We Belong"? (15 minutes)

Give out paper and pens to your singers. Say they will need them later, but to set them aside for now. Begin by asking for verbal definitions of the three terms. Collect suggestions on a white board or digital equivalent. The three different concepts are likely to emerge something like this:

Feeling welcome: If you feel welcome in a choir, you feel comfortable. You are greeted openly and warmly, and your greeting has been thought about carefully to suit you. Welcome can be superficial, of course, and is really the entry stage of any group, a first impression. However, a bit like curb appeal in a house, a well-judged and intentional welcome leaves an impression that can run deep. In the first few seconds with a group, your "blink reflex" instinct can tell you to run a mile if their welcome does not go well. Over time, a group's welcome also needs to be sustained. A singer can later discover that they were less welcome than they first thought. For some singers, this feeling of welcome is enough.

Feeling engaged: People who are engaged have a deeper relationship with a group than simply feeling welcome. If you are engaged, you care about a group enough to give back at least a little extra time or energy. At its simplest, this can take the form of socializing more, and doing simple tasks like pouring the coffee at the break, or helping put out chairs. It can also involve volunteering for leadership roles, taking attendance, raising money, or helping others to sing better. At the next level, highly engaged people manage the group and become advocates for its cause.

Choirs are often volunteer organizations, so we always want more people who are engaged. More engaged volunteers give your group the capacity to do more. Ideally your engaged people should come from the widest possible range of socioeconomic backgrounds, ages, sexualities, genders, and so on, but you may find that your core group skews toward a particular ethnicity, subculture, or age range. Engagement can have its origins in personal involvement, in community, or in a more detached, altruistic belief that "choirs like this are important in society." We can sometimes engage to learn new skills, or because we believe things could be done better if we got involved.

Feeling we belong: Belonging is qualitatively different from engagement, and in some ways deeper. If you feel you belong in a group, then this is your tribe. Belonging involves high levels of emotional trust and cultural comfort. It enables relationship at deeper levels and in a wider and often more personal set of ways. In my group, some members used to spend Thanksgiving together rather than go home to their biological parents. Others established lifelong friendships, and even married others in the group. Kids who feel they belong in a choir go to rehearsal in large part to see their friends. The singing has become incidental to them in that sense. They can also feel that the group's singing expresses who they are.

2) How Do You Personally Feel? (10 minutes)
Next, ask members to pick up their pen and paper, and individually in silence answer all three questions:

> Do you feel welcome?
> Do you feel engaged?
> Do you feel you belong in the group?

They are to do this in two ways. First, for each question, they should pick a number from 1 to 5, where 1 means "I don't feel [welcome] at all" and 5 means "I feel 100 percent [welcome]." Suggest they don't take too long about this. The judgment in each case should come from intuition rather than detailed analysis. Repeat for "feel engaged" and "feel you belong."

Then, after each number, they should think about, and write down any experiences that these questions bring to mind—moments where they perhaps felt especially welcome and engaged or felt they belonged. Some of these moments will be positive ones, but some could be negative. Suggest both will be covered, but ask members to categorize them separately. Also, negative moments must be depersonalized. So if an individual within the group made them feel unwelcome, this is not the time to air that personal grievance. Add that any issues that emerge relating to individuals are valid, and will be collected and noted later.

3) Positive Feelings (20 minutes)
This section and the next take place partly in small groups, and partly in a plenary session. Divide participants into smaller groups of three to five people and seat them in circles around the room. Offer two discussion tasks:

a) **Small Group:** Each person identifies one moment where they felt welcome and engaged or that they belonged. (10 minutes)
b) **Plenary:** Return to the whole group and spend no more than ten minutes sharing those stories.

190 Transforming Choral Singing

4) Negative Feelings (25 minutes)
Use the same format and tasks, depersonalizing stories as you go:

a) **Small group:** Each person identifies one moment where they felt unwelcome, failed to engage, or felt excluded, intentionally or unintentionally (10 minutes).
b) **Plenary:** Return to the whole group and spend no more than fifteen minutes sharing those stories.

5) Wrap-Up and Song (20 minutes)
Finally, wrap up by asking "What have we learned?," and "What issues do we need explore at subsequent workshops?" Make clear that this is not the moment to solve these issues. Today, our job is only to identify them. Ensure issues are listed publicly, so no one feels unheard.

Before you finish, thank those who made themselves vulnerable by sharing experiences. Honor them publicly, and make clear that those insights are valuable, and will help the group to move forward. Perhaps hold hands or sing a song to close.

What proportion of your choir's members would feel they felt welcome? How many would say the felt engaged? And what percentage would say they truly belonged? What does your hunch tell you about who the "belongers" might be?

Discussion

As a leader, this workshop enables you to spot: Who *are* the people who feel unwelcome, find it hard to engage, and tend to feel excluded? How many of them are there? Is it the people you expect? Why is this happening, and what steps should your group take to address these issues? It can also enable the group to begin to help itself. The last activity is clearly more sensitive but crucial. If too sensitive, replace the small group with a plenary format where all cards are first handed to the facilitator, who chooses which ones are appropriate for discussion. Before you start, check in on your members' previous commitments to confidentiality, respect, attentiveness, openness, sensitivity, and *not* making assumptions made in Workshop 1.

Workshop 4: The "One Step Forward, One Step Back" privilege walk (45 mins)

This classic and provocative game is used a lot in community activism and increasingly college contexts. It is adapted from a classic 1989 Peggy Mcintosh article.[16] In its present form, it is designed for adults. Its goal is to heighten awareness of

The Daily Practice of Equity and Inclusion   **191**

intersectionality, and the ways in which society privileges some individuals over others. A typical game involves between ten and forty participants.

1) Play the Game (20 minutes)

Everyone begins by standing in a line shoulder to shoulder, stretching across the middle of the room. There should be space in front of each person to walk forward up to around twenty steps, and behind them the same amount.

The following instructions are read by the facilitator one by one. The participants respond to each by taking one step forward or one back. Some will end up taking many more steps back than others. Below is the complete set of instructions from the college classroom version of the game.[17] If your choir is not based in the US or contains mostly kids or youth, adapt them to suit your location:

> If your ancestors were forced to come to the USA not by choice, take one step back.
>
> If your primary ethnic identity is "American," take one step forward.
>
> If you were ever called names because of your race, class, ethnicity, gender, or sexual orientation, take one step back.
>
> If there were people who worked for your family as servants, gardeners, nannies, etc., take one step forward.
>
> If you were ever ashamed or embarrassed of your clothes, house, car, etc., take one step back.
>
> If one or both of your parents were "white collar" professionals: doctors, lawyers, etc., take one step forward.
>
> If you were raised in an area where there was prostitution, drug activity, etc., take one step back.
>
> If you ever tried to change your appearance, mannerisms, or behavior to avoid being judged or ridiculed, take one step back.
>
> If you studied the culture of your ancestors in elementary school, take one step forward.
>
> If you went to school speaking a language other than English, take one step back.
>
> If there were more than fifty books in your house when you grew up, take one step forward.
>
> If you ever had to skip a meal or were hungry because there was not enough money to buy food when you were growing up, take one step back.
>
> If you were taken to art galleries or plays by your parents, take one step forward.
>
> If one of your parents was unemployed or laid off, not by choice, take one step back.
>
> If you have health insurance, take one step forward.
>
> If you attended private school or summer camp, take one step forward.
>
> If your family ever had to move because they could not afford the rent, take one step back.
>
> If you were told that you were beautiful, smart, and capable by your parents, take one step forward.

192   Transforming Choral Singing

If you were ever discouraged from academics or jobs because of race, class, ethnicity, gender, or sexual orientation, take one step back.

If you were encouraged to attend college by your parents, take one step forward.

If you have a disability, take one step back.

If you were raised in a single parent household, take one step back.

If your family owned the house where you grew up, take one step forward.

If you saw members of your race, ethnic group, gender, or sexual orientation portrayed on television in degrading roles, take one step back.

If you own a car, take one step forward.

If you were ever offered a good job because of your association with a friend or family member, take one step forward.

If you were ever denied employment because of your race, ethnicity, gender, or sexual orientation, take one step back.

If you were paid less, treated less fairly because of race, ethnicity, gender, or sexual orientation, take one step back.

If you were ever accused of cheating or lying because of your race, ethnicity, gender, or sexual orientation, take one step back.

If you ever inherited money or property, take one step forward.

If you had to rely primarily on public transportation, take one step back.

If you attended private school at any point in your life take one step forward.

If you were ever stopped or questioned by the police because of your race, ethnicity, gender, or sexual orientation, take one step back.

If you were ever afraid of violence because of your race, ethnicity, gender, or sexual orientation, take one step back.

If your parents own their own business take one step forward.

If you were generally able to avoid places that were dangerous, take one step forward.

If you were ever uncomfortable about a joke related to your race, ethnicity, gender, or sexual orientation but felt unsafe to confront the situation, take one step back.

If you use a TDD phone system, take one step back.

If you were ever the victim of violence related to your race, ethnicity, gender, or sexual orientation, take one step back.

Imagine you are in a relationship. If you can get married in this state, take one step forward.

If your parents did not grow up in the United States, take one step back.

If your parents attended college, take one step forward.

If your parents told you that you could be anything you wanted to be, take one step forward.

If you are able to take a step forward or backward, take two steps forward.

2) Post-Game Debrief

Discuss the results of the game immediately with the group, sitting in a circle. The two main questions to ask are:

a) **How did it make you personally feel?**
b) What did you learn?

Focus on the use of "I" language throughout. Manage the space so that that those revealing themselves as having less privilege are not cast as victims or made to feel "less than."

Discussion

This game is provocative, and can go in all kinds of different directions, depending on the context and people concerned. If your group is not ready for it, it has potential to reveal strong emotions, and it often needs a long period of post-game discussion. As with Workshop 3 above, it needs careful management by the facilitator, to ensure all those involved feel safe, and especially those who take many steps backward.[18] Expect all kinds of responses. White people will tend to feel guilt and possibly shame. White fragility may lead to defensiveness and denial, and in one game I took part in, there were tears as it played out. It forces some white people to face their privilege openly in ways that can make them feel exposed. For the people of color in the room, feelings can be the same, or very different. There can be anger and sadness. Relief is also frequent—a sense of "At last, these issues are coming to the fore." Also common are more cynical feelings of "Of course, I've known this all my life, this is nothing new." All feelings, and any others, need to be heard and acknowledged in a respectful way, using the framework of Workshops 1 and 2.

The learning is likely to have two components. The first is personal, and concerns what any individual learned about their own privilege and that of others in the room. I remember seeing a close friend whom I assumed had significant amounts of privilege move, as the game progressed, to the back of the room. Thankfully, they were happy to share some of the stories around their upbringing and identity. The second learning component is about privilege in general: how pervasive it is, and how it profoundly denies life opportunities to certain people in systematic ways.

Suggestions and Tips
1) Put Together an Equity and Inclusion Plan

Stats: Publish stats on your website and in your annual report that publicly demonstrate your commitment to transparency, and to creating work that is of, by, and for your community in all its diversity.

HR processes: Review and continually update your HR processes, to ensure DEI values and goals are prioritized and supported. This is likely to include: attention to HR, including staff recruitment, promotion, and succession planning; creating a demographics database; devising policies including a work-from-home policy and a caretaking policy; mentoring and sponsorship.

Diversity goals: Set clear but achievable goals around staffing and volunteer diversity, by, for example, setting a goal by a given date of no more than x percent white, and no more than y percent cisgender male; and likewise for your board if you have one, perhaps z percent BIPOC and no more than v percent cisgender male. Goals can be useful, but quotas less so.

Special needs plan: Devise a plan for audience, staff, musicians, and singers with disabilities of all types—mental and physical. Appoint an officer in the group to keep a confidential record of all those with a verified special need of this kind. They should also be responsible for ensuring that those needs are met by, say, creating larger print scores, or ensuring a chair is placed on stage for the person to sit on as needed.

Languages: Choral singing is all about language, so devise a plan around languages other than English and where and when they will be used, in line with your mission and community demographics.

Ethics: Set goals and ethical parameters around volunteer involvement, internships, and other community partnerships and artistic collaborations.

Signer: Employ a sign language interpreter to sign all your shows, and advertise this in your publicity materials and to deaf community organizations.

2) Auditions and Welcome

What makes a good audition?: A good audition should be relaxed, socially welcoming, and pleasant, but also short, sweet, and efficient. It should be appropriately demanding, with some easy and some harder tasks. It should also be a good first impression that communicates what is unique about your mission, vision, and values.

Who should be involved?: Involve a diverse panel in the room, including some of your existing singers. An equally diverse, observant, and emotionally intelligent welcome team outside the room can also be useful, to chat, manage the process, and provide a second opinion when decisions are taken. A singer should ideally see themselves represented in both groups.

What should an audition include?: After many years of trying different approaches, here is what I currently do:

i) Start with an opening relaxing chat (30 seconds), to establish how they heard about you, their previous experience, and what brings them to your choir.

ii) Next do a short range and tessitura check, and offer a carefully chosen vocalise, taught by ear in the moment, to test musical memory and aural skills. (2 minutes)

The Daily Practice of Equity and Inclusion **195**

iii) Follow this with a short extract from an own choice song. This tests pitch and rhythm accuracy, the style and vocal habits ingrained in the voice, and also performance skill and ability to communicate. (90 seconds).

iv) Finish with a set of tests, covering ability to memorize and match pitches by ear, hear one pitch against another.

Do you have procedures in place if the first language of a singer is not English? Have another song ready, or ask them to sing one of their own. What if they are partially sighted? Know ahead of time, and accommodate them by having enlarged or Braille music ready that they can use. Alternatively, adapt the test. Concentration issues or nerves? Suggest they take a few minutes, and continue when they are ready. Have a peaceful space free of distractions nearby.

Music reading and aural skills: To avoid discriminating against those really talented and musical singers who don't read, first ask how they like to learn their part. If they learn mostly by ear, ask how long that is likely to take them. If they are used to learning from rehearsal tracks, and you think they can learn a part quickly, no problem. I sometimes simply ask, "Do you read music?," and offer three possible answers: a) "Yes, I read music"; b) "No, I don't read music"; or c) "I know when it goes up and down." There can then be a reading test if needed. If they say a), also triangulate. Check if they used music for their song, and how quick their ear seemed elsewhere in the audition. If they say c), make an assessment from their pitch tests as to how quickly they will learn the material.

Assessment: What are you looking for?: Divide your overall assessment into four areas:

i) Musical skills: including musicianship, expressive range, stylistic experience, repertoire choice, and ability to learn quickly, by ear or from the score.

ii) Vocal skills: including vocal quality, ability to blend, level of training, experience, and soloist potential.

iii) Mission "fit": This includes a sense of what is important to them about being in your group, their availability, whether you think they will stay, demographic factors such as age, ethnicity, etc. Also, check for bias, and ensure you judge every singer against the same criteria.

iv) Personal and interpersonal fit: Consider teamwork, social and communication skills, volunteer potential, activism, ability to adapt quickly to the audition setting, and the community and family aspects of choir life. Also, how could membership of the community benefit them?

To make final discussion easier, assign each applicant a single number from 1 to 5 summarizing a view across all these criteria, where: 1 is a complete "no"; 2 indicates future potential; 3 indicates the minimum score for entry; 4 is a solid applicant with minor weaknesses; 5 is a future vocal leader.

3) Inclusion and the Changing Voice

Voice test every member of the group individually every few years: An enabling voice test (not an audition) can help you check that singers are vocally comfortable, and identify how their voice may have changed over time. Health issues, age, and gender identity changes can all impact the voice. As artistic leader, such checks will help you get to know your singers' voices, and deepen your relationship with them as individuals.

Reasons to revoice, moving people from part to part: Revoice if some singers are standing out in the sound or one section is sounding stronger or weaker than others. Revoicing can also help if the color of a section's sound is not what is needed. It can also be useful if individual singers are having technical issues, are in sections that surprise you, or are causing significant social issues within a section.

Older voices: Older voices tend to change color over time and become more prominent and harsher. The solution here may be to place the singer in a lower section, or to run a workshop focusing on the issue. Check mental and physical stamina, acid reflux issues, and any medication taken that can affect the voice. Also ask how they feel about their voice these days, and whether they have noticed any changes recently.

Transgender voices: If a singer is taking testosterone or estrogen, vocal range, resonance, tessitura stamina, and fold quality can all be affected. Done with sensitivity, a monthly verbal check-in and optional voice test can be reassuring, both for you and for the singer. The alignment between vocal part (S, A, T, or B) and gender identity can vary hugely. Some will want the two to align, so, say, a male-to-female transition may coincide with a strong desire to sing alto or soprano. This may or may not enable them to be vocally successful. Likewise a female-to-male transition, if accompanied by testosterone, can result in the voice changing in ways that are unpredictable. This can be similar to those of teenage cisgender boys in some ways, but not in others, because of the age, physiognomy, and vocal health of the person concerned. Others will see themselves on a journey of self-realization rather than transition, within a broad spectrum of gender identity. As with all singers, balance two main concerns:

i) to place them in your group where they can be most successful vocally
ii) to take account of their personal position around their voice, and how they might want it to represent their gender identity and expression.

4) Improving Retention

A buzz: Get a buzz going about what people find fun and impactful in your choir.
Real friendships: Facilitate and then publicize the real friendships of your singers.
Be demanding: Make the learning process demanding but fun.
Punctuality: Start and end rehearsal on time.

Devise a range of social activity: Ours included everything from member-run yoga classes and origami workshops to club nights out, bowling contests, and knitting.

Share digital content: Create digital content that is compelling, and truthfully aligns with your artistic intentions. Ask singers to share it. Sharing on Facebook, Twitter, Instagram, YouTube, and TikTok is the way we reach our audience, and is also a way for singers to own that they are engaged and belong in the group.

Conversations face to face: Encourage old-fashioned personal face-to-face conversations as a means to recruit and retain singers. It can be especially powerful to tell a personal story about an experience, and suggest a person joins in with that experience.

Handwritten notes: A handwritten note expressing passion and enthusiasm to an individual shows you care over and above the norm.

Your organization's ability to deliver transformative change through singing is your most powerful recruitment and retention tool.

5) Leading a Diverse Music Team

Earlier in this chapter, we covered leading your group differently, and allowing a range of voices to be heard. Try these suggestions to implement this approach:

Restructure your artistic team: Devise a more diverse artistic leadership team that you supervise. Offer talented musicians from a variety of musical, ethnic, gender, sexuality, and other backgrounds the chance to lead from the podium, even if it's a single song, or initially just doing a warm-up. Their gifts will surprise you.

Include volunteers as well as paid directors: Share power and empower more voices in your programming and the choral craft of your group's work. In school or college settings, that often means letting your students lead.

Redefine your role: Conduct perhaps 50 percent of rehearsal and performances, and support, supervise, and challenge other leaders the rest of the time.

Appoint an associate director: Find one that specializes in styles you are less skilled in, and perhaps an intern too, from a marginalized background. Use your choral expertise to help them grow.

Hire a vocal coach by the hour: They can come in regularly once a month, or at key moments in your process. I find three times works well: at the start of a rehearsal period, then in the middle, and again right before a performance. They can add value by doing in-depth vocal training, refining choral sound, preparing soloists, and providing a second opinion.

Finally, some questions about your own group. Where are your group on their journey toward equity and inclusion? Are they perhaps feeling fine with where they are now, or feeling that change is needed? Who in your group is raising the issue? Talk to them, and explore what they feel more deeply.

In your own practice as a choral director, what are your cultural or demographic blind spots? Is a particular style of music, age group, or other demographic

198   Transforming Choral Singing

represented in the art you perform? Are there others that just don't appear, perhaps out of fear or ignorance?

Are there people in your group who are being overused as soloists or spokespeople, because of their age, skin color, gender, or cultural background? How can you ensure they do not feel they have to "represent"?

Does your group already have an explicit or unstated set of values around how singers, staff members, and others should behave toward each other? Could you articulate them in a simple document, and build from there?

Notes

1. Kendi (2019: 13) Defines an anti-racist as "one who is supporting an anti-racist policy through their actions or expressing an anti-racist idea."
2. Maya Angelou, interviewed by Anderson Cooper, CNN (uploaded August 28, 2013): https://www.youtube.com/watch?v=UxkTd6BFL1o
3. https://www.statista.com/statistics/383740/antisemitic-incidents-reported-uk-y-on-y/
4. https://www.hrc.org/resources/violence-against-the-trans-and-gender-non-conforming-community-in-2020
5. For more on what privilege is and how it plays out in people's lives, see Peggy Mcintosh's "White Privilege Checklist" here: https://projecthumanities.asu.edu/content/white-privilege-checklist, taken from her seminal 1988 essay: "White Privilege and Male Privilege: A Personal Account of Coming to See Correspondences through Work in Women's Studies." https://www.collegeart.org/pdf/diversity/white-privilege-and-male-privilege.pdf
6. Chris Munce discusses this fear in his podcast, *Choralosophy: A Human Art Form*, Episode 29, Part 1.
7. See especially Robin DiAngelo's (2018) *White Fragility: Why It's So Hard for White People to Talk About Racism* (Boston: Beacon Press).
8. https://www.businessinsider.com/microaggression-unconscious-bias-at-work-2018-6#why-do-you-wear-that-14
9. https://www.theroot.com/he-s-so-articulate-what-that-really-means-1790874985
10. https://lithub.com/but-you-dont-look-trans-a-tale-of-microaggression/
11. https://hbr.org/2020/10/whats-wrong-with-asking-where-are-you-from
12. https://www.ted.com/talks/stella_young_i_m_not_your_inspiration_thank_you_very_much/transcript?language=en
13. https://www.insider.com/microaggressions-against-black-peoples-hair-stop-making-2021-3
14. https://www.ted.com/talks/ashton_applewhite_let_s_end_ageism, 2 minutes 53 seconds.
15. Derald Wing Sue (2010), *Microaggressions in Everyday Life: Race, Gender, and Sexual Orientation* (Hoboken, NJ: Wiley): 352. The term was first coined by Chester M. Pierce (1970) in *Offensive Mechanisms* in Floyd B. Barbour, *The Black Seventies* (Boston: Extending Horizon), DOI: https://dokumen.tips/download/link/offensive-mechanisms-chester-pierce
16. Mcintosh (1989).
17. https://studentaffairs.psu.edu/learningmodules/powerworkshop/privilegewalk.shtml
18. Arao and Clemens (2013), *From Safe Space to Brave Spaces: A New Way to* Frame D*ialogue around Diversity and Social Justice in the Art of Effective Facilitation*, chapter 8, 135, Stylus Publishing. Retrieved from https://sites.lsa.umich.edu/inclusive-teaching/wp-content/uploads/sites/355/2016/06/From-Safe-Spaces-to-Brave-Spaces.pdf

10
An Activist Vision for Choral Singing

Thus far, I have made two overarching points. The first is that choral singing facilitates change by its very nature, and the second is that it needs deep change itself. By exploring the areas of vocal sound, rhythm skills, and improvisation, I've laid out, I hope, how a reliance on well-established but highly specialized norms in our musical and social practices is holding us back as a choral movement. It is preventing our field from embracing the globalized and complex musical culture of the twenty-first century, and preventing us from meeting singers and listeners where they are, in all their musical and cultural diversity.

I've also suggested some clear paths our choral movement can take to rectify the situation, and they have fundamental consequences for our repertoire choices as choral directors, our leadership styles, how we teach choral singing, and how we train choral directors. And I have laid out how in many instances we have simply ignored the social impact of our work, on singers, audiences, and others. There is need for transformation.

I am passionate about choral singing of all kinds, and optimistic about its future. I am excited about its potential to create change-making art, and its ability to change itself. My goal has been to indicate the urgency for change and my passion for it, without denigrating the artistic achievements of the past. There is no doubt that the art music of eighteenth, nineteenth, and twentieth centuries in Western Europe and in particular its choral singing has beauty, complexity, and value. In its day, it compellingly expressed the values and concerns of its time, and engaged both with the musical discourse of its day and with the social practices of its singers and audiences. I am no longer convinced that choral singing does either of those today. Instead, its project is in large part to recreate the musical practices of a former time, regardless of whether current singers and audiences engage in it. It celebrates the discipline of past artistic achievements, but ignores their purpose.

I would go further and say that mainstream musical culture across the world has left those musical practices behind. Most worryingly, the very idea of choral singing no longer resonates as it once did. From talent shows to karaoke evenings, from the Billboard charts to street protests, the evidence all around us is that singing itself is as relevant to people's lives as it ever was. But there are some fundamental features of our musical practices and our social practices as choirs that are excluding many people. Indeed, they prevent them from joining us in what we know are joy-filled and potentially life-changing choral experiences, that can connect people, heal them, inspire them, and have all kinds of personal and community impact. There is much to do.

Transforming Choral Singing. Charles W. Beale, Oxford University Press. © Oxford University Press 2024.
DOI: 10.1093/oso/9780197657775.003.0010

What, then, might a new vision for choral singing look like? So far, I have laid out a theoretical framework for this change, and I have also indicated in some detail the kinds of practical strategies that we can employ as choral directors to achieve it. In this final chapter, I want to draw these various ideas together, around a personal vision characterized by a single concept that takes the idea of purpose and combines it with the idea of action. That concept is activist choral singing.

The Activist Stance

This book opened with the notion that change is the function of all artistic activity, and its inevitable result. In other words, it is impossible to listen to a choir sing, and *not* be changed by it in some way. Ai Weiwei powerfully reminds us: "An artist must be an activist."[1] Seen in this light, the role of the choral director is to seek out and define what change is needed in the world, and then devise choral performances that can achieve it. Their role is to find the biting point in musical culture and then take risks, by pushing at an artistic boundary or telling a story that pushes at a social one.

To reiterate my point from Chapter 1, it is not that you as a choral director have to take any particular position. Mine has been to facilitate singing about the marginalization of LGBTQIA+ people, to tell their stories and celebrate their values, their uniqueness, and their contribution to the world. Yours is likely to be something else entirely. My point is that to be a good choral director, you do have to decide what your unique position is. You must decide what your group's purpose is, and sing with intention from there, in order for your art to have impact within its community ecosystem. You need an activist stance.[2]

In my view, then, there is no need to somehow *become* an activist choral director. You already *are* one. Your work has already created change in hundreds of singers and thousands of audience members, whether you were aware of it or not. Indeed that potential for social change and musical change is always present in our work, and we already measure the success of good choral art by the extent to which that change occurs.

But what exactly is activism in the choral context, and how do we know if we are doing it well, and fulfilling the potential of our artistic work?

Striving, Action, and Communication

First, striving. In a recent interview with Trevor Noah,[3] Barak Obama describes activism as "that constant striving, imagining something better," and elsewhere "a certain impatience, frustration or anger." In the context of race, as I said earlier, all racism needs to survive is inaction, and the same applies in the arts. As artists, all of us have that itch we urgently need to scratch, that feeling that our art is necessary and can do some good in the world. Whether we are preparing a performance of a much-loved standard or a brand new commission, we strive to bring both audience and singers to a new emotional place, and to a fresh understanding. There is always a musical insight that urgently has to be revealed, or a story about a person that needs to be told. I especially like Obama's word "constant" in this context. It is a necessary characteristic both of good art and of good activism to be persistent—to not give up, and to use your art to stand out in a crowd for what you believe in.

Second, embedded in the concept of activism, indeed in the word itself, is the idea of action. As choral directors, we don't simply hold a view. We act. In fact, in common with most activists, we act persistently, again and again. We compose, arrange, rehearse weekly, organize extra sectionals, and refine and polish our performances. We return to our craft iteratively and persistently to refine and improve it, so its impact can grow. As choral directors, we conduct and facilitate singing with energy and passion, and every week communicate with our singers the vital importance of rehearsal. We teach. We lead.

All good choral directors act, from the past greats we admire like Robert Shaw, Weston Noble, Paul Salamunovitch, and David Willcocks (who are all white men) to other more recent leaders like Anton Armstrong, Roberta Laws, or Andrea Ofilada Veneracion. When we program a set of songs, ask a choir to use a specific placement, or ask for a fermata of a particular length, we act through our medium, and aim to elicit a reaction. Try to imagine a context where your intention was for the audience *not* to react in any way, and you'll realize this is true. When we hear audience applause, and even if we hear them boo or shift in their seats with boredom, we know that some kind of reaction is underway. Change has been created.

Later in the same interview, Trevor Noah asserts from his South African experience that there is room in the world for all kinds of activists. From freedom fighters to politicians, and speech-making leaders to quiet administrators, activists use whatever skills they have to change the world. When I began my musical career, I did not see myself as an activist, but my personal journey has taught me that music could not be more powerful as an activist tool, and that I too have things I care about enough to act on them. I use that methodology of persistent action, and have the personal power to facilitate the change I envision in the communities I work in through conducting choirs. The real question is do we have the skills, the focus, and above all the courage to use that transforming power persistently, and if so, what will we use it for?

This brings me directly to the third element in the activist stance, which is that singing is a communication tool. As choral directors, we are guardians of a unique and powerful way of telling stories and spreading messages. As I said in Chapter 1, every choir is, if you like, a glove puppet, with the choral director as its master. Uniquely, our messages enter our listeners' consciousness through the ears, as well as the eyes. Unlike a dry spreadsheet listing numbers of HIV deaths, a choral performance tells the story of how those people lived and died. It can use intimate ballads to put us in touch with how an individual felt in ways that can cause us to connect with them, and it can use spectacular choral anthems to connect us with the way millions across the

202 Transforming Choral Singing

world feel the same. Music has profound power in the life of every human being, and singing gives extra emotional "information" in ways that directly influence hearts as well as minds.[4] Our communication tool is powerful indeed.

At every rehearsal and in every performance, then, choral directors should focus their singers on what their group is communicating. This clear focus will intensify their motivation, increase their learning potential, and so broaden the musical and social impact of their work. Rehearsal becomes more focused, and performances more compelling and fun. Ticket sales increase as your impact widens. Your singers understand *why* they are singing a song, and their work will be harnessed to a clear purpose. They too will become activists.

The Four Principles as Activist

Let's now return to our four principles, and apply these activist characteristics of striving, persistent action, and communication to them.

1) **Connection:** Connection is activist because connections are made that bring people together in new ways. This leads us to questions like:
   - Who do you strive to newly connect with your singing?
   - How exactly should your group act through song to make connection happen, and what do you strive to change when connection occurs?
   - What do you strive to communicate to them, to change and strengthen it?
   - Who are the people who make up the wider community ecosystem around your choir or chorus, that will support its values, come to its performances, and support it financially and artistically? What do they strive for?
   - How can you improve your choral singing, and communicate better to them in and around your music-making, so connection is deepened?

2) **Impact:** If change has come about, there has been impact. This leads us to questions like:
   - What kind of impact do you need your singing to have in the world?
   - How do you measure that impact when it happens?
   - How do you want the behavior, values, and feelings of singers and listeners to be changed as a result of hearing your work?
   - What should your choir do next to make this happen today? How does that differ from earlier eras?

   The most impactful art, then, may not necessarily be the prettiest aesthetically, or even the most technically accomplished. Instead it will be the art that, through being compelling and clear, communicates the best.

3) **Social justice:** All art aligns with a set of beliefs, a set of values that we strive for. These values are in the end around social justice, around being better people and being in more just communities, however we define that. Again, some questions follow:

- What wrong does your choir strive to put right through its singing? What social change do you and your choir stand for?
- What greater good does your singing facilitate?
- Which are the inequalities that are most prevalent in your group, and its surrounding community?
- How can your choir use its music-making to paint a picture of a more just world, and be a safer and braver space for those suffering injustices?
- What kind of singing will heal division, and bring people together in empathy and mutual understanding, as all art does?

4) **Stylistic openness:** Finally, we make change by imagining music that is hitherto unheard, and then getting our choirs to sing it. We take an activist stance in relation to the choral singing that is current. We act persistently to make our own artistic contribution and move the field on. This leads us to questions like:
   - What music is not being heard in your choir, that you feel should be heard?
   - What styles of singing will enable the maximum connection and impact in your community ecosystem, and enable the greatest change?
   - What repertoire is best going to enable your choir to say what it wants to say to the widest possible audience? Is it the repertoire you are currently singing?

Two Kinds of Activism

At the start of this book, I also identified that throughout, I would be making a distinction between a choir's musical practices and its social ones, but that I saw those as overlapping, so that one can result in change in the other and vice versa. Next, I want to examine the concept of choral activism through this lens.

Like any artistic medium, choral singing's practices express a set of values around how music should sound, the kind of music we and our listeners like to hear. It has its clichés, its core repertoires, its niches, and its back alleys. For example, perhaps it has its pianissimo conclusions, its gorgeous chords, its hackneyed octavos, its triumphant endings, its money notes, its ways of using vibrato, and so on.

As choral directors, we live within the norms of the field, but to make our music interesting to audiences, that field must at some level contain something unique and previously unheard. Those musical practices must continually evolve. In this sense, we are activists both in our program design, for example, and in our in-the-moment design of previously unheard choral gestures in sound. If we are performing the premier of a commission from a new Latinx composer from our community ecosystem, our activism will be more palpable. But even if we are singing Mendelssohn's *Elijah* for the fiftieth time in the same venue, with the same cast of soloists, most of the same singers, and the same audience members, every performance will be, to a limited extent, a brand new musical creation. Is that enough? All music contains

204 Transforming Choral Singing

something fixed and something free, and although the score will provide a fixed structure, we are not just free but actually required to make new decisions—about tempos, ornamentation, the sound of each voice and instrument, the blend, and so on. We are never without creative agency, and choral directors have huge creative freedom if they choose to use it. How will you use yours to transform your choral singing? What will your statement be?

Choral composers are especially concerned with uniqueness and musical change. They envision brand new ways of saying things in music, and they design whole new musical languages and then realize them. For example, William Byrd conceived his gorgeous masses in three, four, and five parts (1592–1595) for a secret meeting of faithful Catholics, in an austere Protestant culture.[5] In the richness of his innovative and virtuosic counterpoint, he was being highly innovative, very unique, and taking huge musical risks by communicating a powerfully subversive Catholic vision in his masses. They could have ended his career. He could have been cancelled. In fact, they changed the direction of choral singing forever.

Another example of this approach is the ground-breaking "Re-imagining the Choir" project led by André de Quadros and Emilie Amrein. They see themselves as rethinking choral practice from the ground up as an "equitable and just social space where divided and displaced communities can dismantle systems of oppression, transform conflict, and build bridges across difference with story and song." They see current choral singing as a "site of violence as much as a site of beauty," where acts of symbolic and structural violence occur.[6]

Another recent and highly successful example of musical activism is the work of Bill Bankes-Jones, whose UK-based opera company Tête-à-tête has been challenging the norms of opera for over twenty years. Persistently innovating in over five hundred new productions large and small, Tête-à-tête have been devising new formats for operas, performing in new kinds of spaces, varying opera lengths, musical styles, instrumentations, and voices, and actively facilitating under-represented and marginalized writers to get involved. He creates evenings of five-minute operas, devises opera with two singers and a backing track on park benches, and works with world class performers and companies. Their very special mission is to produce "extra-ordinary opera in extra-ordinary places" and work "to make an inclusive exciting future for opera makers." Every piece I have seen of theirs has said something new, either about a social issue or about what opera itself can be.

Though musically radical and socially relevant in its time, these days the Byrd is more likely only to have impact with certain college-educated listeners, who have an awareness of history, can think symbolically and are already encultured into church music and a certain form of Christianity. The musical practices Byrd employed and indeed those of Mendelssohn's above are likely to be seen as "great art" rather than activist music. Likewise, even Tête-à-tête's work is of its time.

So when my group were considering what to sing on a June 2011 Pride march in New York City, a Byrd Mass was not on my list of activist singing to use. Instead, to return to my earlier story from Chapter 6, we sang Lady Gaga's "Born This Way."

It had come out in February that year, and was the protest music of the moment, most likely to have impact with LGBTQIA+ revelers and campaigners on the streets. We can certainly discuss whether "Born This Way" is great art, and whether it will still speak to future generations. No one that day was even faintly concerned with those questions. Nor were those who first sang Handel's *Messiah* or Byrd's Masses. In these new times, much older music will gradually become increasingly irrelevant, outdated, and even offensive to some. And that's OK. It doesn't mean that it was bad music in its time, or that it isn't still "great" on some level, to music professionals, historians, and choral nerds. My point is that given our principles, and once both start as equally valid options, it makes much less sense to perform the Byrd or Handel now to many communities and in many contexts. Instead, it makes more sense to lean into the repertoire and, for example, the vocal resonance choices, of our time.

We can begin to summarize the role of the activist choral director, then. First, we use the main criteria of impact and connection to choose what to program. Then we check the choral arrangement works for the context, which in the case of the Lady Gaga was outside on 5th Avenue to choreography of 150 rainbow fans in sweltering heat. Next, we have to teach it well, so that all singers are included and can learn efficiently, the choral sound is resonant, and the singers sing safely and in tune outside on the street, over many repetitions. We also need to convince our singers that this is the most relevant and apt song for the moment.

Is this TTBB choral singing? Absolutely. Does it involve high levels of vocal expertise and artistic skill to have maximum impact. Undoubtedly. Will it connect with an audience? We sang to 250,000 people that day, and they were responding by singing, dancing, waving flags and in some cases hugging us as we marched. Do many mainstream choral directors see these kinds of musical practices as part of what they do? Not so much. Have they been trained in how to get a TTBB chorus to sound like Lady Gaga? It's not on many choral curricula that I have seen.

Earlier I introduced the idea of "educate" as coming from the Latin "educare," literally "to draw out." In Chapter 3, that was about drawing out the natural voice of the individual singer, their vocal "mother tongue." As well as teaching their singers in this way, activist choral directors should have the skills, vocal knowledge, and leadership skills to draw out from whole communities the singing they have within them. That Lady Gaga song was the perfect fit here too—in the LGBTQIA+ community of New York that year, it was hard to *stop* them singing it! What, I wonder, is your equivalent song?

About ten years back, I attended a high level meeting of mainstream choral arrangers and publishers. The main topic of the session was that arrangers should write more SAB arrangements, because there was an international shortage of tenors, and sales of SATB arrangements were dropping. At the time, I had 120 tenors in my group, all queer, who I frankly could not get to stop singing(!). By contrast, we see that many parts of the world are characterized by gradually emptying churches and concert halls, and languishing school choirs and choruses. If your local singers and audiences are no longer engaged, if your school choir has no energy and is going

206 Transforming Choral Singing

through the motions, perhaps they need you to facilitate the music that belongs to them, and that makes them feel they belong.

Alongside musical activism, there is a second form of activism possible in choral singing around *social and political change*. To many non-specialist musicians and singers, these non-musical values are at least as important as musical ones.

Let's revisit the kinds of social and political values that tend to be expressed in the choral field. Previously they were often embedded in religion, and specifically in Christianity. Even today, if you are running a choir in a community of faith, you will perhaps be singing songs about the glory of particular sort of God or a particular season (harvest?), and telling stories about a particular moral or ethical issue. If your starting point is Biblical, this means you might be singing about "othering" people, about homelessness, about how to treat "foreigners," or about what to do with people who do "wrong," however that is defined.

If you are managing a school choir, you might be singing about how teenage love feels, about rebellion and transgression, about celebrity, about gender fluidity, misogyny, and homophobia, about drugs and alcohol, about racial inequity, or about climate change. Meanwhile, college, pro, and semi-pro choirs may have a more specialized musical focus, but their repertoire too will still be "saying something." An inexperienced college choral director will find out very fast if the values of their students prevent them from being comfortable singing a certain song. In every case, a set of social and political values relating to the context is articulated. This is the basis of social and political activism.

Choral Singing in an Era of Activism

We are now in a new era. It is a more divided time where clearer decisions have to be made about where we stand on all kinds of issues. Rethinking is underway on many levels, and the turbulence we feel is a sign that more and more people on all sides of the spectrum are becoming activists. The choirs that thrive in this new activist era will seize the moment and take an unequivocal and new position on what is important to them. They will have what in fashion is called a "point of view." Their activist stance will be clear, and, as many arts organizations and groups around the world are doing right now, they will not only change themselves, but facilitate change in others.

They will be prepared to modify aspects of their musical and social practices in fundamental ways. They will use new vocal sounds, stand and sing in new ways, hire new instrumentalists to work with them, sing in new venues to new audiences, sing new repertoire, wear new concert attire, recruit and retain new kinds of singer, and above all tell new stories that better represent the ideas of the moment in their work.

The choirs and choruses I worry about are the ones that think they are doing fine. Without self-awareness, they are singing the same repertoire to the same audience in the same venue with the same singers and same soloists as always. They are not yet having those messy conversations with their cautious boards, their school and college department managers, or their church staff and minority singers about what change is appropriate. They do not yet feel connected. They are puzzled because the talented BIPOC singers who could transform their sound and re-energize their programming are not in their groups, and if accepted, they tend to leave after three to six months. They are unsure why talented younger singers are not seeing the artistic opportunities they provide as relevant to them. They believe that there are no gay people in their groups, while their queer singers are hidden in plain sight. They have no disabled singers in their groups. These choirs are especially vulnerable right now to reduced impact, diminishing audiences, less motivated singers, and attacks from social media and elsewhere, around artistic narrowness and a lack of clarity on social justice issues. If yours is one of those groups, I believe it is now urgent that you ask itself why. If social justice is not yet something you see as concerning you, think again. If singing the repertoire that surrounds and engages your community is not important yet, take your own decisions, but without doubt, dust off the cobwebs around your purpose, and think carefully and critically.

Open your doors and let all these singers in at every level, so they too can contribute, and live their lives joyously through song. Show up for them, and embrace their communities as human beings. Embrace their songs, their vocal sounds, and their musical practices. Embrace their social and political values and their causes, and see the world through their eyes. Trust and empower them. Sing with them and about them, and allow them the space to lead your group's art forward themselves. They may not initially trust you back, and why should they? The work will be hard, and will require persistence and deep systematic change, that will affect every aspect of your choir or chorus. It is also work that never really ends, and some people may even leave your group as a result. But once underway, it will bring huge benefits to your art, the communities around your art and to society as a whole.

An Activist Vision in Practice

To focus this vision further, I present next a series of broad statements, that encompass both its musical and social aspects:

Vocal pedagogy: An activist vocal pedagogy should be holistic and persistently person-centered. It should aim to grow the voice of the singer and deepen their sense of who they uniquely are. It should also give every singer a range of vocal strategies to enable them to sing in their own style with authenticity, safety, and joy, and to sing in the styles of others with competence, and with a deep awareness of the technical similarities and differences between them.

Voice parts: To fully empower and celebrate minority singers, and enable all voices to fully engage, all choirs should do at least some singing where SATB and other conventional choral structures are dismantled, along with the gender binary. All tenor and bass singers should explore their falsetto and other higher pitch

208   Transforming Choral Singing

options, and all female identifying singers should be auditioned as tenors and in some cases baritones as well. Amongst its many social benefits, this would also be practical, helping solve shortages in some vocal parts. Male identifying singing also needs significant innovation, so that, regardless of gender, children approaching puberty continue to feel that singing is an engaging and culturally attractive activity, that they feel they belong in. Changes in repertoire and vocal sound could go a long way toward rectifying this, as could honest and authentic discussion of masculinity and gender in general, with focus on the voice.

Choral programming and repertoire: An activist choral pedagogy should start not from a particular repertoire and canonical approach, but from a place of creativity, innovation, community, and openness. Every choir should devise an approach to repertoire, programming, and vocal sound appropriate to their culture, experience, and their community ecosystem. After such a long period of canon-based choral singing, choral programming in the next few decades should catch up, by truly centering a range of new stories from those whose voices have not been heard, and especially heard less in choral singing.[7] This is likely to include the stories of disabled, black, queer, gender non-binary, neurodivergent, and other marginalized groups. Choirs should be able to sing any kind of song that exists out in the world, including songs that were only composed last week. Every choir, then, needs an arranger.

Choral directing: Activist choral directors should be demanding and skilled in all styles. They should run efficient, productive, and joyful rehearsals, and take singers to new artistic places that continually excite them and confound their expectations. They should also run kind, compassionate, open, and loving rehearsals that meet their singers where they are, bring them together in new ways, and engage them in two-way conversations. Activist choral directing should be inclusive, egalitarian, and collaborative rather than privileging expertise around given musical texts. Directors should hold brave spaces where singers can own the social and political messages embedded in their singing, and have messy conversations, knowing they will be heard and respected regardless of background.

Music education: At every level from elementary school to professional, music education should reflect the full stylistic diversity of the real-world music-making that surrounds us. It should give all students the culturally appropriate tools to recreate good, impactful music in all styles. It should encourage them to have opinions, and be both reflective and critical about the songs they sing. It should enable them to create new music that expresses who they are and how they want their world to be. Music is intrinsic to being human, and every child and adult should have opportunities to sing, play an instrument in any style, compose, and improvise. Music-making should not suddenly stop when we leave school, but should continue throughout our lives, online and offline, alone and in groups, through singing and playing.

Where we sing: Choirs should sing from balconies and rooftops, at political rallies, at elections, at major festivals, on stages supporting rock bands, and with orchestras;

in railway stations, in the open air, in homeless shelters, elementary schools, dance clubs, supermarkets, shopping malls, hospitals, schools, colleges, churches, and other faith community contexts; in drug rehab facilities, mental hospitals, and dementia wards. Choirs also have a place in adverts, in corporate contexts, and on social media. Choirs should collaborate with all kinds of arts organizations at their level, including rock bands, dance companies, theater groups, poetry and literature readings, museums, and as part of multimedia installations. They should sing at births, deaths, marriages, birthdays, religious festivals, parties, and other social events.

To summarize, we need a period of radical experimentation in choral singing, a time where every norm is taken out, examined, dusted off, and replaced afresh. We also need to reconnect it at all levels to our social and political purpose, recognizing that choral singing is in the end about people as well as music. Once that is in place, people will again engage in choral singing.

Four Statements

Finally, here are four even broader vision statements, that paint a picture of what this new world of activist choral singing might look like.

1) The arts are centrally important to all our lives, and a diverse range of choral singing opportunities is plentifully available to all in an equitable way.

The arts are a central part of what it is to be human, and music is important to every single one of us in so many different ways. Our lived experience as choral directors tells us this, our experience of people the world over supports this, and research backs it up. Whether we sing, dance, act, mold clay, paint or make video games, the ability to create a non-functional artistic object "for its own sake" is a uniquely human activity, and one of huge value to us all. We do not need music to survive, but we do need it to thrive. Singing is one of the easiest ways into artistic activity, because it does not require an instrument or other external medium of some kind. It can be done in groups, and promotes crucial, civilizing understandings of the world, that make us better individuals and create a better society. It is empowering, it enables us to articulate who we are, and makes us aware of ourselves and others in new and powerful ways. It has immeasurable value.

The first element of this activist vision then is that choral singing is plentifully and equitably available to all, and widens stylistically, so that people of all races, backgrounds, vocal styles, and repertoire knowledge sing in choirs. In this new world, many more people can see the good that it does, and experience being in a choral community. Choral singing comes to people where they are; engagement and participation in choral singing is vastly increased for all kinds of people, and those benefits accrue to us all. There are trans choirs, black choirs, Spanish-speaking choirs, choirs that sing in Tagalog, choirs in offices, choirs for older people, choirs for seven-year-olds, choirs in all schools. There should also be choirs that welcome everyone, and other choirs that curate new and innovative vocal spaces specially designed for unheard voices and new kinds of choral writing.

In the 1970s and '80s, it went without saying in many Western countries that that the arts should be available throughout every level of the education system and through thriving and vibrant subsidized arts sectors. It was not a perfect system. White, straight, educated, middle-class people benefited much more than others from that, but it was at least a given that governments had a role in facilitating the arts. We understood that all children should be able to sing, dance, and take part in other artistic activity as part of their schooling.

Those adults who had trained at their choral craft for fifteen to twenty years and put in the 10,000 hours it takes to achieve mastery were recognized as having something special to offer the world, and got paid fairly. Freedom of speech and the democratic benefits of amateur and professional artistic activity were seen as self-evident and essential. I use the word "essential" here in both its meanings, in that it is the essence of being human to make art, and also that it is essential that we act, to ensure this is the case.

It's time to wake up. The act of making art and indeed free speech itself is under threat. We can no longer rely on the state or philanthropy to support us. Society in the US and Western Europe is also in such a state of division that we are highly sensitized. Even if we do believe in freedom of speech, almost all of us find some forms of artistic activity offensive. The concept of education has narrowed, and many schools do not even have music lessons, or a school choir, orchestra, or band. Of course STEM subjects are valuable, but as we are discovering in the current mental health epidemic, the arts help us feel part of something bigger than ourselves. They are potent tools for sharing our feelings and our understandings. Tweeting is simply not the same, and in many ways drives us apart. We are stronger together, and choral singing can facilitate that.

Performer or teacher, if you believe in the power of the arts, recognize that you are now an outsider, and effectively an activist. If you have not yet seen the need to speak out, become an activist to prevent this essential part of being a human being from dying a death, submerged by the digital revolution, the COVID pandemic, economic pressures, and a deluge of other divisive voices and financial needs. Choral singing is *our* lived experience. We see with clarity its huge benefits to everyone's lives. Let's own those benefits, demonstrate them, and fight for them.

In my activist vision, then, choral directors and singers are out there all the time, persistently striving and acting. They model the value of the arts by singing proudly and with passion about what is important to them. Around their music-making, all choral directors advocate. They insist that choirs takes place in their organizations and institutions. Their singers are not just singing, but advocating too. They grow the

An Activist Vision for Choral Singing   **211**

ecosystem, by telling their families and friends what an impact singing has had on their lives, and insisting they come and join the choral party.

2) Choirs are interactive and flexible, and sing all kinds of music in the widest possible range of live and recorded contexts and spaces.

Alongside community choirs, choral music in the past has sat firmly in the domains of communities of faith, schools, and colleges. All three of those contexts can be centers of choral excellence, but all are limited in the kinds of stories that can be told, the sizes of their audiences, and the styles they can employ, by concerns either of religious belief or pedagogy. Many churches have no choir these days, and both UK and US church choirs and their congregations are also in decline.[8]

My vision is more all-embracing than that. It starts above all with stylistic openness and artistic flexibility. We need to divest ourselves of purist high art notions of the venues in which choral singing occurs, and be prepared to sing anywhere where we can have impact. We should divest ourselves of gendered vocal parts, and allow all genders to sing the part that suits their voice best. We should use all available technologies to help. Every choir should have its YouTube channel or its podcast, and have video and audio experts as part of its artistic team.

When my choir sang at the Skirball Center in New York, the space was in essence a dry lecture hall and a theater space, but the sound designer used his iPad and digital mixer to create us a reverb-filled sound stage, which at times could sound like a recording studio and at others like a Broadway stage or a concert hall. The technology supported us and made us flexible. We could segue from Orff's *Carmina Burana* to Michael Jackson's "Thriller," and we could follow Eric Whitacre's "Lux aurumque" with a rendition of "Light" from Tom Kitt and Brian Yorkey's "Next to Normal." With ingenuity, technology and a practical, make-it-work attitude, choral singing can work artistically, sound incredible and have impact in all kinds of spaces. During COVID, some choirs[9] rehearsed in parking lots, and the most intrepid choirs already sing in shopping malls,[10] railway stations,[11] offices,[12] and any number of other places where people congregate. When we were doing our show about HIV, choral clinician Mollie Stone told us of how in South Africa, when a patient left a doctor's office in shock after a positive HIV diagnosis, a choir would follow them home. Once there, they would sing songs to them and their families, that were not only about how they felt, but also taught them how to live with HIV, through eating their carrots, exercising, and taking their medication.

Choral singing should be open to *any* style that is relevant to committed people who want to sing together and sing well. If they are BIPOC communities, then one repertoire and set of themes may be needed. If they are, say, a community of older queer people, or Mexican immigrants, then another entirely is the right direction. Again, it is our job as choral directors to be flexible. We should know those

212 Transforming Choral Singing

repertoires, have hundreds of songs at our fingertips, and be able to teach them by ear as well as from notation. Our training should enable us to respond to the needs of those communities with practical and culturally appropriate choral strategies, that will enable the songs of those communities to sound good and tell their stories with resonance.

Continuing the theme of flexibility through technology, COVID lockdowns forced choral directors themselves to become video producers, editors, studio engineers and digital sound designers. All of us spent nearly two years where our main mode of communication was Zoom. Circumstances have forced us, often against our will, to learn new rehearsal skills, deal with latency issues, use more backing tracks, and get good at teaching parts online. While this has taken many of us outside our comfort zones, COVID has actually forced choral singing into the twenty-first century. This is a massive creative opportunity.

During lockdown, YouTube showed us how musicians and educators of all kinds used recording, composition, and arranging facilities on their laptops and tablets to create singing that was unheard of in previous generations. Smart teenagers from Lil Naz X to Craig David[13] in the early 2000s, have been creating whole albums in their bedrooms, many without formal musical or vocal training. World-class jazz musicians like Emmet Cohen[14] are streaming their own chamber concerts and jazz gigs in their apartments, and making enough money through weekly shows to pay their rent and support their musicians. Top a cappella ensembles from VOCES8 to Pentatonix regularly produce excellent videos with quality sound. One choral video can reach millions, and can vastly expand your audience size beyond your local church or concert hall, helping your live audiences to grow. Zoom singing was only our first limited stab at this new and open field of digital choral singing. In this activist vision, we do better, because communication is what singing is about.

Once your audience is activated, interaction online will be key in this new world. Listeners love to engage, and this too connects them. They love to comment and say what they liked and hated about your choir's content. Rather than close them down, start a real conversation with your choir's ecosystem. Henry Timms, current CEO of the Lincoln Center in New York and leading influencer on the phenomenon of social media, talks about this interactivity as part of the exciting world of "New Power." No longer can artists hoard their power and control their message. What he calls "new power" operates differently, like an electric current: "It is made by many. It is open, participatory, and peer-driven. It uploads, and it distributes. Like water or electricity, it's most forceful when it surges. The goal with new power," he says, "is not to hoard it but to channel it."[15] Your community ecosystem just learned to bite back, and we as choirs must be the ones making those waves.

3) Choral directors have transformed skills, repertoire knowledge, and cultural experience, both as musicians and educators.

In this activist vision, directors show leadership by having specialist understanding of a wide range of repertoire, songs, and arrangements, and can respond with ease to the Tagalog speakers, gospel singers, early music nerds, or R&B aficionados in their groups. They also have the latest skills in crafting choral sound, and can conduct and shape musical gestures with authenticity in a range of styles. They own the pedagogical skill and the cultural understanding to facilitate the learning of their singers in a range of formal and informal ways, appropriate to their learning styles. They can all use the latest technology, from microphones, PA systems, and lighting and sound, to video and recording and mixing software, so that all choral musicians are studio musicians. This makes them simply better musicians, better conductors, and better educators. We need choral musicians out there in our communities, actively creating new choirs for singers, teaching all our kids in schools, and creating amazing complex choral performances in all styles and in all kinds of venues, that tell today's stories and take our musical and social discourse to new places.

In this new vision, choral directors have the vocal and idiomatic understanding not only to know and understand but to engage. Constantly striving to stay ahead of real-world music-making and social movements, they can get inside the musical gestures of all repertoire equally, and using the principle of social justice, they can consider all repertoire with the same level of intentionality and analytical rigor. They know how to collaborate respectfully with culture bearers to find authentic arrangements, and make space for them to lead. They can support a range of knowledgeable team members with different cultural backgrounds to direct their groups, so their choirs can sing many kinds of repertoire stylishly and with commitment to its messages. They also have a wide repertoire of strategies to support choral learning, and can grow singers with different learning styles in both formal and informal ways.

This necessitates a wholesale change both in choral leadership structures, but also in choral pedagogy in colleges. Choral directors should be in touch with the latest developments in their new stylistically broader field, and be continually be updating their musical, technological, and cultural skills. Student cohorts and faculties would also include a wide range of black and brown people, challenging them and supporting them as they grow. Racism and discrimination against nonwhite music is baked into many curricula in K–12 music education, and in many college programs training future choral leaders. It will not go away overnight, and leveling the playing field will involve persistence and a massive educational initiative over many years.

This is partly the responsibility of the schools and colleges that train directors, and partly on directors themselves. We all need regular refreshers on the latest

214 Transforming Choral Singing

developments on vocal pedagogy, which is a fast developing field, transformed in the last twenty years. Ask your choir to send you on courses regularly, to keep you in touch with others. "Vocalprocess"[16] is one interesting example of a YouTube channel devoted to supporting choral directors and vocal coaches, but there should be many more. The internet is fast becoming the backbone of formal and informal teaching of all kinds, and online courses are often helpful—short and long, free and paid. Remember too that the educational needs of our singers will change over time, and within our groups we will have a much wider range of gender, race, and age. This new more diverse singer base will be singing at many levels of expertise, and will have a variety of vocal needs and ways of singing, to which we should be able to respond with pedagogical incisiveness and deep cultural understanding.

Finally, in this new world, choral directors are in closer touch with their *own* cultures, and their own inner motivation as musicians. They have the tools to practice self-care, so they can nurture their personal physical, mental, and emotional resources, and have energy to share. They embody their personal passion for choral singing in all they do. They have the courage and critical skills to take risks smartly, and be assertive in the face of voices telling them to be conservative in their thinking and to repeat older, less impactful music-making. They continually strive for the choral singing that they believe in, and are respected for the courage, vulnerability, and leadership it takes to do so.[17]

4) Choral singing creates and embodies community and change.

Community is key to activist choral singing. A choir that is not a community cannot listen to itself, blend well, and lead vocally as a single person. Divided, it lacks the power to act or to sing well. Also, wherever anyone can see a community developing, there should be a choir, and wherever there is a choir, there will always be a community that surrounds it. Singing creates new community and energizes and galvanizes those who do it and hear it. When someone outside a community hears them sing, new bonds are formed. In this vision of choral singing, choral directors understand the community power built into their work, and use it with intention.

Choral singing also empowers and changes communities, so they become more themselves. Choirs are living, breathing organisms that expand and contract, have their own needs, issues, and struggles, and often survive for decades under many directors. Directors are definitely entitled to express themselves through their work, but their main satisfaction should come primarily from service, from empowering whole communities to express their *own* purpose. In this vision, choral conducting is an especially refined form of social and political leadership. It turns individual singers into more expressive versions of themselves, and then bonds those singers into choral groups that express with radical honesty who those groups are, what they have in common, and what they believe. Choral singing becomes a catalyst in this context. It causes change in the way we think and feel about our identities, and our future.

In closing, I have a couple of particularly cherished memories that I want to share. One is of a group of three five-year-olds dancing on the street to one of our groups singing Katy Perry's *Firework*. The light shone in the five-year-olds' eyes, and they giggled as they danced. My singers could not stop themselves from smiling and pointing as they sang, and nor could I. The singers felt empowered, the kids danced, and everyone laughed. The most jaded of tenors in my choir wrote me an email afterward, saying that watching those kids had re-energized him, and reminded him why he sings.

A second memory is of a Lower East Side day care center, where people with cancer were facing death. As they listened to us singing Lauridsen's "Sure on this Shining Night," I saw subtle change in the faces of those in wheelchairs with drips in their arms, in the day room where we sang. There were tears, from both singers and listeners. Then there was a long silence at the end of the performance and much hugging—singer to singer, singer to patient, and patient to patient. The next day, the carers gave us astonishing feedback in their thank-you email. They wrote movingly and with authenticity about how hard it often was to improve the well-being of people in such tough situations. They described our singing as miraculous in its healing, and said it was continuing to make a noticeable difference to the patients twenty-four hours after the performance.

One final memory: Fred (his real name) had been in his time an uncompromising activist for what were then LGBT rights in the 1970s and '80s, and was HIV positive for over twenty years. When I first joined our group, he was already a community elder. His body was twisted and marked by disease, but he remained relentless, mischievous, formidable, reliable in his attendance at rehearsal, and a passionate activist for LGBTQIA+ quality through and through. I used to take him to lunch at a local diner once or twice a year.

Over lentil soup, he told me stories about what being in the group meant to him, and what he thought it should mean to me, as the newcomer and British outsider. During the AIDS epidemic, the group had lost 150 of its singing members, and before anti-retroviral drugs, they were at one point singing for a funeral every week. When he struggled into rehearsal, he said he sang primarily for those 150 singers. He saw them singing next to him, and felt their presence. They were his purpose.

This story, for me, is the most powerful expression of what activist choral singing can be. It is in the end a group expression of the change-making potential of community love.[18] Fred's uncompromising activist stance gave me a sense of the awesome responsibility I carried as a community leader, when I took on the role directing the group. I will always love the New York singers individually and collectively from whom I learned such a lot, and am proud of the change we brought to the lives of thousands of people over many years. That impact will stay in our hearts, and in the hearts of those we sang to. That love grew directly from music-making. It came from teaching them, conducting them, learning from them, getting to know them as people through their voices, and, I hope, binding them together into an often messy but tightly bonded community.

My experience is that the power of choral singing to transform people's lives is limitless. This is not idealistic white guy bullshit, but the daily truth of the impact of my work with activist choirs. I believe that the methods, principles, and practices I learned to use in my work have the potential to reinvigorate choral singing itself. My hope is that they will lead to better and more impactful choral art, sung by more people with greater commitment, in a wider variety of contexts, in a wider variety of styles. They will lead increased participation and engagement, and indeed an outpouring of relevant, joyful, and stylistically diverse choral singing. They will lead to a choral art performed by a larger, more energized, and more diverse group of singers, and consumed by a wider range of listeners, who see singing as more relevant to their lives.

The radical power of choral singing can create a more equitable and more integrated society—one which celebrates all its members, allows them all to lead, and is more equitable, tolerant, diverse, and at peace with itself. The connective power of this kind of singing can heal division and integrate and unify communities once more. I have seen it happen. And if ever there was a time when such transforming change was desperately needed, it is right now.

Notes

1. Weiwei (2020).
2. Hess's (2019) concept of activist music education is in some ways similar to mine, creating perhaps an "activist choral singing." She draws on Higgins's stylistically open concept of "musicking," and Freire's concept of continually reinventing "critical pedagogy" (12), and summarizes her definition of activist music education as addressing injustice, "fostering connection, honoring and sharing lived experiences, and engaging in critical thinking" (38).
3. President Obama, "Inspiring Future Leaders and 'A Promised Land,'" *The Daily Social Distancing Show*, December 16, 2020 https://www.youtube.com/watch?v=vy3IsfyS2Ng
4. COP26 is a shining example of a group that makes innovative music in the cause of climate change activism with nursery children, schools, neighborhood groups, choirs, local councils, youth groups, and artists in Scotland. https://letitgrow.scot/.
5. Marius Bahnean, "William Byrd: Catholic Masses for Three Voices, Four Voices and Five Voices in Protestant England," *Bulletin of the Transylvania University of Braşov—Supplement Series VIII: Performing Arts* 9, no. 2 (2016).
6. Amrein and De Quandros (2020).
7. Specifically on disability in schools, Fuelberth and Todd (2017) write: "The success of students with disabilities in the choral classroom hinges on the educator's desire to know and support every individual learner. Of equal importance is the educator's ability to understand the strengths and weaknesses of the whole student, and create opportunities through which each individual can contribute as an important member of the school's choral community."
8. "The numbers are not adding up," https://www.theguardian.com/commentisfree/2021/oct/26/the-guardian-view-on-the-church-of-england-the-numbers-are-not-adding-up

An Activist Vision for Choral Singing   **217**

9. Columbus Gay Men's Chorus; also Epsom Choral Society: https://www.getsurrey.co.uk/news/surrey-news/surrey-choir-rehearses-multi-storey-20842667

10. https://www.youtube.com/watch?v=SXh7JR9oKVE

11. Imusicacapella from the Philippines. https://www.youtube.com/watch?v=uem0UDoMLN8

12. Office Choir of the Year 2016 https://www.youtube.com/watch?v=4dcBRy_t-Ag

13. https://www.bbc.co.uk/hampshire/content/articles/2008/10/31/craig_david_feature.shtml

14. https://emmetcohen.com/live-from-emmets-place

15. Henry Timms, "Understanding 'New Power,'" *Harvard Business Review*, December 2014

16. https://www.youtube.com/c/Vocalprocess

17. Hess's (2019) concept of "Activist Music Education" points to one powerful way forward here, though it is focused more on general music education than on choral singing specifically.

18. Jennifer Rodgers (2019) summarizes this well: "In current times, we as choral directors would be wise to seek a more active relevancy based on dynamic, specific relationships with the actual people in our communities. Further, these relationships need not only be reserved for the special projects and partnerships; they need to become the foundation of our organizations. When that happens, they will change us for the better and we, in turn, will be able to have the impact that we seek.

11
Calls to Action

To finish, here is a list of calls to action, specific things you can do right away to start changing your practice. You may be doing some of them already. They are grouped under the headings of the four principles.

Connection

Nurture a friendship: Bring a friend to rehearsal, and get a choir member to chat to them. Then ask your singers to bring a friend next week.

Create a new social activity: Offer a meal in the venue before rehearsal, or plan a bake sale at the break. Organize a picnic, bowling trip, yoga retreat, or gaming night.

Make yourself and your team available: Set up a time when singers or listeners can reach you, or a regular interactive chat in person or online.

Break the fourth wall: In your next performance, talk to your audience more than usual. Sing to them, but also sing with them.

Hold hands and sing: Sing one song in a circle while holding hands. Then spend five minutes talking about how it made you feel.

Turn up the lights and ask a question: During a show, turn up the house lights. Ask a question, and ask for a show of hands, so all can see. Then sing a song about the question, and ask the audience to join in.

Invite your community in: Invite an expert or community leader to rehearsal to talk about a concern. Stand them on your podium, and make them feel valued by singing something to them.

Articulate what is meaningful about singing: Share a five-minute personal story from the podium about what singing has meant to you, and how it has changed your life.

Use your art to draw people in: If you need younger singers, find and program one song that will engage them. Advertise that you are singing it.

Strengthen your group's groove: Groove in the body bonds your singers. Regardless of style, embed one groove warm-up in your next rehearsal.

Keep a relationship fertile: Write an unexpected thank-you note to a person outside your organization, who did something that you think made a real difference.

Transforming Choral Singing. Charles W. Beale, Oxford University Press. © Oxford University Press 2024.
DOI: 10.1093/oso/9780197657775.003.0011

Impact

Catch the eye: Add color by changing one thing about your lighting, design, or concert dress.

Use more audio and video: Make a teaser recording or video about the theme of your concert.

Reach out to a like-minded group: Contact a choir like yours but in another city. Sing something with them in one of their shows.

Call a *non*-musical group: Identify local communities and causes you believe in: nurses, sports people, people from local ethnic groups, other marginalized groups, schools, churches, colleges. Call one, and ask how your group could help.

Start from a story: Find one new story to sing about, rather than one new song. Then find the one song that fits.

Add a storytelling gesture: In rehearsal, give your singers one simple thing to do with their bodies or faces, to make a story more explicit.

Share: Take a picture of one thing that happens at rehearsal every week. Add a caption saying how you all felt, and share it on social media.

Sing and rehearse more from memory: If new to memorization, decide which song you are going to sing from memory for the first time. Teach it by ear and from notation from the first time your group sings it. Teach your choir to look at the audience while they sing it.

Put your art first: Go through every meeting your organization has. Cancel the least important, so you have more time to focus on impactful music-making.

Change venue for one rehearsal: Find a new venue to rehearse in for one evening. See what new contacts you can make there.

Find out how others see your group: Call several trusted and frank audience members, and ask them what others say the impact of your group really is. It may surprise you.

Social Justice

Lean in to strong emotion: Which is the song that makes your singers and listeners laugh or cry the most? Sing that change-making song more. Don't be afraid to repeat it, so it becomes an audience favorite. Then find another one.

Name one big change: Name the one big social change you want to see in the world. Share that idea with your singers and leadership often.

Find your majority and minorities: Do you skew old, white, heterosexual, or able-bodied? Are there too many basses or sopranos? Identify your demographics by age, gender, ethnicity, income, disability, neurodiversity, and voice part. Now you know.

Check your alignment: Is everyone equally enthusiastic about your equity and inclusion position? Talk to one person who has their doubts.

220 Transforming Choral Singing

Find one microaggression: Identify one common microaggression occurring in your group. Ensure your members are alert for it, and explain how to respond.

Celebrate the personal uniqueness of a singer: We are all individuals—tall, gay, shortsighted, shy, Latinx, dyslexic, seventy but still climbing mountains, First Nation, nineteen and non-binary . . . Find one singer, and celebrate their uniqueness in a song.

Find one small issue that matters: What is wrong in your neighborhood today? Call one organization that is also campaigning for that change. Sing a song about it, in collaboration with that organization.

Solve one challenge around access or mobility: Identify a barrier to singing in performance some singers face, and find a way around it. Is it wheelchair access? Performance attire?

Change one thing about your audition process: What one thing in your audition process could be excluding good singers unnecessarily? Take it away.

Do an exit interview: Think of someone who left your group recently. Call them, and ask them why. Also ask a friend of theirs, who can get a more in-depth answer.

Celebrate an activist: In every choir, there are singers who are especially passionate about your group, because of the change it creates in the world. Give them a space in rehearsal to talk about why they are in the group. Ensure they get a big round of applause.

Say "no": Turn down a gig that is not part of your mission.

Take courage: When you prepare your next show, monitor your artistic choices. Find a song that you feel it would be too risky to try. Feel the fear, but sing it anyway. Allow it to spark debate.

Show up to everyone in your choir equally: Show up to everyone in your group in small ways, initially by simply asking how their day went. Work out who you are not doing that with so much, and do it with them too. Feel the trust deepen over time.

Sing for a present reason: In your next program, sing a song for someone who did something great for your group recently, or in honor of someone who passed away. Celebrate a change in the law, or the opening of a new building.

Stylistic Openness

Connect with a local musician: Contact with a local musician accomplished in a non-classical style. Go to their gig. Then invite them in, and let them teach your group one of their songs.

Get hip to new repertoire: Program one pop song that is less than six months old, also a classical one, if you like.

Choose one new song: Find an attractive song in an unfamiliar style that you would usually pass by. Learn how to rehearse it.

Singer favorites: Poll your singers about their favorite singers, bands, and shows. Program one song they like, in a new arrangement. Get them to introduce it.

Buy a book: Buy a book about being a pro drummer, and research one unfamiliar groove in either jazz, pop music, or Latinx styles.

Round out your musical knowledge: Find a composer or song you absolutely hate, or know nothing about. Ask a trusted colleague to explain what they love about it and how it works musically.

Establish a debate around an aspect of vocal sound: Choose a specific vocal technique you are working on in the current program, like belt, low larynx, or diction. Provoke singer discussion by dropping it into your rehearsal language regularly, and discuss in depth.

Share early singing experiences: Ask a singer to reveal how they first learned to love singing. Ask them to choose one positive and one negative early experience.

Employ a wider range of vocal sound in your programs: Program two songs with contrasting vocal sounds in mind, and point out the differences.

Free the voice by improvising: Do one warm-up that involves singers making their own pitch or rhythm choices.

Mix up your group work to empower your singers: Do an exercise where singers listen to each other in pairs or standing in small groups.

Singer and Choir Appendix

Singers

Classical Singers

Enrico Caruso ("O sole mio," Eduardo di Capua and Alfredo Mazzucchi, 1916): One of the first bel canto opera stars of the recording age, Caruso's voice was bright and at the same time exceptionally full sounding even at high pitch. Described at the time as exceptionally resonant, his became the model for operatic tenor sound for generations. Interestingly, Caruso was also a strong influence on the vocal and trumpet sounds of jazz musician Louis Armstrong.

Joyce DiDonato ("Lascia ch'io pianga," Handel, 2013): DiDonato is currently a leading US mezzo-soprano at the time of writing, and also an outstanding supporter of opera students and advocate for the classical singing tradition. Her vocal color is simultaneously warm, sweet, and ringing in timbre. With her *Songplay* (2019) album, she has also ventured into the world of cabaret, classical sound largely intact.

Bryn Terfel ("Non più andrai," Mozart, 1998): This Welsh bass-baritone's sound is richer and speechlike in its core sound. Mainly an opera star, he is also a fabulous actor, and has not shied away from crossing over into musical theater territory, most notably in *Sweeney Todd* (2014).

Emma Kirkby ("But Who May Abide," Handel, 1982): With the ultimate in bright and sparkling soprano voices, Kirkby's reputation in 1980s early music was unrivaled. Her vibrato was especially fast, and the sound lacked the weight of a Romantic tradition soprano, while retaining unparalleled brightness, agility, cry, and a simple twang-related sheen.

Jessye Norman ("Der Abschied," from *Das Lied von der Erde*, Mahler, 1985): The ultimate contrast with Kirkby, Norman's voice was dark, rich, and full of sob—perfect for Mahler and Richard Strauss. Like DiDonato, we hear thin folds at work at lower pitch, combined with extraordinary breath control. We also hear an almost pop-style uniqueness, authenticity, and personal warmth in the sound— a master connector. Norman often sang gospel music—"Give Me Jesus" (1990) for example—mainly with classical inflections.

Renée Fleming ("Fable," from *A Light on The Piazza*, 2019): Fleming is another world-class singer, primarily in opera, who has nevertheless done several critically acclaimed albums in popular styles. For even more detail on "Fable," compare this performance with that of Victoria Clarke on the 2003 original cast recording. Fleming has also produced an entire rock album, *Dark Hope* (2010), and starred in a Björk project in 2017 with the Stockholm and New York Philharmonic orchestras. In both, she kept her pingy classical resonance in some places, but in others completely recolored her voice, showing her cultural roots from Indiana, Pennsylvania. She also used vibrato much less, and vowels became much more conversational at times in Björk's *All Is Full of Love*.

Musical Theater Singers

Kelli O'Hara ("If I Loved You," Rodgers and Hammerstein, 2016): Broadway star Kelli O'Hara often produces a sweet, rounded, vibrato-filled sound that has made her a go-to voice in classic Broadway, and crosses over well into classical singing. At the same time, raised in Oklahoma, O'Hara knows how to produce the "twangy" straight tone of a country sound, and has done so professionally with an orchestra on "They Don't Let You in the Opera, if You're a Country Star."

Elaine Stritch ("Ladies Who Lunch," 1970): Stritch's sound here is grounded in a gritty thick folds speech voice, with the darker harmonics of a low larynx and some brighter twang too—conversational overall, but with hints of singerliness at the edges. In the "call" of her resonance, you can tell she could sing unamplified in a 1950s Broadway theater. This is a vocal performance of huge expressiveness and intensity, with moments of growling, creaking, and extreme vocal effects that are regarded as unskillful by some, but take great skill to do well, eight shows a week.

224 Singer and Choir Appendix

Bernadette Peters ("No One Is Alone," 1987): Peters is a natural mezzo, with a free and unaffected upper register, and a lighter sound lower down. Often singerly, she has the instrument to sing classic Broadway with classical legato lines, but is also a natural belter. She is perhaps vocally at her most easeful in Sondheim's *Into the Woods*.

Billy Porter ("Not My Father's Son," 2013): Here Billy Porter combines the belt and twang of pop-style Broadway with gospel/RnB phrasing and resonance. Success in contemporary Broadway requires stylistic openness, and Porter is a virtuoso, sounding just as confident and politically charged on his 2020 club hit "Love Yourself." Porter could not be more accomplished, charismatic, and political, all in a good way. In doing so, he utilizes the widest possible range of vocal color choices, attracts the widest audience, and remains utterly himself .

Judi Dench ("Send in the Clowns," 1995): With regard to timbre and resonance, Dench's unconventional vocal performance of this song is acknowledged as one of the greatest, paradoxically because it is superbly acted. Long notes falter, breaths are short, and the sound carries in the theater but is rarely resonant in the conventional sense. Instead, the broken character's sound is mostly spoken (thick folds and breathy), and on the verge of tears (so naturally retracted at the level of the false folds). The vocal interpretation is highly colorful, expressive, and technically sophisticated, yet conversational, intimate and in the final analysis tragic. She sings with great interpretive power, but rarely sounds like a "singer."

Cynthia Erivo ("The Impossible Dream," 2017): A singer with crossover powers of a different kind, Erivo has transcended style and culture by combining a Grammy-winning musical theater career with Nigerian British roots and virtuoso-level skills in gospel and soul music. From "The Impossible Dream" to "And I Am Telling You, I'm Not Going" (2015), she can adapt her vocal sound and vibrato, so it sits well in a range of stylistic contexts. These changes do not damage her voice nor do they compromise her ethnic identity.

Rock/Pop Singers

Elvis Presley ("Love Me Tender," "Hound Dog," 1956): A darker, lower voice in pop music, Presley's ballad singing is often very sweet-toned, with low larynx, thin folds, and some thyroid tilt. By contrast, "Hound Dog" sits in a straight-tone, speech voice, semi-belt much of the time, and also features some safe growling.

David Bowie ("Changes," 1971): Unconventional but authentically British, Bowie's baritone voice, even with bright pop vowels, is hugely successful commercially because it is instantly recognizable. Bowie uses his voice with great flexibility of color and pitch, from soft speaking through to high belting and falsetto. His voice is naturally much less spacious and retracted than Presley's.

Billie Eilish ("Bad Guy," 2020): Eilish's young, transgressive voice was pop flavor-of-the-month in 2021. It combines thin-fold sweetness and high-larynx childlike fragility with breathiness and some vibrato. As with other good pop voices, it is instantly recognizable for what Barthes would call its "grain." As with, say, Madonna's voice, you recognize the singer within the first five seconds, which is pop music skill in itself.

Michael Jackson ("Billie Jean," 1983; "You Are Not Alone," 1995): A high tenor with extraordinary rhythmic articulation, Jackson uses percussive clicks and fry/creak sounds to add emotion and expression. Note the very high larynx, thick folds, and a bright pop vocal sound with AES (Aryepiglottic Sphincter) on the chorus of Billie Jean. On ballads like "You Are Not Alone," by contrast, he engages a sweetly thin-folds long note sound, and uses vibrato liberally but not at all times.

Jon Anderson ("Heart of the Sunrise," 1972): Like Bruno Mars, Anderson is a master technician with a high tenor voice that will "mix" naturally up and up into soprano territory. High levels of skill are needed to keep the voice even, in tune, and easeful across such a wide range. Compared to Michael Jackson, he uses less vibrato but like Jackson, much AES, and larynx height is generally high.

Whitney Houston ("Love Will Save the Day," 1987): Church-trained, her bright-toned and pingy sound is all you would want in a gospel choir soprano, but she also gives depth of tone and "cry" when needed. Compare with an equally pingy Emma Kirkby (see Classical Voices above). You can hear an especially wide range of color, from Houston's sweet-thin folds voice up high to her more belty middle register tones. She also has amazing technical agility in both her embellishments and runs, moving from one register to another at great speed without compromising color.

Karen Carpenter ("We've Only Just Begun," 1970): A darker voice, with both speech and singerly elements and an extraordinary rich timbre, perfect on microphone. Her upper register also has a darker quality that still cuts through a band texture, which makes it especially effective on ballads, and an excellent example for your altos. There is always a sweetness there, which implies she naturally tilts her thyroid cartilage and finds it natural to retract. Compare to an equally dark Jessye Norman (see Classical Voices above).

Celine Dion: ("All by Myself," 1996, "Las Vegas," 2016): This is a fascinating example of a versatile pop voice with evident classical training, French Canadian vowels, and emotional nuance. Her upper register can switch from belt-quality on a "money note" (such as the key change here) to more "mix" and even "fluty" classical soprano tones at will. She also has excellent microphone technique, and sings both pure and more breathy sounds quietly without losing her tonal center. She can vary her vibrato, using it in the conventional classical way at times. At others, she sings only straight tone, and moves from one to the other in surprising ways on a single note. Her distinctive vowels also add unique character to her sound, engaging soft palate on her "u" vowel and her "o," as in the French word "non."

Choirs and Vocal Ensembles

There are so many fabulous groups to choose from. Here, I have focused on only a handful of examples of choirs that demonstrate the qualities I note above, at various levels of difficulty, voice combinations, and ages. I also note how most also implement the four principles in some way. In this list, I have also tried to cover as many sounds and styles as possible, offering archetypal and freely available "primary color" examples of choral sounds. Several code-switch, attempting to combine vocal qualities from different singing traditions. In each case a single performance or possibly two are given, and all are available for free at the time of writing on YouTube.

Jason Max Ferdinand Singers, "Jerusalem" (2020): Church choral singing of spirituals, from this new African American group, but using the color and nuance of classical singing to create excellent ensemble.

Stellenbosch University Choir, "The Rainmaker" (2020): This South African choir won the recent World Choir Games, and this set is an inspiring example of an adult social justice choir in action. Repertoire is uniquely of its place and communities, and the ethnic diversity of this majority black choir is striking, also matched by stylistic diversity. This is also a fantastic example of a large choir really belting.

Color Music Children's Choir, Ukraine, "Something Just Like This" (2018). This highly disciplined, committed, and energized children's choir have been well trained to produce a wide range of vocal color and melodic phrasing on this Coldplay song, in unison and parts. They move their bodies naturally to the groove in an informal way. Highly creative dance backing tracks and visual backgrounds show a similar deep understanding of presenting pop styles attractively.

VOCES8, "Sleep" (2020): A smaller classical ensemble, whose core sound is again sweet and singerly thin folds, with conventional church diction for unamplified spaces. Superb blend, and again a clear sense of purpose.

Ely Cathedral Choir, "Lux aurumque" (2017): This high Episcopalian UK cathedral choir has a fantastic sound, and is an inspiring but also very practical example of best practice equity and inclusion work. They allow boy and girl choristers to sing at the cathedral both together and separately, without any compromise in the quality of the sound, or the excellence of the ensemble.

Les Double Six, "Fascinating Rhythm" ("Le Pas Qui Plaira") (1962); "Doodlin'" ("Tout En Dodelinant") (1960): This late 1950s and 1960s French jazz vocal ensemble transformed the style of jazz singing, and was highly influential on later groups including the Swingles, New York Voices, and Manhattan Transfer. Vocal color and dynamics here are perfectly suited to close-miked performing, and complement the swing phrasing.

Crouch End Festival Chorus, "Songs from Liquid Days" (Philip Glass) (1986); "Saving Private Ryan" (John Williams) (2006); *Locus Iste* **(Bruckner) (2019); "Waterloo Sunset [choral version]"**

226 Singer and Choir Appendix

(The Kinks) (2012): Initially a conventional oratorio-singing community choir based in the UK, Crouch End Festival Chorus reinvented itself in the 1990s, and is now a poster child choir for stylistic openness. They appear in major venues as a session choir in a huge variety of contexts, with pop stars from The Kinks to Coldplay, and on Oscar-winning movie scores, as well as singing conventional classical repertoire.

Take Six, "Spread Love" (1988); "Quiet Place" (1988): Creating another step change in jazz and gospel singing, virtuoso a cappella group Take Six use vocal sound, mixing, and close-miking to create a unique African American TTBB take on close harmony. Note the straight-tone, thin-folds work, with pop vowels, and extensive use of onset variety to create tension and release over a groove. Their blend is second to none.

PS22 Chorus, "True Colors" (Cyndi Lauper) (2012); "Old Town Road" (Lil Naz X) (2021): This Staten Island children's choir shows the kind of impact you can have from a mixed ability group of ordinary elementary school children from an especially diverse New York City. The choral educator is inspiring, the children move naturally, the music is in their bodies, and there is a feeling of commitment, authenticity, and color in the voices that have made this group justly famous across the US.

The Hi-Los, "Lulu's Back in Town" (1957); "Life is Just a Bowl of Cherries" (1957): This early jazz vocal quartet phrased like a big band, using shakes, doits, and falls, and their vocal tone was equally brassy and tightly phrased. They used mainly straight-tone singing, with complex control of speed and depth of vibrato, over a range of pitch that would rival many SATB groups.

Perpetuum Jazzile, "Africa" (Toto); "Don't Stop Me Now" (2015): A large adult SATB choir from Slovenia, Perpetuum Jazzile have really mastered how to sing pop music a cappella, with over fifty singers and two beatboxers. Each singer is individually miked.

Angel City Chorale, "The Rising" (2020): A Los Angeles–based mixed-ability community choir, that sings with a rock band and orchestra. Recognized in a recent season of *America's Got Talent*, they also have excellent social media presence, and an inclusive approach to repertoire, recruitment, and community that has won them plaudits and a dedicated fan base.

Gospel

I have included here an additional section for gospel choirs, as they are often under-represented on lists of great choirs. I also wanted to highlight the variety of their work as community choirs with social justice underpinnings, and their excellence in groove-based styles. So many mainstream choirs try and fail to sing spirituals well. There is much to learn from these groups, around clear purpose and distinctive vocal color.

The Original Five Blind Boys of Alabama, "You Got to Move" (1953): A highly influential early gospel tenor and bass small group, combining vocal freedom and intense groove with a wide range of vocal color.

Brooklyn Tabernacle Choir, "Worthy Is the Lamb" (2009): A more recent, well established and huge New York gospel choir with a worldwide following of millions worldwide, because it sings to pro standards while also representing a community.

Manchester Inspirational Voices, "Swing Low, Sweet Chariot" (2016): This majority black UK-based gospel choir shows that it is possible for all races to sing gospel music with authentic vocal sound and phrasing, if they are well taught, in this case by their charismatic director, Wayne Ellington. Often on national TV, this group communicates infectious sense of fun and religious commitment.

Richard Smallwood Singers & Vision, "The Highest Praise" (1999): Smallwood helped invent the contemporary gospel sound of the early 2000s, and in its time, this professional group was much praised for its artistic innovation while also focusing on a slickly commercial singing and recording style.

Broadway Inspirational Voices, "A Whole New World" (2019): This joyous New York choir is one of the top gospel groups in the US, managed by Michael McElroy. It is uniquely made up of working Broadway actors, who give up their time to support other causes at very expensive fundraiser performances. Their sound is a fascinating combination of highly tuned gospel nuance with an energized New York musical theater sound. The group shows how pro singers can code-switch, adapting their sound to suit the context.

Bibliography

Abrams, Stacey. *Minority Leader: How to Lead from the Outside and Make Real Change*. New York: Henry Holt and Company, 2018.

American League of Orchestras. *Of and for the Community: The Education and Community Engagement Work of Orchestras*. New York: 2014. https://americanorchestras.org/knowledge-research-innovation/youth-education-and-community/of-and-for-the-community-edce-report.html

Amrein, Emily, and André De Quadros. "Re-imagining the Choir." *Chorus America*, 2020. https://www.thechoralcommons.com/blog/reimagining-the-choir

Anzaldua, Ahmed F., Abbie Betinis, and Tesfa Wondemagegnehu (eds.). *Justice Choir Songbook*. Minneapolis, MN: Self-published, 2019. https://www.justicechoir.org/

Bailey, Betty A., and Jane W. Davidson. "Effects of Group Singing and Performance for Marginalized and Middle-Class Singers." *Psychology of Music* 33 (2005): 269.

Balén, Julia. *A Queerly Joyful Noise: Choral Musicking for Social Justice*. New Brunswick, NJ: Rutgers University Press, 2017.

Bath, Naomi, Alison Daubney, Duncan Mackrill, and Gary Spruce. "The Declining Place of Music Education in Schools in England." *Children and Society* 34, no. 5 (September 2020): 443–457.

Beaumont-Thomas, Ben. "Third of British Musicians May Quit Industry Amid Pandemic." *Guardian*. September 22, 2020.

Beckett, Samuel. *Endgame: A Play in One Act; Followed By, Act without Words I: A Mime for One Player*. New York: Grove Press, 2009.

Beheshti, Setareh. "Improving Studio Music Teaching through Understanding Learning Styles." *International Journal of Music Education* 27 (2009): 107.

Bernstein, Basil. *Pedagogy, Symbolic Control and Identity: Theory, Research, Critique*. London: Taylor and Francis, 1996.

Bond, Vanessa L. "Culturally Responsive Education in Music Education: A Literature Review." *Contributions to Music Education* 42 (2017): 153–180. https://www.jstor.org/stable/26367441.

de Botton, Alain, and John Armstrong. *Art as Therapy*. London: Phaidon Press, 2013.

Brett, Philip, Elizabeth Wood, and Gary Thomas (eds.). *Queering the Pitch: The New Gay and Lesbian Musicology*. New York: Routledge, 2011.

Bunch Dayme, Meribeth. *Dynamics of the Singing Voice*. New York: Springer-Verlag Wien, 2009.

Burrack, Frederick W., Phillip Payne, Dale E. Bazan, and Daniel S. Hellman. *The Impact of Budget Cutbacks on Music Teaching Positions and District Funding in Three Midwestern States*. National Association for Music Education, 2014.

Chapman, Janice L. *Singing and Teaching Singing: A Holistic Approach to Classical Voice*. San Diego, CA: Plural Publishing, 2006.

Chernoff, John Miller. *African Rhythm and African Sensibility: Aesthetics and Social Action in African Musical Norms*. Chicago: University of Chicago Press, 1979.

Cleese, John. *Creativity: A Short and Cheerful Guide*. New York: Penguin Random House, 2020.

Cole, Brittany. "How Stacey Abrams Can Teach All Citizens to Be Resilient Leaders." *Tennessean*, January 8, 2021. https://www.tennessean.com/story/opinion/2021/01/08/stacey-abrams-resilient-leader-georgia-senate-elections/6585327002/

Collins, Jim. *Good to Great and the Social Sectors: Why Business Thinking Is Not the Answer*. Harper Business, 2005.

Crossick, Geoffrey, and Patrycja Kasynska. *Understanding the Value of Arts and Culture: The AHRC Cultural Value Project*. Arts and Humanities Research Council, 2016. https://ahrc.ukri.org/documents/publications/cultural-value-project-final-report/

Csikszentmihalyi, Mihaly. *Flow: The Psychology of Optimal Experience*. New York: Harper Collins, 1990/2008.

Di Grazia, Donna M. *Nineteenth Century Choral Music*. London: Routledge, 2013.

228 Bibliography

DiAngelo, Robin. *White Fragility: Why It's So Hard for White People to Talk About Racism*. Boston: Beacon Press, 2018.

Dreyer, Les. "Is Classical Music Dying?" *New York Times*, 2012.

Elpus, Kenneth, and Carlos R. Abril. "High School Music Ensemble Students in the United States: A Demographic Profile." *Journal of Research in Music Education* 59, no. 2 (2011): 128–145. http://www.jstor.org/stable/23019481.

Ester, Don. "Taking Advantage of Learning Styles in the Choral Rehearsal." *Choral Journal* 35, no. 4 (November 1994): 21.

Estill, Jo. *A Programmed Introduction: Anatomy of the Vocal Instrument*. Santa Rosa, CA: Estill Voice Training Systems, 1997.

Evans, Dafydd. *Film Showing Male Voice Choir's Bond to Hit the Cinema*. BBC.com. November 4, 2021. https://www.bbc.com/news/uk-wales-59160353

Ewell, Philip. *Music Theory's White Racial Frame: Confronting Racism and Sexism in American Music Theory*. Presented at the Society for Music Theory Annual Meeting, November 2019.

Feng, Phyllis. "Is Classical Music on the Decline?" *Affinity Magazine*, January 12, 2019.

Floyd, Samuel A., Jr. "Ring Shout, Signifyin(g), and Jazz Analysis." Edited by Robert Walser. *Keeping Time: Readings in Jazz History*. Oxford: Oxford University Press, 1999: 401–409.

Forbes, Guy W. *The Repertoire Selection Practices of High School Choral Directors in Florida, Georgia, South Carolina, North Carolina, and Virginia*. PhD dissertation. University of Florida, 1998.

Forbes, Guy W. "The Repertoire Selection Practices of High School Choral Directors." *Journal of Research in Music Education* 49, no. 2 (2001): 102–121.

Frederickson, Scott. *Popular Choral Handbook: New Techniques for Pop, Jazz, and Show Choir Directors*. ScottMusic.com, 2013.

Freire, Paulo. *Pedagogy of the Oppressed: 30th Anniversary Edition*. Translated by M. Bergman Ramos. New York: Continuum, 2000/1970.

Frith, S. *Performing Rites: On the Value of Popular Music*. Oxford: Oxford University Press, 1996.

Fuelberth, Rhonda, and Christy Todd. "'I Dream a World': Inclusivity in Choral Music Education." *Music Educators Journal* 104, no. 2 (2017): 38–44. https://www.jstor.org/stable/26588617.

Gates, Henry Louis, Jr. *The Signifying Monkey: A Theory of African-American Literary Criticism*. New York: Oxford University Press, 1988.

Gersema, Emily. "Researchers Find That Children's Brains Develop Faster with Music Training." *Medical Xpress*, 2016. https://medicalxpress.com/news/2016-07-children-brains-faster-music.html

Gioia, Ted. *The History of Jazz*. New York: Oxford University Press, 1997.

Goodkin, Doug. "Learning through Music and Art." TEDxConejoSalon, 2013. https://www.youtube.com/watch?v=zKZAfDcU6BQ

Green, Lucy. *Music, Informal Learning and the School: A New Classroom Pedagogy*. Burlington, VT: Ashgate, 2008.

Green, Lucy. *Music on Deaf Ears: Musical Meaning, Ideology and Education*. Bury St Edmunds: Arima Publishing, 2008.

Gumm, Alan. "The Effect of Choral Student Learning Style and Motivation for Music on Perception of Music Teaching Style." *Bulletin of the Council for Research in Music Education*, no. 159 (Winter 2004): 11–22.

Guthe, Emily. "The Choral Process: Enhancing the Success of Students with Disabilities within the Choral Structure." *Choral Journal* 57, no. 10 (2017): 51–56.

Hallam, Susan. "The Power of Music: A Research Synthesis of the Impact of Actively Making Music on the Intellectual, Social and Personal Development of Children and Young People." *International Journal of Music Education* 28, no. 3 (2001): 269–289.

Hamilton, Darren. "#BlackMusicMatters: Dismantling Anti-Black Racism in Music Education." *Canadian Music Educator* 62, no. 2 (Winter 2021): 16–28.

Harley, Arreon. "How Choirs Have the Capacity to Change Lives." TEDxWilmington, Delaware, 2015. https://www.youtube.com/watch?v=-heVqNNqI_w

Harvey, Adrian. *Funding Arts and Culture in a Time of Austerity*. London: Arts Council England and New Local Government Network, 2016.

Hebdige, Dick. *Subculture: The Meaning of Style*. London and New York: Routledge, 1979.

Heimans, Jeremy, and Henry Timms. *New Power: How Power Works in Our Hyperconnected World—and How to Make It Work for You*. London: Doubleday Penguin Random House, 2019.

Hesmondhalgh, David. *Why Music Matters*. Oxford: Wiley-Blackwell, 2013.

Hess, Juliet. *Radical Musicking: Challenging Dominant Paradigms in Elementary Music Education*. PhD dissertation, University of Toronto, 2013.

Hess, Juliet. *Music Education for Social Change: Constructing an Activist Music Education* London and New York: Routledge, 2019.

Higgins, Lee. *Community Music in Theory and Practice*. New York: Oxford University Press, 2012.

Hodges, Donald A. "Implications of Music and Brain." *Research Music Educator's Journal* 87, no. 2 (2000): 17–22.

Interaction Design Foundation. "Design Iteration Brings Powerful Results," 2020. https://www.interaction-design.org/literature/article/design-iteration-brings-powerful-results-so-do-it-again-designer

Janmohamed, Hussein. "Choral Music: The Road to Harmony." TED Talk. Canada: also University of British Columbia, 2012. https://www.youtube.com/watch?v=L0q0buX3fmM

Jansson, D. "Choral Singers' Perceptions of Musical Leadership." Edited by G. F. Welch, D. M. Howard, and J. Nix. *The Oxford Handbook of Singing*. Oxford University Press, 2019: 865–885.

Johnson, Julian. *Who Needs Classical Music? Cultural Choice and Musical Value*. Oxford: Oxford University Press, 2002.

Jordan, James. *Fundamentals of Choral Conducting*. 2nd edition. Chicago: GIA Publications, 2009.

Jordan, James. *The Musician's Soul: A Journey Examining Spirituality for Performers, Teachers, Composers, Conductors, and Music Educators*. Chicago: GIA Publications, 1999.

Jorgensen, Nancy S., and C. Pfeiler. *Things They NEVER Taught You in Choral Methods*. Milwaukee, WI: Hal Leonard, 1995.

Kat, Katie. "Finding Your Voice: The Necessity of Singing." TEDxJerseyCity, 2014. https://www.youtube.com/watch?v=d8rmKXbYljw

Kendi, Ibram X. *How to Be an Anti-Racist*. New York: Random House, 2019.

Kinzer, Charles E. "The Tios of New Orleans and Their Pedagogical Influence on the Early Jazz Clarinet Style." *Black Music Research Journal* 16, no. 2 (1996): 279–302. https://doi.org/10.2307/779332.

Klimek, Mary McDonald, Kerrie Obert, and Kimberley Steinhauer. *Estill Voice Training System*. Santa Rosa, CA: Estill Voice Training Systems International LLC, 2005.

Kolb, David A. *Experiential Learning Experience as the Source of Learning and Development*. Englewood Cliffs, NJ: Prentice Hall, 2005.

Lawrence-McIntyre, Charshee Charlotte. "The Double Meanings of the Spirituals." *Journal of Black Studies* 17, no. 4 (June 1987): 379–401.

Lee, Don. "Choruses and Community Wellness." *Chorus America*, 2013. https://www.chorusamerica.org/singers/choruses-and-community-wellness

Lind, Vicki R. "Adapting Choral Rehearsals for Students with Learning Disabilities." *Choral Journal* 41, no. 7 (2001): 27–30.

Livermore, Ann. *Artists and Aesthetics in Spain*. Wolfeboro, NH: Longwood Publications, 1988.

Lundquist, Barbara R., and Winston T. Sims. "African-American Music Education: Reflections on an Experience." *Black Music Research Journal* 16, no. 2 (1996): 311–336. https://doi.org/10.2307/779334.

Marafioti, P. Mario. *Caruso's Method of Voice Production: The Scientific Culture of the Voice*. London: D. Appleton and Company, 1922.

McAfee, Barbara. "Bringing Your Full Voice to Life." TEDxGustavusAdolphusCollege, 2015. https://www.youtube.com/watch?v=Ze763kgrWGg

Mcintosh, Peggy. *White Privilege: Unpacking the Invisible Knapsack*. Peace and Freedom Magazine, July–August 1989, pp. 10–12. Women's International League for Peace and Freedom, Philadelphia, PA. https://psychology.umbc.edu/wp-content/uploads/sites/57/2016/10/White-Privilege_McIntosh-1989.pdf

McKay, George, and Ben Higham. "Community Music: History and Current Practice, Its Constructions of 'Community' Digital Turns and Future Soundings." *Connected Communities*. Arts and Humanities Research Council, 2017. http://www.ahrc.ac.uk/documents/project-reports-and-reviews/connected-communities/community-music-history-and-current-practice-its-co

230   Bibliography

Menehan, Kelsey. "Building Community While Doing Research: The Community of Voice Senior Choir Project." *Chorus America*, 2014. https://www.chorusamerica.org/singers/building-commun ity-while-doing-research-community-voices-senior-choir-project>

Middleton, R. *Studying Popular Music*. Philadelphia, PA: Open University Press, 1990.

Miller, J.R. "Creating Choirs That Welcome Transgender Singers." *Choral Journal* 57, no. 4 (2016): 61–63.

Nevala-Lee, Alec. "Coco Chanel Rule." Author's own website, 2016. https://nevalalee.wordpress.com/2016/04/05/the-coco-chanel-rule/

Nhan Dan Online. *The Colours of Love*. Hanoi, Vietnam, July 26, 2019. https://en.nhandan.org.vn/cult ure/item/7736002-the-colours-of-love.html

Núñez, Francisco. "Is Diversity Enough in Choruses?" *Chorus America*, August 11, 2020, https://chorus america.org/publications/blog/diversity-enough-choruses and https://www.franciscojnunez.com/news-press/s5hj2pt8rkf7759e793fk6fx99wjcl

Oshiro, Shana. "Race on the Path to Choral Conducting That Milky White Way." *Chorus Connection* blog. October 21, 2020. https://blog.chorusconnection.com/race-on-the-path-to-choral-conduct ing-that-milky-white-way

Osman, S.E., V. Tischler, and J. Schneider. " 'Singing for the Brain': A Qualitative Study Exploring the Health and Well-Being Benefits of Singing for People with Dementia and Their Carers." *Dementia (London)* 15, no. 6 (2016): 1326–1339. doi:10.1177/1471301214556291

Peretz, I., S. Cummings, and M.P. Dubé. "The Genetics of Congenital Amusia (Tone Deafness): A Family-Aggregation Study." *American Journal of Human Genetics* 81, no. 3 (2007): 582–588. doi:10.1086/521337

Pearce, Eiluned, Jacques Launay, and Robin I.M. Dunbar. "The Ice-Breaker Effect: Singing Mediates Fast Social Bonding." *Royal Society Open Science* (2015). http://doi.org/10.1098/rsos.150221.

Philips, Kenneth H. *Directing the Choral Music Program*. New York: Oxford University Press, 2004.

Prtoric, Jelena. "Revolutionary Road: How the Activist Choirs in the Balkans Are Reviving Partisan Songs." *Calvert Journal* (December 9, 2016). https://www.calvertjournal.com/articles/show/7318/balkan-activist-choirs-partisan-songs

Rodgers, Jennifer. "A Rubric for Choral Relevance." *Choral Journal* 59, no. 9 (2019): 22–29. https://www.jstor.org/stable/26662728.

Ross, Malcolm. *The Creative Arts*. London: Heinemann Educational Books, 1978.

Ross, Tyler. "Singing in the MRI with Tyler Ross: Making the Voice Visible." YouTube, 2017. https://www.youtube.com/watch?v=J3TwTb-T044

Seelig, Tim. *Perfect Rehearsal*. Los Angeles: Music Sales, 2007.

Seelig, Tim. *Perfect Blend*. Los Angeles: Music Sales, 2007.

Seelig, Tim. *Tale of Two Tims: Big Ol' Baptist, Big Ol' Gay*. Macon, GA: Nurturing Faith Inc., 2020.

Shuker, Roy. *Understanding Popular Music*. London: Routledge, 1994.

Siadat, Fahad. "Reflections on Segregation and Representation in Choral Music." *NewMusicUSA*. June 18, 2020. Newmusicusa.org/newmusicbox

Sieck, Stephen. *Teaching with Respect Inclusive Pedagogy for Choral Directors*. Milwaukee, WI: Hal Leonard, 2017.

Simon, Nina. *The Art of Relevance*. Santa Cruz, CA: Museum 2.0, 2016.

Simons, Harriet. *Choral Conducting: A Leadership Teaching Approach*. Champaign, IL: M. Foster Music Co., 1983.

Sing Up. "Joined Up Thinking." *Sing Up* website. London, May 2, 2018. https://www.singup.org/blog/article/1330-joined-up-thinking/

Slobin, Mark. *Subcultural Sounds: Micromusics of the West*. Middletown, CT: Wesleyan University Press, 1993.

Sloboda, John A. "Music and Everyday Life: The Role of Emotions." In *Handbook of Music and Emotion: Theory, Research, Applications*. Edited by P.N. Juslin and J.A. Sloboda, 493–514. Oxford: Oxford University Press, 2010.

Small, Christopher. *Music, Society, Education*. Hanover, NH: University Press of New England, 1996/1977.

Smith, Brenda, and Robert T. Sataloff. *Choral Pedagogy*. San Diego, CA: Plural Publishing, 2013.

Stone-Davis, Férdia J. *Music and Transcendence*. Farnham: Ashgate, 2015.

Suttie, Jill. "Four Ways Music Strengthens Social Bonds." *Greater Good Magazine*. January 15, 2015. https://greatergood.berkeley.edu/article/item/four_ways_music_strengthens_social_bonds

Swanwick, Keith. *Teaching Music Musically*. London: Routledge, 2011.

Talbot, Brent C. (ed.). *Marginalized Voices in Music Education*. New York: Routledge, 2018.

Trecek-King, Anthony. "A Conductor's Journey." TEDxBoston, 2012. https://www.youtube.com/watch?v=I-MBqr4KWjo&t=410s

Tucker, Mark. *The Duke Ellington Reader*. Oxford: Oxford University Press, 1995.

UCLA Williams Institute School of Law. *How Many Adults Identify as Transgender in the United States?* June 2016. https://williamsinstitute.law.ucla.edu/publications/trans-adults-united-states/

Varvarigou, M., and L. Green. "Musical 'Learning Styles' and 'Learning Strategies' in the Instrumental Lesson: The Ear Playing Project (EPP)." *Psychology of Music* 43, no. 5 (2015):705–722.

Vennard, William. *The Singing Mechanism and the Technic (revised)*. New York: Carl Fischer, 1968.

de Voogt, Alex. "Dual Leadership as a Problem-Solving Tool in Arts Organizations Montreal." *International Journal of Arts Management* 9, no. 1 (2006): 17–22.

Wallas, Graham. *The Art of Thought*. Kent, England: Solis Press, 2014/1926.

Weiwei, Ai. "An Artist Must Be an Activist." *Guardian*, March 22, 2020. https://www.theguardian.com/artanddesign/2020/mar/22/ai-weiwei-an-artist-must-be-an-activist

Wierson, Arick, and Beau Draghicui. "Call off the Requiem: The Classical Music Business Is Not Dead Just Yet." *Observer*, September 11, 2019.

Williams, Roderick. *A Choral History of Britain*. BBC Radio 3, 2017.

Wilson, Greg. "Singing and Stuttering: What We Know." Stuttering Foundation website, 2013. https://www.stutteringhelp.org/content/singing-and-stuttering-what-we-know-0

Wright, Rayburn. *Inside the Score: A Detailed Analysis of 8 Classic Jazz Ensemble Charts by Sammy Nestico, Thad Jones, and Bob Brookmeyer*. Delevan, NY: Kendor Music, 1982.

Young, James Webb. *A Technique for Producing Ideas*. New York: McGraw Hill Professional, 1939.

Youth Music. *Music in Healthcare: Evidence Review*. London, September 2017. https://network.youthmusic.org.uk/file/25179/download?token=PNChjGF1

Zander, Ben S. *The Art of Possibility*. New York: Penguin Books, 2002.

Zander, Ben S., and Rosamund Zander. *The Transformative Power of Classical Music*. 2008. https://www.youtube.com/watch?v=r9LCwI5iErE

Zander, Ben S. "Saint-Saens: Violin Concerto no. 3 - 1st Movement. (Benjamin Zander - Interpretation Class)." December 10, 2015. https://www.youtube.com/watch?v=YtsMevGpgQE

Index

For the benefit of digital users, indexed terms that span two pages (e.g., 52–53) may, on occasion, appear on only one of those pages.

Figures are indicated by *f* following the page number

Accentuate the Positive, 99, 111–16
activism, 110, 200–9
   activist stance, 9, 200
   auditions and, 195
   choral singing as, 2
   new era of, 206
advocacy, 8. *See also* activism
After the Rain, 116
age, 11, 21n.1, 42, 71, 118, 139, 197–98
   ageism, 13
   changing voice and, 196
   community ecosystem and, 36
   DEI and, 174, 184, 213–14, 219
   micro-aggression and, 187
America, 81
Amrein, Emilie, 204
Arbery, Ahmaud, 175
Armstrong, Anton, 201
Armstrong, Louis, 94–95
art, 8, 13, 175, 207
   connection through, 1–3
   groove in choral, 71
   intrinsically activist as, 199–202
   jazz as, 71
   leading from, 156–58, 219
   organizational values and, 38
   organizational vision and, 37–38
   purpose and, 156
artistic change, 17
   marketing and, 44
   programming and, 35, 44
artistic leadership, 152–55, 156–58
   age and ethnicity and, 36
   collaboration in (*see* collaboration)
   mission and, 39
artistic strategy, 20–21, 39–45
   See also arts organizations; choral art; performing arts, arts the,
artistic team, 197, 211
arts organizations, 9, 25*f*, 162–63, 206, 208–9
arts the, 209–11
   education in, 210
   under threat, 210
   See also art

audience, 1–2, 6, 7, 11, 123*f*, 124*f*, 149–50
   activism and, 200–1
   Big Gay Sing and, 99, 108–9
   changing tastes, 29, 111
   choral backings, 167–68
   community ecosystem and, 25*f*
   connection and, 154, 205
   creating change in, 120
   day of the week and, 111
   decline and 35, 206–7
   demographic data on, 179
   encores and, 116
   exclusion and 17
   expectations and, 112–13, 114
   friends and family, 35
   growing new, 161
   hopeful close, and, 116
   impact and, 37
   improvisation and, 94
   leaving the stage and, 169
   licensed bar and, 111
   looking at, 219
   memorization and, 219
   newly constructed performances and, 148, 203–4
   participation through groove, 72–73, 74–75
   party atmosphere and, 110
   programming for engagement of, 205–6
   projecting the words and, 110
   purpose and, 40–41
   race and, 13
   relationship with choral director and, 153
   shocking the, 115
   size, 119
   social media activation and, 212
   special needs plan and, 194
   vision, mission and values and, 33
   visual impact and, 104
auditions, 20, 74, 161, 179, 194–95, 207–8, 220
aural skills, 194, 195

Baby Shark, 13–15, 71
backbeat, 80, 81
backing tracks, 84, 212

234 Index

Bankes-Jones, Bill, 204
Barnwell, Ysaye, 114
Beach Boys The, 52–53
Beatles, The, 8–9
Bechet, Sidney, 133–34
Beckett, Samuel, 115, 117
belonging, 3–4, 188–90
    BIPOC and marginalized singers and, 173
    cliché and, 109
    levels of, 36
    microaggression and, 187
    ownership of repertoire and, 134, 171, 205–6
    pressure to belong, 159
    singalong and, 111
    voice parts, gender and, 207–8
    welcome, engagement and, 174
Berlin, Irving, 58
Bernstein, Basil, 132
Bernstein, Leonard, 48
Beyoncé, 35
Bigard, Barney, 133–34
Big Gay Sing, 44, 99, 107–11, 112
Billie Jean, 70
Blues in Bb, 113
Bolero, 71
Bond, Justin Vivian, 121
bonding, 2, 4, 5–6, 34, 76, 214–15, 216
    choral singing as generating unified group, 178
    college choirs and, 26
    groove through, 218
    rehearsal and, 127
    singalongs and, 107
    story-telling by choral directors and, 159
Born This Way, 106, 204–5
Both Sides Now, 139
Britten, Benjamin, 52
Brown, James, 82
Burke, Tom, 52
Burns, Ken, 4, 177–78
Byrd, William, 7, 143, 204–5

Capital Children's Choir, 49–50
Carmina Burana, 210
Carreras, José, 47
Centerpiece, 80
change, 1–2, 4–6, 8, 10, 19, 199–200
    choral singing as change-making, 13, 21, 214
    music education as, 127
    organizational vision and, 37–38
    See also activism; artistic change; social change
changing musical tastes, 19
choral art, 12, 30*f*, 161, 216
choral directing, 208, 213–14
    backings, 167–68

in breaths, 165
conducting gestures, 170
conducting the beat, 166, 168
conductor position, 169
count-ins, 165
directing the groove, 166
education of, 16, 164
focus, 168
form and routine signals, 167–68
groove texture, 166
inhibitor as, 161
Italian terms, 166
learning practice flexibility, 134
majority white, 13
moving to the groove in, 168
relationship with rhythm section, 166
repeats, 167
repertoire choice, 161
rhythmic gesture, 165
rhythm section position, 167
round and round signals, 167
choral leadership, 160, 164–71, 213
    collaboration as, 152–54, 156, 163
    DEI collaboration and, 180–81
    leading a community and, 171
    leading popular styles, 164
    musical aspects of, 164–71
    need for change within, 164
    racism and discrimination within, 213
    social aspects of, 199
    structures in, 213
    See also leadership
choral music education, 16, 46
    myths within, 15–16
    need for change within, 19
    treatment of non-classical music within, 16, 164
    See also choral pedagogy; vocal pedagogy
        choral pedagogy, 18, 208, 213
        activist, 208
        artistic literacy and, 17
        college contexts, in, 213
        hierarchical, 141
        learning style variety in, 127–31
        top down, 67
choreography and movement, 170–71
classical music, 15, 204–5
    dominant culture as, 10
    exceptionalism, 14–16, 49
    high art as, 41, 50, 111
    organizational mission and, 33
    vocal pedagogy of, 48–50
    vocal sound of, 48
    warm-ups in, 47, 58–61

Cleese, John, 102, 104
Cohen, Emmet, 212
collaboration, 44, 107, 120–21, 152, 162–63, 208–9
Collins, Jim, 5, 9
communication
    activism in, 200–2
    choir and audience between, 169
    choral directing as, 153, 154–55, 202
    choral singing as, 7
    skills, 137, 147, 149–50
    tool, choral singing as, 9, 212
    two-way within choral organizations, 156, 165–66
community, 1, 5–8, 34, 215–16
    art as reflecting issues in, 159–60
    auditions and, 155
    BIPOC, 10–11
    choir as looking like, 160
    choir as voice of, 40
    choral activity and, 34, 127, 137, 214
    classical music as global, 48
    ecosystems, 26–27, 45, 118
    elders within, 162
    influence on programming, 156–57
    LGBTQIA+, 11, 108, 177
    musical community, 27
    musical style as enabling, 203
    organizational mission and, 39
    outside perceptions, 28
    problematic term as, 5, 159, 177–78
    respect and, 178–79
    singalongs as building, 111
    singing about social issues in, 119
    two-way relationships within, 154
    welcome, engagement and belonging, 188–89
connection, 2–4
    activism and, 202
    choral singing as facilitating, 3
    connected artistic leadership, 152
    as defining good art, 46, 154
    groove and, 69–70, 72–73
    learning strategies and, 127
    musical style and, 99
    performing without conductor via, 169
    preparation and, 148
    pulse and, 75
    purpose and, 26
    purpose of all music, 71
    singers with each other, 150
    video content and, 41
    warm-ups and, 137
Coro Gai Ciudad de México, 106–7, 163
Crazy in Love, 113–14

David, Craig, 212
Davis, Miles, 69
default positions, 48–50
    belt and, 52
    conversational diction and, 52
    legato and, 51–52
    straight tone and, 53
DEI. See diversity; equity; inclusion
dementia, 6–7
Dench, Judi, 53
disability, 11, 132, 173, 179, 187, 192
disability, 179
diversity. *See* diversity; equity; inclusion
diversity, equity and inclusion, 174, 175
    brave spaces, 178–79
    changing voice and inclusion, 196
    diversity as 'major step', 10
    equity and education as vehicles, 10
    equity and inclusion plan, 193
    exclusion in choirs and, 13, 36
    healing through, 178
    homophobia, 12–13
    inclusion, 174
    intersectionality, 177
    in musical practices, 55
    need to change, 175
    pedagogical variety and, 131
    practices as ongoing, 179
    privilege, 176
    pulse, rhythm and groove education and, 74
    racism, 12
    setting standards, 178
    unintentional exclusion, 12
    white leadership and, 135

ear, working by, 80, 94, 95, 211–12
    improvising by ear in rehearsal, 86
    less valued in formal education, 16
    rehearsing by ear, 127–29, 130–31, 133–34, 136–37, 140, 141–44
    riffing and, 92
elders, 136, 162
Elijah, 203–4
Ellington, Duke, 14, 18
empowerment, 5, 34, 160–62, 214–15
    BIPOC and marginalized singers of, 173
equity, 174. *See* diversity; equity; inclusion
Estill, Jo, 56
Estill model, 56–58
    aryepiglottic sphincter (AES), 51, 57–58, 65, 66
    cricoid Cartilage, 58
    false folds, 57, 59, 60
    fold mass, 49, 52

236 Index

Estill model (*cont.*)
head, neck and torso, 57, 59, 61–62, 63, 168
jaw, 57, 72
larynx position, 47, 51, 57–58
lips, 57
onsets and offsets, 48, 49, 51–52, 57
soft Palate, 47, 51, 57
thyroid Cartilage, 58, 60
tongue, 52–53, 57, 58, 59, 60, 61, 66
ethnic identity, 174
auditions and, 195
BIPOC singers, 10–11
communication style of choral director
and, 135
current singers of, 40
data collection on, 219
fellowship and, 159
groove-based music and, 73, 74
leadership roles and, 36
microaggression and, 195
musical practices and, 20
musical training of choral directors and, 164
music team and, 197
privilege and, 191
purpose and, 26
queerness, and, 12–13, 177
social practices and, 20
ethnicity. *See* ethnic identity

Firework, 215
Florence and the Machine, 49–50
Floyd, George, 175
formal and informal learning, 131–34, 213
See also learning
Four Choirs and a Cathedral, 163
Franklin, Aretha, 8–9
Freire, Paulo, 132
function of choral singing, 2, 9, 10, 12, 17–18,
26, 28, 45
level and, 18
See also purpose of choral singing
funding, 2–3, 9, 27, 119, 122, 131, 156

Gay. *See* LGBTQIA+
gender, 11, 174, 191
assumptions and, 185
cisgender, 12, 13, 154–55, 174–75, 176,
177, 184
cross-section, 118
data collection, 40, 219
gender binary, 207–8
gendered voice parts, 211
gender-fluid, 108–9, 110, 176, 206
gender pronouns, 119, 183

leadership team and, 197
See also transgender
Gjeilo, Ola, 8–9
glove puppets, choirs as, 9, 201–2
gospel, 6, 26, 33, 53, 54, 67, 81, 84, 133, 213
greatness in arts organizations, 5, 9
Green, Lucy, 130–31, 134, 141
groove, 30*f*, 69–71, 88, 92
backbeat, 80
backing tracks and, 84
bodily engagement, 72–73, 76, 83, 165, 168
choral education in, 69
choral leadership and, 164
choral warm-ups and, 56
classical singing and, 48, 128
directing pulse, beat and tempo in, 165
foldback and, 84
group participation and, 72–73
improvised harmony through, 96
improvised melody through, 96
leading a rhythm section in, 166–67
locking in, 82
mood change and, 71
musical material, as, 84
pulse and, 75
swing, 80
voice and, 72
walking in time to, 97–98

Hadestown, 53
Happy Birthday, 159

I See Fire, 121
identity, 3–4, 154–55, 173, 193
assumptions and, 184–85
identity performance, 159, 174
intersectional as, 177
microaggressions and, 187–88
See also DEI; ethnic identity; gender
impact, 5–9, 219
activism and, 203–6
activist stance and, 200, 202
art and, 1, 202
artistic strategy and, 43
choir's financial bottom line and, 154
community ecosystem within, 43
groove and, 71
inequality and, 13, 175
musical and social as, 28, 29
musical practices in, 20*f*–21
programming and, 18
programming repertoire and, 106, 107
purpose and, 10–11, 29
riffing through, 92

singers who work by ear and, 129
song meaning through, 149–50
story-telling and, 139
vocal sound and, 51, 67
improvisation, 86, 94–97
aural skills in, 92
BIPOC communities and, 86
seen as hard, 87–88
inclusion. *See* diversity; equity; inclusion
inputs and outputs, 9
intersectionality, 11, 174, 177–78, 190–91
community and, 178
Isley Brothers, 70
It's Your Thing, 70

Jackson 5, 115
Jackson, Michael, 70, 110, 211
Jazz, 47, 52–53, 67, 107, 113, 221
count-ins, 165
default positions in, 48
directing the groove, 166
formal and informal learning in, 133–34
improvisation, 86, 88, 92, 97
individuality in, 166–67
learning styles in 127–29
mindful engagement in, 150
onsets in, 51–52
othering of, 16
refinement within, 15
rhythm skills in, 69–70, 71, 72, 74, 78–81
Emmet Cohen streaming performances
of, 212
vocal safety in, 15–16
Jordan, James, 55, 135–36

karaoke, 54, 88, 199
Kitt, Tom, 211
Kodaly method, 74
Kuti, Fela, 70

Lady Gaga, 204–5
Lambert, Hendricks and Ross, 52–53
Lauridsen, Morten, 58, 112–13, 215
Laws, Roberta, 201
leadership
antiracist, 179–80
diversifying your, 197
equitable, 154–55
leading from the art, 156–58
learning leader, 179–81, 215–16
'New Power' and, 212
personal and organizational aspects, 152–63
vulnerability and, 157
See also choral leadership

learning, 20
autonomous, 141
choreography, 171
externalizing pulse, 72
leadership style and, 154
musical practices and, 45
new material, 138–44
partially sighted, 179
pitches, 141
recognizing what you do not know, 69
rehearsal tracks, 146, 195
reviewing, 144–47
rhythmic, 168
singing through, 138
small group, 94–95
strategies, 127
See also learning style; teaching and learning
learning style, 11, 15, 71, 127–31, 213
aural, 87, 127–28, 129–30, 142, 144–45, 147
intersectionality and, 177–78
kinesthetic, 71, 87, 127–28, 130, 146–47
popular music in, 74
reading, 87 (*see also* reading music)
visual, 127–28, 129–30, 134, 145, 147
warm-ups in, 137
See also learning
LGBTQIA+ people, 1, 117, 159, 204–5, 208, 215
appropriate mission language for, 38
changing priorities within, 120
choirs, choruses and singers, 6, 154, 182,
206–7
chosen family, 159
coalitions, 162–63
community, 1, 108, 113–14, 176, 182,
183, 205
dress, 112
hiding in choirs and choruses, 11, 206–7
intersectionality within community, 11, 177
issues, 110
internalized low self-worth, 16
marginalization of within choral singing,
12–13, 16
Pulse nightclub tragedy, 106
Safer spaces, 173
themes, 44, 211–12
youth, 26
Life is a Celebration, 113, 120
Light, 106, 211
Lil Naz X, 212
lived experience, 1–2, 12–13, 36, 106, 154–55,
176–77, 209
choral directing and, 159, 180–81
microaggressions and, 178–79
Lux Aurumque, 78, 211

238   Index

Madonna, 35, 109
mainstream choral singing
   improvisation in, 86
   lack of tenors in, 205–6
   learning style and, 128
   mainly white as, 10–11, 179–80
   mainstream musical culture and, 199
   rhythmic education and, 71, 73
   unchanged as, 17
   vocal color and, 46
Mamamoo, 140
McDaid, Tony, 175
McIntosh, Peggy, 190–91
memorization, 128, 129–30, 133, 142, 144–45,
      194, 219
Mendelssohn, Felix, 203–4
Mercury, Freddie, 66
microaggressions, 178–79
   oops and ouch, 186–88
   songs as, 180–81
mission. See mission; values; vision
mission. See values, mission and vision; vision,
      mission and values; vision, mission
      and values
Mitchell, Joni, 139
Mulligan, Gerry, 113
music education, 73–75, 127–34, 208
   music as aural medium in, 131, 201–2
   benefits of, 33
   change, and, 127
   classical music exceptionalism in, 14–60, 71
   formal and informal learning, 131–34
   groove and, 73
   need for subsidy, 210 (see also funding)
   rhythm in, 72, 73–75
   provision patchy, 2–3, 17
   schools in, 2–3
   stylistic bias within, 18
   stylistic diversity, need for, 208
musical theater, 5, 15–16, 58, 67
   amplification, 53
   belt in, 58
   choral pedagogy and, 74
   connection and, 17
   conversational diction in, 52
   count-ins in, 165
   developments in vocal teaching in, 52
   groove-based, 71
   improvising in, 71, 166–67
   learning style in, 133
   onsets in, 51–52
   othering of, 16
   resonance in, 54
   vibrato in, 53
   warm-ups in, 47, 61–64

musical practices, 18, 37, 204, 205, 207
   by ear work versus staff notation, 128–29
   expressing purpose as, 34–35
   improvising and embellishment dropped
      out of, 86
   formal and informal learning as part
      of, 133–34
   less bodily movement in classical, 73
   loving approach intrinsic to, 136
   rhythm and groove step change
      required, 74–75
   vocal sound as an example of, 47
   See also musical and social practices in choirs
musical and social practices, 18, 19–20, 37, 45,
      152, 199, 203–4, 206
   analogue, 164
   choral leadership and, 152
   follow-through and disability, 179
   learning practices as embedded in, 20
   norms in need of change, 199, 206
   overlapping as, 20, 127, 203
   purpose, 25
   in rehearsal, 127
   social justice principles in, 181
   songs as microaggressions, 180–81

Next To Normal, 53, 211
New Year's Carol, 77–78
New York, 140
Noah, Trevor, 200–1
Noble, Weston, 201
Non, Je ne Regrette Rien, 115
Non-Western styles, 15, 16–17, 47, 67
Nuñez, Francisco, 9

Obama, Barak, 200–1
O Fortuna, 110
O'Hara, Kelli, 52
Orff, Karl, 110, 211
Our Lady J, 115
overlaps in musical styles, 17, 52, 67, 164

participation and engagement, 46, 129, 209–
      10, 216
Pasek Benj, 5
Paul, Justin, 5
Pears, Peter, 52–53
pedagogy. *See* choral pedagogy *and* vocal
      pedagogy *and* music education
Pentatonix, 212
performance skills, 147–50
performing arts, 5, 12, 103
Perry, Katy, 143, 215
Piaf, Edith, 115
pop music. *See* popular music

Index   239

popular music
  artistry in, 75
  belt in, 52
  BIPOC singers and, 50
  choral arrangements in, 107
  classical music exceptionalism and, 74
  diction in, 52
  groove-based as, 46
  home musical style as, 50
  impact of, 15–16
  improvisation in, 47, 86
  lack in choral pedagogy, 49
  learning styles in, 74, 134
  pulse and groove, 74–75
  vocal style, 55
  warm-ups in, 64–66
positivity, 136
Powell, Jeremy, 52
practices, musical and social, 19–21
privilege, 13, 176–77, 193
  art and, 176–77
programming
  artistic choices and, 220
  creativity and, 100, 105
  good judgement and, 117
  innovation in, 109
  non-canonical, 208
  taking risks and, 117
  tension release and, 117
proprioception, 130
purpose of choral singing, 1, 2, 10–11, 13, 19, 20–
    21, 200, 206–7, 215
  choral activism and, 200, 202
  collaborations as enabling, 163
  community purpose, 214–15
  impact and, 18, 107, 156
  saying something, 7–8
  social purpose, 6
  song choice and, 160
  story-telling in rehearsal, 136–37
  See also function of choral singing

Quadros, André de, 204
Queen, 58
queer. See LGBTQIA+

racism, 13, 114, 174–75, 180, 200–1, 213–14
  See also DEI; ethnic identity
Ravel, Maurice, 71
reading music, 16
  auditions in, 195
  equity and, 174
  formal learning in, 133
  popular music conventions, 128–29, 133
  learning style and, 133, 141

rehearsal
  learning styles in, 134
  story-telling in, 139–40
rehearsal tracks, 129, 136–37, 141, 144,
    146, 195
relevance, 1, 13, 16–17, 20–21, 37, 38, 44, 46, 111,
    199, 204, 206–7, 211–12, 216
Rent, 53
repertoire, 2, 19, 30*f*, 33–36, 45
  activist, 208
  artistic strategy and, 42
  audience development and, 203
  choral programs in, 213
  Christian, 8, 10, 17
  classical, 18, 49
  community-based, 206–7
  contemporary, 204–5
  director control of, 161
  greatness, 9
  groove-based, 76
  impact, 107
  mission and, 39, 41–42
  new, 119, 220
  norms, 199
  preserving, 38
  quality, 110
  range of vocal sound and, 46
  repeating, 206–7
  saying something through, 206
  singers encultured, 132–33
  story-telling, 112
  stylistic openness, 18, 47
resonant, art as, 1, 3, 5, 18
respectful social space, 97
riffs, 70, 92, 96
Rogers and Hammerstein, 53
Ross, Malcolm, 100

safer space, 173, 178, 203
  for beginner improvisers, 87–88
  choirs as, 11, 26
  music as, 12
  rehearsal as, 159
  the arts as, 12
Salamunovitch, Paul, 201
'saying something', 1, 7–9, 13, 18, 26, 173,
    204, 206
Send in the Clowns, 53
Sesame Street, 113
sexual orientation. See LGBTQIA+
Sharon, Deke, 137
Shaw, Robert, 137, 201
Sheeran, Ed, 121
Single Ladies, 81
So in Love, 52

240 Index

social change, 112, 200
  activism and, 9, 206
  context change, 119
  leaders denying need for, 12
  musical excellence and, 34
  reason for singing as a, 29–32
  singing and, 34
  systemic, 12–13, 207
social justice, 13
social practices, 18, 19–21, 26, 36, 55
  DEI work as change in, 173
  social justice principles in, 181
  vocal warm-ups as, 137
  See also musical and social practices
solfège, 56, 69, 73–74, 95, 130, 133–34, 142
Somewhere Over the Rainbow, 109
Sondheim, Stephen, 8–9, 35
song choice
  explanation to singers and, 140
Speed, Ann-Marie, 52
Spring Awakening, 114
stakeholders, 1, 26, 27–28, 38
Stellenbosch University Choir, 54
Sting, 116
Stone, Mollie, 211
Stop: The Love you Save (May Be Your Own), 115
stylistic openness
  music education, and, 16
  popular styles and, 164
  structural issues preventing, 39
Sure on this Shining Night, 58, 59–61, 78, 116, 120, 183, 215
Surrey with a Fringe on Top, 69
swing, 69, 78–81

taste choices, 48–54
  fold mass, 52
  legato, 51
  tongue position, 52–53
Taylor, Breonna, 175
Teacher, Don't Teach Me Nonsense, 70
teaching and learning, 2
  embedded in musical and social practices, 20
  See also learning
Te Kanawa, Kiri, 47
Tête-a-Tête, 204
The Bucket's Got a Hole in It, 94–98
theory
  See also theory and practice
There's No Business Like Show Business, 58, 61–64
Thriller, 110, 211
Timms, Henry, 212
tongue
  feeling rhythm through, 72
  high, 52–53

Totally Fucked, 114, 120, 140
transgender, 11, 44, 175
  communities of musicians, 17–18
  composers, 121
  intersectionality and, 177
  LGTBQIA+ community focus, 112
  microaggressions and, 186–87
  performers, 121
  privilege and, 176
  transgender voice, 208
  voice tests and auditions, 179, 196
Trecek-King, Anthony, 10
Turner, Tina, 108–9
Twelve, 113

values, 27–28, 33–35, 37–39, 159, 194, 198, 200, 203, 206, 207
  activist singers and, 155–56
  art as aligning with, 202
  choral leader as expressing, 154
  choral singing as a public statement of, 6, 8, 12, 26, 199
  Christian values, 10
  equity and Inclusion plan and, 194
  expressed in a song, 139
  funders attracted to, 156
  respect practices as expression of, 182
  transgressive, 4
  See also mission; values; vision; saying something,
Varvarigou, Maria, 130–31
Veneracion, Andrea Ofilada, 201
Vienna Boys Choir, 53
vision, 27–29, 33–34, 37–39, 43–44, 119, 194
  activist vision for choral singing, 200, 207–16
  artistic vision, 156
  See also mission; values; vision
vision, mission and values, 37–39, 43, 119
vocal mechanism, 51
vocal pedagogy, 15–16, 47
  activist, 207
  classical music, 48–50, 52–53
  code-switching in, 54–55
  cricoid cartilage in, 58
  diction in, 52–53
  fold mass in, 50
  home style, in, 54
  inclusive, 67
  larynx position in, 67
  legato in, 51
  older voice and, 196
  person-centered, 207
  recent developments in, 50–51, 213–14
  soft palate, 57
  stylistically open, 50–55

taste choices in, 53
transgender voice and, 196
vibrato in, 53
vocalprocess, 213–14
vocal resonance, 16, 47, 49, 52, 53, 54, 57–58, 67, 168–69, 170, 221
classical, 50–51
fellowship, 160
repertoire choice and, 204–5
speech voice, 141
swing, 81
transgender singers and, 179
VOCES8, 212
Vogue, 109
voice parts, 41, 205–6, 207–8
volunteers, 104, 119, 135, 154, 155, 159, 182, 188, 194, 195, 197
vowels, 47, 49–50, 52–53, 55–56, 57, 60, 63, 65–66, 93, 141

warm-ups, 47, 55–66, 137–38
improvisation in, 86, 88
learning style in, 137
rhythm warm-ups, 75
We Are The Champions, 58, 64–66
Weiwei, Ai, 200
West Side Story, 47
Whitacre, Eric, 78, 211

white folks, 10, 12, 36, 201, 210
'being white', 179–81
in classical music, 14
college choral programs and, 213
control, 16–17
enabling diversity, 181
foregrounding, 174
fragility, 180
groove and, 73
guilt, 193
humility, 180–81
leaders as mainly white, 177
likely to make mistakes, 180
microaggression, 186
privilege and, 13, 74, 176, 181, 193
speaking for other races, 180–81
vocal sound, 49, 67
white choral directors, 154–55, 164
white gay men, 114
white gaze, 10–11
white majority, 13, 140, 173, 177, 179–80
Willcocks, David, 201
Williams, Clarence, 94–98
Would You Harbor Me?, 114

Yorkey, Brian, 211
You Can Be as Loud as the Hell You Want (When You're Makin' Love), 115

Printed in the USA/Agawam, MA
October 18, 2024